FOR REFERENCE

Do Not Take From This Room

Modern Slavery

Recent Titles in the

CONTEMPORARY WORLD ISSUES
Series

Modern Slavery

A REFERENCE HANDBOOK

Christina G. Villegas

ABC-CLIO®

An Imprint of ABC-CLIO, LLC
Santa Barbara, California • Denver, Colorado

Library of Congress Cataloging-in-Publication Data

Names: Villegas, Christina G., author.

Title: Modern slavery : a reference handbook / Christina G. Villegas.

Description: Santa Barbara, California : ABC-CLIO, [2020] | Series: Contemporary world issues | Includes bibliographical references and index.

Identifiers: LCCN 2020011965 (print) | LCCN 2020011966 (ebook) | ISBN 9781440859762 (hardcover ; alk. paper) | ISBN 9781440859779 (ebook)

Subjects: LCSH: Slavery. | Slavery—History—21st century.

Classification: LCC HT867 .V554 2020 (print) | LCC HT867 (ebook) | DDC 306.3/620905—dc23

LC record available at https://lccn.loc.gov/2020011965

LC ebook record available at https://lccn.loc.gov/2020011966

ISBN: 978-1-4408-5976-2 (print)
      978-1-4408-5977-9 (ebook)

24 23 22 21 20   1 2 3 4 5

This book is also available as an eBook.

ABC-CLIO
An Imprint of ABC-CLIO, LLC

ABC-CLIO, LLC
147 Castilian Drive
Santa Barbara, California 93117
www.abc-clio.com

This book is printed on acid-free paper ∞

Manufactured in the United States of America

Contents

Slavery has been banned throughout the West for more than 150 years, and hundreds of international treaties and conventions have outlawed the various manifestations of slavery and the slave trade worldwide. In 2007, Mauritania became the final country to remove explicit protection for the institution from its legal code. Although it is no longer openly condoned or legally sanctioned, the eradication of slavery is nevertheless far from accomplished. Today, an estimated 21–45 million people are enslaved—more than at any other point in history—and the institution continues to thrive across the globe.

The scourge of modern slavery exists most acutely in war-torn, poverty-stricken, politically unstable, and totalitarian countries where the rule of law is nonexistent or has been severely compromised—yet even affluent, free-market democracies, such as the United States and Great Britain, are not exempt from its reach. Most major towns and cities worldwide have a booming trade in girls, boys, women, and men of all ages. Some of these slaves are brought across international borders, while others are born into servitude or groomed for it domestically. In recent decades, profits from the sale of human beings for sex, labor, and other purposes have risen to be among the highest sources of illegal income, ranking just below drug dealing in breadth and profitability. In several regions, profits in human beings have surpassed those of the black-market arms trade.

The abuses associated with slavery of the past often receive more attention than those of the present, but the severity of slavery has not subsided with time. As the personal accounts of slaves and survivors illustrate, modern slavery is at least as brutal in its violations of fundamental human rights as slavery of previous generations (Bales 2012). Slavery—the subjection of human beings to absolute, uninhibited, and unaccountable power—remains, in the words of former slave and abolitionist Frederick Douglass, "the most abject, the most terrible bondage ever imposed on any portion of mankind." As in centuries past, its "grand aim . . . always and everywhere, is to reduce man to a level with the brute" (Myers 2008, 25). Evidence exists and is indisputable—the need for individuals, organizations, and governments to take up the mantle of abolition domestically and internationally remains just as relevant as ever (Batstone 2010).

Modern Slavery: A Reference Handbook is a valuable resource for students and general readers seeking to identify the key issues of the worldwide epidemic of modern slavery and the various abolitions efforts. The book presents a discussion of the scope and nature of modern slavery and its various aspects, including its evolution, geographic and socioeconomic contexts, and contributing factors. The book additionally evaluates ongoing and proposed prevention, eradication, and rehabilitation efforts and provides a listing of key actors and resources as a foundation for further research and engagement of the topic.

Modern Slavery is organized into seven chapters. Chapter 1, "Background and History," highlights the importance of the topic by reviewing the scope and nature of modern slavery. It introduces the various manifestations of modern slavery, explores the growth of slavery in the twentieth and twenty-first centuries, and overviews the various international treaties and conventions aimed at eliminating the practice. It then examines the geographic, political, cultural, and economic contexts of modern slavery and discusses various factors that contribute to the crisis.

Chapter 2, "Problems, Controversies, and Solutions," outlines the most common controversies in responding to modern slavery as well as legal, social, cultural, and economic barriers to prevention and eradication. It further highlights specific prevention, eradication, and rehabilitation efforts taken by governmental and nongovernmental agencies and individuals and discusses proposed solutions to the various manifestations of modern slavery.

Chapter 3, "Perspectives," includes nine essays written by authors from a variety of viewpoints and professional backgrounds on a range of topics related to the issue of modern slavery. These essays are intended to supplement and enrich the presentation of the crisis laid out in chapters 1 and 2.

Chapter 4, "Profiles," lists and describes key governmental and nongovernmental organizations involved in a wide array of prevention, eradication, and rehabilitation efforts.

Chapter 5, "Data and Documents," offers data and primary source documents, including conventions, laws, executive orders, speeches, and testimonies, to provide readers with first-hand information on the following: What is the scope of modern slavery? Who is enslaved, and what patterns are emerging? Who or what is responsible? What insights can be learned from survivors? What is being done at the local, national, and international level to address the continued growth of modern slavery? And how can slavery be eradicated and, in the future, prevented?

Chapter 6, "Resources," provides an annotated list of selected books, articles, and reports on a variety of topics related to modern slavery, which offers readers a starting point for further research. Several nonprint sources are listed and annotated as well.

Chapter 7, "Chronology," offers a concise timeline of defining moments and major events affecting slavery in the twentieth and twenty-first centuries.

The book concludes with a glossary of key terms relating to modern slavery and its various contexts.

References

Bales, Kevin. 2012. *Disposable People: New Slavery in the Global Economy.* 3rd edition. Berkeley, CA: University of California Press.

Batstone, David. 2010. *Not for Sale: The Return of the Global Slave Trade—and How We Can Fight It.* Revised and Updated Edition. New York: HarperCollins.

International Labour Organization (ILO) and Walk Free Foundation. 2017. "Global Estimates of Modern Slavery: Forced Labour and Forced Marriage." Geneva. Accessed November 15, 2019. https://www.ilo .org/global/publications/books/WCMS_575479/lang--en /index.htm

Myers, Peter C. 2008. *Frederick Douglass: Race and Rebirth of American Liberalism.* Lawrence, KS: University Press of Kansas.

Acknowledgments

I would like to thank Catherine Lafuente and Robin Tutt of ABC-CLIO, who assisted me in various stages of this project, and Martha Elwell, who reviewed drafts of several of the chapters. I relied heavily on the data provided by the International Labour Organization (ILO) and Walk Free Foundation (2017), from their most recently published *Global Estimates of Modern Slavery*, and am appreciative of the extensive work these organizations have put into providing reliable estimates of the nature and scope of modern slavery. I am additionally thankful to Brian Janiskee, chair of the political science department at California State University, San Bernardino, for his professional support and mentorship, and to Marilyn Gareis, the political science administrative support coordinator, for her assistance in various administrative tasks. Above all, I am grateful to my husband, Manuel, and our four children, Alexander, Anna, Izabella, and Sophia, for their support and for the profound joy they bring to my life.

Modern Slavery

1   Background and History

Introduction

At present, slavery is illegal in every country, and it would be nearly impossible to find anyone willing to publicly defend the institution. As one unknown author writing for *The Economist* observes, "Slavery is like polio. Most westerners associate it with earlier, darker times in human history. Its eradication is a sign of human progress" (2005). Accordingly, members of today's cognoscenti tend to focus much of their attention on how to properly condemn and make amends for the harms inflicted by historical slavery.

The atrocities committed against slaves of generations past and their descendants should never be dismissed or forgotten, but anyone concerned with justice and human dignity must also recognize that slavery and the horrific crimes associated with it did not end with abolition in the nineteenth century. Slavery not only continues to exist—it is alive and well. At this very moment, millions of living, breathing men, women, and children are oppressed and brutalized under various contemporary forms of slavery that are prevalent across the globe. Over the past several decades, slavery has metastasized faster than

Slavery has been banned throughout the West for more than 150 years, and hundreds of international treaties and conventions have outlawed the various manifestations of slavery and the slave trade worldwide. Yet, the institution continues to thrive across the globe. Today, an estimated 21–45 million people are enslaved—more than at any other point in history. (Choat Boonyakiat/Dreamstime.com) any other form of illicit activity, and the trade of human beings has surpassed weapons as the second most lucrative commodity for crime syndicates, behind drugs. This disturbing trend is exacerbated by the fact that even those from the most developed, high-GDP nations, who would never support slavery in speech, often unwittingly do so in deed by contributing to its sustenance and growth.

The illegality of modern slavery and other factors make it difficult to identify the exact number of slaves, but contemporary estimates suggest that there are more slaves today than at any point in human history. The United Nations' (UN) International Labour Organization (ILO) and the Walk Free Foundation (2017) estimate that on any given day, 40 million people are victims of modern slavery. This includes 25 million people in forced labor and 15 million in forced marriage. In some places, slavery—while not openly condoned or legally sanctioned—is carried out with impunity in broad daylight with the implicit sanction of state authorities. And while most of today's slaves are not sold in public slave markets or held through legal documentation, they are every bit as trapped, oppressed, and dehumanized as the slaves of previous generations. Several scholars, including Bales (2012) and Batstone (2010), have observed that in contrast with slaves of the past who were often viewed as long-term investments, today's slaves are cheap, easily moveable, require little care, and are consequently viewed and treated as disposable.

Defining Modern Slavery

One of the greatest difficulties in exposing and fighting the scourge of modern slavery involves disagreement over the very definition of slavery itself. Slavery in its contemporary form is not always easy to recognize. In contrast with chattel slavery, which involves the capture or purchase and full legal ownership of human beings, many of the current manifestations of slavery are far subtler in nature. In fact, among activists and policy makers alike, the definition of slavery is often disputed. In political discourse, for instance, the condition of slaves and wage laborers are frequently conflated. But not all who face economic mistreatment are slaves. Using slavery as a metaphor for those who are underpaid or overworked has the deleterious effect of concealing the uniquely malevolent violation of humanity that slavery entails in comparison to other forms of exploitation.

Another complication that arises in providing a clear picture of modern slavery is that the terms "trafficking in persons" and "human trafficking," which people typically understand to include movement across borders or great distances, are used interchangeably with the term "modern slavery" to describe various forms of compelled service. The image that generally comes to mind in reference to modern slavery is that of women and children being trafficked into prostitution rings. But many victims of modern slavery are never transported outside of their own communities, and although individuals trafficked and forced into prostitution make up a significant percentage of today's slaves, sex trafficking is only one of many forms of slavery in the modern world. It is thus important to note that "trafficking in persons," "human trafficking," and "modern slavery" are umbrella terms used to refer to sex trafficking and compelled labor whether or not they involve movement, and the victims include all those who are born into a state of servitude, are exploited in their own community, or are transported into an exploitative situation (U.S. Department of State n.d.).

Although modern slavery is not explicitly defined in law, there are certain common legal concepts that arise in various attempts to delineate the issue. One of the most succinct and precise definitions of modern slavery promulgated by modern slavery expert Kevin Bales (2005) holds that slavery consists in "the complete control of a person, for economic exploitation, by violence or threat of violence" (462). Free the Slaves, the world's oldest human rights organization, similarly defines slavery to include those forced to work, held through fraud, under threat of violence, for no pay beyond subsistence (Skinner 2008). The U.S. State Department defines slavery to exist any time a person has been recruited, transported, or compelled to work by force, fraud, or coercion (U.S. Department of State n.d.). For purposes of this book, slavery is understood to occur in the following circumstances: when an individual is bought or sold as property; when an individual is forced to work for no pay beyond subsistence through coercion or threat; when an individual is physically constrained or restricted in movement; or when an individual is owned or completely controlled by another individual through the exercise or threat of abuse. This slightly more comprehensive definition of modern slavery encapsulates a variety of configurations of both forced labor and forced marriage.

Forced Labor

Most of what is considered slavery today falls under the category of forced labor. Forced labor includes any work or services that people are compelled to do against their will under deception, abuse of the legal process, or the threat of violence or other severe punishment. Exceptions include prison labor and compulsory military service. Forced labor can exist in the private economy or be state imposed. It comes in a variety of forms, but it is most often found in industries that are low skilled and labor intensive and is frequently used to produce many of the products in global supply chains. Some of the categories of modern slavery that involve forced labor include traditional chattel slavery, state-imposed forced labor, debt bondage, domestic servitude, sex trafficking and exploitation, and child slavery.

Chattel Slavery

Chattel slavery is a form of slavery in which a person is treated under the law as the wholly owned property of another.

Unlike in debt bondage, chattel slaves cannot pay a debt to be freed, and they can be traded, bought, or sold. Chattel slavery includes hereditary or descent-based slavery, in which people are born into slavery because their ancestors were captured and enslaved and they remain in slavery by descent. Under chattel or descent-based slavery, any children born are also considered the master's property.

While chattel slavery—the type of slavery that existed during the era of the Transatlantic Slave Trade—is less common today than other forms, it hasn't vanished from the globe. Today, racialized chattel slavery is still prevalent in Mauritania, Niger, Sudan, and other parts of Northern Africa. Slavery is technically illegal in these countries, but cultural practices support a system in which slave status is inherited and law enforcement officials will return escaped slaves to their slave holders just as if the practice were legal. Mauritania, for instance, legally made slavery a crime in 2007, and the government officially denies that it exists, yet 10–20 percent of the population remains enslaved. Slavery is deeply rooted in the country's cultural and social caste system, and the practice continues to receive state support. The slave-owning classes continue to dominate the judicial and executive system. Consequently, only one slave owner has ever been successfully prosecuted, and activists opposing the practice are frequently arrested (Sutter 2012).

In Libya, which has always been a notorious hub for slavery in the Arab world, formal slave trading made a comeback in the wake of the overthrow of the Muammar al-Gaddafi regime in 2011. In 2017, CNN journalists traveled to a town not far from Tripoli and obtained cellphone video footage of an old-style slave auction involving the sale of 12 Nigerian men, and they uncovered evidence that similar auctions have occurred in other locations as well (Elbagir et al. 2017). Following the release of this shocking footage, Libya banned Western journalists from entering the country, but the return of slave markets is not isolated to Libya. The International Organization for

Migration (2017) has similarly reported the torment of hundreds of young African men in slave markets on migrant routes throughout North Africa.

State-Imposed Forced Labor

According to the ILO and Walk Free Foundation (2017), in 2016, there were approximately 4.1 million victims of state-imposed forced labor, which occurs when governments enslave their own citizens or others. State-imposed forced labor includes situations in which national or local authorities force otherwise-free citizens to work as a means of mobilizing labor for economic development or when state authorities force prisoners or detainees to work in breach of ILO Forced Labour Conventions. The ILO Forced Labour Convention 1930 (No. 29) specifies that forced or compulsory labor includes "all work or service which is exacted from any person under the threat of a penalty and for which the person has not offered himself or herself voluntarily." Notable exceptions listed in the convention include compulsory military service, normal civil obligations, prison labor (under certain conditions), work in emergency situations, and minor communal services (within a community). The Abolition of Forced Labour Convention (No. 105), adopted by the ILO in 1957, specifically prohibits the use of forced labor as punishment for the expression of political views, for the purpose of economic development, as a punishment for participation in strikes, or as a means of racial, religious, or other discrimination.

The Democratic People's Republic of Korea (DPRK, or North Korea) is the worst offender of state-imposed forced labor. Under North Korea's authoritarian regime, forced labor is an essential component of the political and economic system. The entire population is tightly controlled, and more than 2.6 million people, about one in every 10, are forced into forms of labor slavery (Walk Free Foundation 2018). Testimony from defectors and information from various intelligence sources reveal that the North Korean Kim Jong Un regime relies on several methods of forced labor (U.S. Department of State 2019; Walk Free Foundation 2018).

The first is the repeated mass mobilization of men, women, and children for mandatory, unpaid several monthlong "communal labor" campaigns, which involve intensive labor in agriculture, road building, and construction. The campaigns are especially detrimental to children, who can experience physical and psychological injuries, malnutrition, exhaustion, and growth deficiencies. In addition to these seasonal mass labor campaigns, the North Korean government operates regional, local, and subdistrict-level labor training camps for individuals who are suspected of engaging in simple trading schemes or who have been unemployed for more than 15 days. Detainees at these "training" camps are forced to engage in unpaid hard labor for long hours with little food and are subject to routine beatings and other forms of abuse. Tens of thousands of North Koreans have been sent to the even harsher political prison camps. In most cases, the prisoners sent to these camps do not receive notification of formal criminal charges or any kind of judicial hearing. Prisoners, including children, are subject to long hours of labor in harsh conditions, unhygienic living conditions, torture, rape, and insufficient food. Many do not survive.

The North Korean government additionally exports thousands of its nationals each year for government-contracted forced labor abroad. These individuals, who are conscripted to work excessively long hours in unsafe conditions and extreme temperatures for foreign governments and companies, live under constant surveillance, are restricted in their communication, and face government threats of reprisal to themselves and their families back home if they try to escape. These laborers primarily work in the logging, mining, textile, and construction industries in China and Russia, but they are also conscripted for various jobs throughout Africa, Asia, the Middle East, and Eastern Europe. The North Korean government withholds 70–90 percent of the workers' wages, which generates hundreds of millions of dollars annually in foreign currency for the regime. This foreign currency makes up about a tenth of the country's total economy and helps fund its programs for the development of weapons of mass destruction and ballistic missiles and various other illicit activities (Mendoza 2018; U.S. Department of State 2019).

In 2017, the UN banned countries from authorizing work permits for outsourced North Korean workers, but the ban is widely flouted. There are still nearly 100,000 workers earning revenue for the North Korean regime, the bulk of whom are in China and Russia (U.S. Department of State 2019). Over the past couple of years, several reports have revealed that American manufacturers may have inadvertently supported modern slavery and helped finance North Korea's nuclear program by purchasing materials produced by North Korean workers. In 2017, an Associated Press investigation documented North Korean workers processing seafood in Chinese factories, which ended up in American supermarkets, including Aldi and Walmart (Sullivan 2017).

The North Korean government is not alone in subjecting an extremely high percentage of its population to servitude. Other countries—Eritrea, Burundi, Uzbekistan, and Turkmenistan, for instance—have similarly high rates of state-imposed labor. The Global Slavery Index estimates that in Eritrea 93 out of every 1,000 subjects are living in a form of modern slavery created by its compulsory national service conscription system (Walk Free Foundation 2018). Under this system, individuals ranging in age from 18 to 50 are forcibility conscripted into military training, where they are exploited and forced to labor unpaid for indefinite periods of time, often decades, on projects unrelated to military service. Burundi likewise uses civil service as a cover to force its subjects—men, women, and children—to engage in unpaid labor in agriculture, mining, charcoal production, and construction on behalf of the state. Continuing a practice first initiated during the Soviet era, the governments of Uzbekistan and Turkmenistan force their citizens to leave their families, jobs, and schools to pick cotton during the harvest months every year. More than a million children and adults in Uzbekistan and tens of thousands in Turkmenistan are compelled to slave away in hot, hazardous, unsanitary conditions to help line the pockets of the country's elites who rely on finances from cotton production (Skrivankova 2015). In recent years, a coalition of human rights groups referred to as the Cotton Campaign have been actively working to end the practice by encouraging multinational businesses to stop using Uzbek and Turkmen cotton in their products and by attempting to convince Western governments to cease from promoting business, investment, and trade with the two countries.

Bonded Labor

Half of all victims of forced labor imposed by private actors are in bonded labor, often referred to as debt bondage, making it the most prevalent form of modern-day slavery (ILO and Walk Free Foundation 2017). Bonded labor occurs when a person is forced to work indefinitely in an attempt to pay off a debt, which is often impossible to repay because of low wages, deductions for food and lodging, and high interest rates. Bonded labor thus differs from standard labor contracts, in that the conditions of the loan are such that the laborer is never able to repay the principal and interest. Many people who fall victim to bonded labor take an initial loan because they are desperate to provide basic sustenance or medicine for their family or to travel in pursuit of promised work. Often, they will get an offer of a job abroad or in another region and will borrow money from traffickers to pay for travel and accommodation. When they arrive at the agreed-upon location, they find that the work they applied for does not exist or that the conditions are not as described. By this point, an individual or family is trapped. Their documents are often taken away, and they are forced to work until their debt is paid off—but with no clear contract, their debt only grows as they incur outrageous fees and interest for food, shelter, and medical supplies. This debt is frequently passed down to children or to other family members who then find themselves forced into bonded labor. Individuals bonded by debt they can never repay face coercion, violence, and intimidation if they try to escape. Thus, bonded labor becomes, in effect, a form of chattel slavery.

Following the abolition of the Transatlantic Slave Trade, bonded labor was used to trap laborers into working plantations in Africa, the Caribbean, and Southeast Asia. Today, bonded labor is by far the most widespread and common form of slavery in the world. It is most common in South Asia—predominantly in India, Pakistan, Bangladesh, and Nepal—where individuals caught in debt bondage and their children are forced to work in extreme conditions in agriculture, brick kilns, rice mills, mines, and carpet and textile factories. In recent years, the rampant practice of debt bondage in the fishing industry has received international attention. Debt bondage in the fishing industry is particularly acute in Thailand, the world's third-largest seafood exporter. Thailand's multibillion-dollar seafood sector, including its fishing boats and onshore food processing factories, has been a source of widespread trafficking, violence, and slavery for decades. One investigative study by the Issara Institute and the International Justice Mission (2017) found that more than three-quarters of migrants working on Thai fishing vessels were in debt bondage.

Bonded labor is also common in the context of employment-based temporary work programs in which workers are afraid to seek legal redress because their legal status in a destination country is tied to their employer. For example, under the kafala system operational in the Middle Eastern Gulf States and Lebanon and Jordon, migrant workers are required to have a national sponsor. The sponsors, either individuals or companies, control the mobility of migrant workers through their ability to prevent them from changing jobs or exiting the country. The system has created systemic abuse and exploitation of workers and in some cases facilitates slave labor.

Domestic Servitude

Domestic servitude, another common form of forced labor, exists when a worker living and working in a private residence is not free to leave and is abused, underpaid, or not paid at all. Because domestic servitude takes place within private homes, it often remains hidden from the public view, making it one of the hardest forms of modern slavery to identify and track. Moreover, employment in private homes increases the isolation and vulnerability of domestic slaves who are restricted in their freedom of movement and often experience severe forms of exploitation and assault. Even in countries where workers enjoy significant legal protection, authorities charged with overseeing regulations governing wages, work hours, safety conditions, and so forth generally do not have the authority to inspect private homes like they do for formal workplaces. Victims of domestic servitude usually do not raise suspicion because they appear to outsiders to be working as legitimate nannies or other types of live-in domestic help when in reality they are being exploited and controlled. Common warning signs of domestic servitude include individuals who do not possess identification, documentation, or any control over their own finances and individuals who appear abused, scared, and reluctant to interact with others.

Migrants are common victims of domestic servitude and are particularly vulnerable to sustained exploitation because they are geographically isolated from friends and family and often do not speak the language of the destination country or understand how to navigate the legal system. Such migrants often become victims of debt bondage and are forced into domestic servitude when, after reaching a destination country, they incur debt for their travel and a recruitment fee. Their recruiter or employer will then impose additional debt for food and housing costs that can never be repaid.

While more rampant in developing nations, domestic servitude occurs with frequency in wealthier, industrialized nations, such as the United States and Great Britain, as well. In fact, domestic slaves make up the second highest percentage of human trafficking victims in the United States after those trafficked for prostitution and sex services (Bales and Soodalter 2009). U.S. immigration policies, which tie a worker's residence status to a particular employer, give exploitive employers a powerful means of controlling migrant workers, particularly if exploitive employers have diplomatic status and are thereby immune from civil and criminal jurisdiction if their case becomes public. Bales and Soodalter (2009) point out that foreign diplomats and employees of international agencies such as the World Bank and UN legally import thousands of domestic servants on work visas each year, many of whom are enslaved. If their exploitation is exposed, diplomats can escape prosecution either by claiming immunity or by returning to their home countries.

Sex Trafficking and Exploitation

Sex trafficking refers to the action or practice of illegally recruiting, obtaining, harboring, or transporting people from one country or area to another for the purpose of sexual exploitation, which occurs when an individual is forced to perform a commercial sexual act, such as prostitution, as the result of force, threats of force, fraud, or coercion. According to the ILO and Walk Free Foundation (2017), sexual exploitation accounts for nearly 20 percent of the world's victims of forced labor.

While traffickers recruit victims in a variety of venues, advances in social media, technology, and various online back channels have made it much easier for traffickers to identify and groom vulnerable individuals. Adult victims of sexual trafficking are often ensnared by the promise of employment opportunities in major cities or abroad. Women may be offered jobs as models, nannies, waitresses, or dancers, and men may accept employment in construction or agriculture. Upon arrival at their intended destination, however, they are abused, threatened, and forced into the sex industry. Sexual exploitation also commonly occurs in the form of debt bondage, in which traffickers compel individuals to work as prostitutes to pay off unlawful debt for their transportation, recruitment, and upkeep. Sometimes adults initially consent to enter into prostitution or other commercial sexual activities, but they are then prevented from leaving the trade by psychological manipulations and physical force. Others are ensnared after becoming romantically involved with someone who then forces or manipulates them into prostitution. Sex trafficking victims face an added threat, in comparison to other victims of forced labor, in that they can be detained and prosecuted by local law enforcement for engaging in criminal activities (i.e., prostitution and other illegal sex acts). In addition, victims typically suffer from sexually transmitted diseases, drug addiction, and other physical and psychological trauma resulting from their exploitation.

Sex trafficking occurs in every country across the globe, and sexual exploitation is practiced in a wide range of venues, including brothels, strip clubs, fake massage businesses, escort services, private residences, truck stops, hotels, and outdoor public settings. Exploitation might also involve remote, live, interactive commercial sex acts in which webcams, text-based chats, and phone sex lines simulate remote contact between a buyer and victim. According to a recent study by Polaris (2018), based on calls received by the National Human Trafficking Hotline and analysis of numerous publicly available data sets, massage parlors accounted for the largest number of sex trafficking cases in the United States. The study revealed how this lucrative industry is able to operate legally, while hiding massive criminal enterprises. Analysis of collected data suggests that victims controlled through force, fraud, and coercion generate $2.5 billion in annual profits for criminal networks in over 9,000 illicit massage businesses operating in plain sight throughout the country.

Sex trafficking may be carried out by a variety of actors, but it typically falls into three distinct types: pimp controlled, gang controlled, and family controlled. The most well-known type of trafficking, pimp-controlled trafficking, occurs when an individual or group controls and financially benefits from the commercial sexual exploitation of victims. Pimps may act alone or as part of sophisticated criminal networks. Pimps typically recruit vulnerable and isolated individuals whom they are able to connect with, easily manipulate, and exploit. One of the most common tactics pimps use to recruit and groom victims is "lover boy syndrome." Using this method, a "lover boy" or "Romeo" pimp will identify an individual with significant vulnerabilities, such as being alienated from friends and family, having a history of sexual abuse, or being homeless or in the foster-care system. The pimp or trafficker will then work to take the place of a missing father figure, boyfriend, or caregiver in the targeted victim's life and will attempt to bond with the victim through false love and affection, gifts, and promises of a better life. Once a victim is completely dependent on the trafficker, he will push the victim into prostitution and will eventually control every aspect of the victim's life through psychological manipulation and/or physical violence.

A second common type of trafficking occurs when street gangs recruit, groom, and exploit victims. In a review of the recent growth of gang involvement in sex trafficking, Frank and Zerwilliger (2015) explain that sex trafficking has become an appealing source of revenue for street gangs because it is highly profitable, it entails relatively minimal risk of detection by the police, and gangs already possess many of the connections and tools, including structure, discipline, networking skills, and a reputation for violence, necessary to operate a profitable sex trafficking venture. Moreover, gang-controlled sex trafficking cases are particularly difficult to prosecute because victims are highly unlikely to snitch on a gang.

Gangs typically recruit victims using the same tactics as pimps—that is, offering a romantic relationship or promising security in the form of shelter, food, and clothing—or they might abduct victims, lure them with false promises of opportunity, or purchase them from human smugglers. Gang trafficking is particularly prevalent in areas with high levels of poverty, violence, and corruption, such as the northern triangle of Central America, which includes El Salvador, Guatemala, and Honduras. In this increasingly unstable and violent region, it is common for women and minors to pay everything they have to a smuggler who promises them a better life in the United States only to be handed over to gangs who force them into the sex trade or another form of forced labor to pay off their debts for the journey north (Sadulski 2019).

A third type of sex trafficking, family-controlled trafficking, occurs when young people are sold or coerced into commercial sex by their parents or other relatives. Parents, stepparents, grandparents, and the like may make the decision to sell their children temporarily or for a long term to make extra money to provide for more valued children (i.e., boys or non-step children), to provide sustenance or a higher standard of living for themselves, to pay off a debt, or to support a drug or alcohol addiction. According to the Counter Trafficking Data Collaborative (CTDC n.d.), almost half of identified cases of child trafficking begin with some family member involvement, and 36 percent of these cases involve sexual exploitation. Family-controlled trafficking is especially prevalent in poverty-stricken countries, such as India, Thailand, the Philippines, and Cambodia, where cultural tradition supports the selling of a loved one to pay off family debt. In Cambodia, it is not uncommon for mothers to sell their daughters' virginity and then to pressure them to work in a brothel to support the family (Hume et al. 2013). In Thai society, custom dictates that the youngest unmarried daughter of a family is obligated to care and provide financially for her parents. In practice, this leads many parents, who expect financial support, to pressure their daughters into prostitution (Kara 2017). This is particularly true among poor rural and hill tribe families, who are denied citizenship and the rights associated with it, are often uneducated, and face difficulty finding wage-paying jobs.

Child Slavery

Although children may legally engage in some forms of employment and work, child slavery, sometimes referred to as forced child labor, occurs when a person under the age of 18 is required to engage in exploitative or forced labor. Today, children make up a quarter of those held in modern slavery and account for about one-fifth of the bonded labor workforce (ILO and Walk Free Foundation 2017). Child slavery takes many forms and can include unskilled forced labor, child domestic slavery, child forced recruitment for armed conflict or other illicit activities, and child trafficking for sexual exploitation. Children become victims either because they are forced to work with their parents for the same employer or because they have been individually forced to labor on their own as a result of abduction, deceptive recruitment, or other coercive means.

Industries rife with forced child labor include coffee, cocoa, and other forms of agriculture, mining, carpet and textile production, and brick making. While most forced child labor exists in the shadows, victims of the most prolific form of nonsexual child labor exploitation, forced begging, operate in plain sight. This widespread form of child exploitation is particularly acute in Senegal and other West African countries, where tens of thousands of boys from poor rural backgrounds, known as talibés, live far away from their families in Koranic schools called daaras (Cohen 2019). Parents in the region commonly send their children to schools to learn the Koran, but daaras in Senegal are not regulated by the government, and the boys who attend them typically live in extremely squalid conditions and are vulnerable to abuse. Boys as young as five years old are forced to beg and are typically physically or psychologically abused by their Koranic teacher if they fail to meet their begging quotas of money, rice, or sugar. Many parents are unaware of the conditions to which they have subjected their sons, but a large percentage cannot afford to raise them and do not want them back even after learning of their abuse.

The second most common form of forced child labor is domestic servitude. Financial destitution and violence in poverty-stricken nations frequently leads children to migrate from rural areas to cities in search of work. Many find employment in private households. Far from their families and vulnerable to exploitation, these children are often denied a salary and forced to work long hours with little chance of attending school. A large percentage of children in domestic servitude suffer physical and sexual abuse as well. Forced domestic servitude of children is especially systemic in Haiti as a result of the restavec system. Under this system, poverty-stricken parents send their children to work in another household as an unpaid domestic servant because the parents lack the resources necessary to support them. The parents are told that their children will receive care and educational opportunities. Most of the time, however, restavecs do not receive basic care or education and are severely mistreated physically, psychologically, verbally, and sexually.

Another prominent form of child slavery occurs when children are forced to take part in armed conflicts. This includes children who are coerced by government armed forces, paramilitary organizations, or rebel militias to serve as soldiers, but it also includes children who are made to work as porters, cooks, guards, servants, messengers, or spies and girls who are taken as "wives" for soldiers and militia members. Both female and male child soldiers are often sexually abused or exploited by armed groups. In Afghanistan, the practice of *bacha bazi*, which involves the conscription of adolescent boys into sexual slavery, is widespread among the military, the police, and the higher echelons of government. In 2008, President George W. Bush signed the Child Soldiers Prevention Act (CSPA) into law, requiring publication in the annual Trafficking in Persons

Report of a list of foreign governments identified during the previous year as having governmental armed forces or government-supported armed groups that recruit and use child soldiers, as defined in the act. The 2019 CSPA list included governments in Afghanistan, Burma, Democratic Republic of Congo, Iran, Iraq, Mali, Somalia, South Sudan, Sudan, Syria, and Yemen.

In recent years, the commercial sexual exploitation of children (CSEC) has become a matter of growing international concern. Anytime a child under the age of 18 is recruited, transported, provided, patronized, solicited, or maintained for the purpose of child pornography, prostitution, or child sex tourism, the actions classify as sexual exploitation and can be prosecuted as human trafficking regardless of the use of force, fraud, or coercion. Over the past three decades, the loosening of moral and legal standards regarding the production and sale of pornography and the development and growth of the internet have contributed to a continually expanding international market for child pornography (Miers 2003). The decreasing cost of international travel coupled with global internet connectivity has additionally enabled the expansion of the child sex tourism industry, which has outpaced every attempt to restrict it at international and national levels (Hawke and Raphael 2016).

Forced and Sham Marriages

Forced marriages are a form of slavery that occur when individuals are married against their will and cannot freely leave the marriage. Individuals who are compelled to marry as a result of physical, emotional, or financial duress, physical abuse, deception, death threats, or other threats of abuse by family members or others are considered victims of forced marriage. Such arrangements can involve a mix of various forms of slavery, including forced labor, sexual exploitation, or domestic servitude. Child marriage is considered a form of forced marriage given that children are unable to express full, free, and informed consent. Exceptions include 16 and 17 year olds who wish to marry and are granted legal permission following a judicial ruling or parental consent. More than a third of victims of forced marriage are under the age of 18, and children under the age of 15 account for 44 percent of child victims (ILO and Walk Free Foundation 2017). In many places, cultural practices support forcing girls as young as 9 into arranged unions (Vogelstein 2018). As of 2018, only 38 countries have criminalized forced marriage in line with the UN Trafficking Protocol (Walk Free Foundation 2018).

While forced marriages occur in both the developing and developed world, rates are much higher in countries—particularly in Africa, the Middle East, and Asia—whose longstanding cultural and religious traditions support the practice and are antithetical to the dignity and rights of women and girls. Victims may be forced to marry for a variety of reasons. According to some social and religious customs, women are inherited by a brother or other family member of a deceased husband, and in others, rapists can escape criminal sanction by marrying their victims. In addition to being steeped in detrimental social, cultural, and religious practices, forced marriages may be carried out for economic or other pragmatic reasons. Families may agree to force a daughter, or son, into a marriage in exchange for payment or the settlement of a debt or to secure opportunity such as entry into a country. In regions with significant levels of armed conflict, forced marriage is frequently used as a tool of war. In recent years, militant groups in Asia and Africa and Islamist terrorist groups in Iraq, Syria, Somalia, and Nigeria have forced thousands of women and girls into marriage as a guise for systemic sexual trafficking and exploitation. In a speech before the UN Security Council, president of the Malian branch of the NGO Working Group on Women, Peace and Security Saran Keïta Diakité testified that in Mali "Islamists perform religious marriages in order to escape the clutches of international criminal justice" for their use of women as both sexual and domestic slaves (Paterson 2013). In certain conflict situations or humanitarian crises, such as those occurring in Syrian refugee camps, parents may sell their daughters into wedlock with foreign men in hopes of protecting them from poverty, violence, and rape, not realizing that their daughters may face extreme exploitation and violence within the marriages themselves (Ghafour 2013).

Sham marriages are marriages in which two individuals consent to enter into a legal union, without intending to create a real marital relationship, subject to certain conditions such as an exchange of financial or other benefits in order for one party to obtain permanent residency in another country. Sham marriages differ from forced marriages in that victims consent to enter into a legal union because they believe that it will benefit them in some way. Experts have recently noted the growing trend of sham marriages as a form of human trafficking, particularly in Europe (U.S. Department of State 2019). Traffickers, typically members of organized crime syndicates, lure victims from impoverished or destitute backgrounds looking for economic opportunity and a better life to marry men they have never met with false promises of financial remuneration, accommodations, job opportunities, and divorce procedures. Once victims are trapped in a foreign country with no means of supporting themselves, they are forced to engage in a range of exploitive activities, including sex trafficking, domestic servitude, or criminal activities. Traffickers typically use debt bondage to trap victims of sham marriages indefinitely.

Key Moments

During the twentieth century, significant attempts were made to recognize and address the issue of modern slavery through international laws and conventions. The League of Nations—established after World War I to promote peace, disarmament, and global welfare—was the first international body to sponsor major conventions regulating contemporary slavery. In 1924, the League of Nations established the Temporary Slave Commission to determine the continued existence and extent of slavery. The commission concluded that slavery is widespread throughout the world and called on member states to consider the "abolition of the legal status of slavery." Based on this assessment, the League of Nations sanctioned the creation of the Slavery, Servitude, and Forced Labour and Similar Institutions and Practices Convention of 1926 (Slavery Convention; OHCHR 1926) signed at Geneva on September 25. The Slavery Convention established a basis by which states could measure slavery within their borders, defining slavery as "the status or condition of a person over whom any or all the powers attaching to the right of ownership are exercised" and the slave trade to include "all acts involved in the capture, acquisition or disposal of a person with intent to reduce him to slavery." Entering into force the year after its signing, the Slavery Convention required on paper that all signatory states enact and enforce laws against slavery, forced labor, and the slave trade in their territories, intercept slave traffic in their territorial waters and on ships flying their flag, and assist other states in antislavery efforts. In 1930, the ILO adopted the Convention Concerning Forced or Compulsory Labour requiring signatories to take effective measures to prevent and eliminate the use of forced labor. In 1948, three years after the UN was established as the successor of the League of Nations, the UN General Assembly adopted the Universal Declaration of Human Rights, identifying fundamental rights that ought to be universally protected. Article 4 of the Declaration states that "no one shall be held in slavery or servitude; slavery and the slave trade shall be prohibited in all their forms."

In spite of these self-imposed international mandates, an agency for effectively monitoring and responding to instances of modern slavery did not exist, and there were still no written laws or protocols clearly defining the various manifestations of slavery. While chattel slavery obviously fell under the definition, the language of previous conventions left the nature of servitude and other slave-like practices under debate. In 1956, the Supplementary Convention on the Abolition of Slavery, Slave Trade and Institutions and Practices Similar to Slavery represented an effort to better acknowledge the complex nature of contemporary slavery. This convention expanded the definition of slavery and updated the 1926 Slavery Convention to criminalize practices involving debt bondage, the sale of wives, serfdom, and child servitude. Like its predecessors, however, the 1956 Convention provided no international monitoring body or enforcement mechanism, nor did it establish any meaningful obligations for countries to report abuses. In an effort to respond to the lack of credible information and reporting mechanisms, the UN Working Group on Contemporary Forms of Slavery was formed in 1974 with the task of monitoring the existence of slavery, collecting information from state parties, and making recommendations on slavery and slavery-like practices around the world.

These initial international efforts were important means of defining and drawing attention to modern manifestations of slavery, but their impact was minimal due to lack of enforcement. Furthermore, Suzanne Miers (2003) points out that in reality moralizing pronouncements accompanied by promises to combat slavery at the UN were often forgotten when they interfered with the political and economic interests of the ruling elites in individual countries. This was compounded by the actuality that during the latter half of the twentieth century, little scholarship was conducted on the nature and extent of modern slavery, and pressure on governments to act was nominal. World-renowned antislavery scholar Kevin Bales points out, for example, that when he first began to seek funding to conduct research on modern slavery in the early 1990s, few foundations recognized the need for such research because of the predominantly held belief that "slavery ended long ago" (Bales 2007, 5). In the late 1990s and early years of the twenty-first century, however, the emergence of a generation of young activist, journalists, and scholars and growing public outrage, resulting from growing awareness of international human trafficking, contributed to an explosion of interest in and work on modern slavery and led to significant national and international legislative action. Bales himself drew international attention when he published the first edition of *Disposable People* in 1999 in which he provided evidence that at least 27 million slaves existed worldwide.

At the outset of the twenty-first century, the United States took the lead in the fight to end modern slavery. In 2000, Congress launched major U.S. anti-trafficking efforts with its passage of the Victims of Trafficking and Violence Protection Act, today known as the Trafficking Victims Protection Act (TVPA). The law, which has been reauthorized and expanded several times, most recently in January 2019, created the Office to Monitor and Combat Trafficking in Persons within the State Department. The office is charged with investigating and creating programs to combat human trafficking domestically and internationally. Each year, the office releases the Trafficking in Persons (TIP) Report, which ranks countries according to their compliance with minimum standards for eliminating trafficking in persons.

Shortly after Congress passed the TVPA, the UN approved the Protocol to Prevent, Suppress and Punish Trafficking in Persons, Especially Women and Children (commonly referred to as the Palermo Protocol or UN Trafficking Protocol) as part of the Convention against Transnational Organized Crime in November 2000. Signed by 117 countries, the protocol became the first legally binding global agreement with an internationally agreed-upon definition of trafficking in persons that establishes international guidelines for investigating and prosecuting traffickers and protecting and aiding victims.

In 2003, President George W. Bush made history in a speech delivered before the UN, by becoming the first world leader to call on the General Assembly to fight modern slavery and by pledging $50 million to the cause. Nevertheless, Bush's speech focused almost exclusively on sex trafficking as opposed to other more prevalent forms of modern slavery. E. Benjamin Skinner (2009) points out that the speech, and U.S. trafficking policy generally, "reflected the loudly articulated opinion of a small but powerful coalition of academic feminists and religious, predominantly evangelical conservatives" who had first shared common cause a decade earlier in the war on pornography and who had together pushed for passage of the TVPA (36). This coalition largely set the international tone, and for the first few years of the twenty-first century, counter-trafficking campaigns were almost entirely focused on the issue of modern slavery within the sex industry. Not until Bush's second term were U.S. counter-trafficking efforts broadened to include a focus on all forms of bondage.

The first two decades of the twenty-first century have been marked by continued growth of international and national legislation, by a dramatic upswing in research and reporting on contemporary slavery, and by a significant expansion of the scope and nature of antislavery NGO activity. On September 25, 2015, the UN General Assembly officially adopted 17 Sustainable Development Goals (SDGs) intended to be achieved by 2030 to guide their global development efforts and policies. Target 8.7 of the SDGs called on all governments to "take immediate and effective measures to eradicate forced labor, end modern slavery and human trafficking and secure the prohibition and elimination of the worst forms of child labor, including recruitment and use of child soldiers, and by 2025 to end child labor in all its forms." In spite of dozens of universal conventions, hundreds of international treaties and national laws, and numerous NGO and intergovernmental campaigns against modern slavery, in many places the political will and ability to enforce change has remained weak. A report released by the UN Office of Drugs and Crime (UNODC) in 2009, for instance, found that a majority of the 155 countries studied had never registered a single trafficking conviction

(Skinner 2009). In 2019, the Walk Free Foundation published its *Measurement Action Freedom* report providing an independent assessment of whether meaningful action has been taken to achieve Target 8.7 of the UN SDGs. The report identified encouraging examples of governmental action that have led to increased prosecutions and victim support services, but overall the report found that global progress in tackling modern slavery has been disappointing. According to the report:

> 47 countries globally still do not recognize human trafficking as a crime in line with international standards; nearly 100 countries fail to criminalize forced labor or, if they do, the penalty for exploitation amounts to nothing more than a fine; and less than one-third of countries protect women and girls from the exploitation inherent in forced marriage.

The report concludes that if progress is to be made in eradicating modern slavery, governments will need to redouble efforts to identify victims, arrest perpetrators, and address the driving factors. Thus, although the last decade has witnessed a dramatic increase in awareness of the problem of modern slavery and an upward trend in the number of victims identified and traffickers convicted, the evolving global scourge of modern slavery continues to pose a major obstacle in the promotion and protection of basic human rights.

Where Does Slavery Exist, and Who Is Affected?

Geographic Contexts

Contemporary slavery exists in some form in every country across the globe, but there are particular regional contexts in which it is more widespread with regard to its prevalence and absolute number of victims. Modern slavery is most prevalent in Africa, where available data suggests that there are approximately 7.6 victims for every thousand people, followed by

Asia and the Pacific (6.1 per 1,000), Europe and Central Asia (3.9 per 1,000), the Arab States (3.3 per 1,000), and the Americas (1.9 per 1,000). (Unless otherwise cited, all the figures provided in this section are based on data compiled by the ILO and Walk Free Foundation in the *2017 Global Estimates of Modern Slavery*.) The ILO and Walk Free Foundation (2017) report, however, that because of critical gaps and limitations in the gathering of data, the numbers presented may actually underestimate the extent of modern slavery in the Arab States and Latin America and overestimate its prevalence in Europe.

In terms of raw numbers, Asia and the Pacific are home to more than 60 percent of the total victims of modern slavery worldwide, followed by Africa (23 percent), Europe and Central Asia (9 percent), the Americas (5 percent), and the Arab states (1 percent). The Asia Pacific region is home to the highest share of victims of all forms of modern slavery, and most of the world's slaves live and work in India, Nepal, Pakistan, and Bangladesh in a form of bonded labor (Skinner 2008).

According to the 2018 Global Slavery Index published by the Walk Free Foundation, the top 10 countries with the highest prevalence of modern slavery are North Korea, Eritrea, Burundi, the Central African Republic, Afghanistan, Mauritania, South Sudan, Pakistan, Cambodia, and Iran. This list indicates a strong connection between modern slavery and highly repressive regimes and conflict. The index cautions, however, that improvements in data collection and methodology suggest that the prevalence of modern slavery in highly developed, high-income countries is higher than previously understood. Nevertheless, the governments in countries such as the Netherlands, the United Kingdom, and the United States are among those taking the most action to respond to the scourge of modern slavery. On the other hand, countries including Qatar, Singapore, Saudi Arabia, and the United Arab Emirates have taken limited action despite possessing high levels of resources.

Gender

Women and adolescent girls make up 71 percent of all modern slavery. While women and girls are at much greater risk of being enslaved overall, modern slavery is prolific across genders, and the demographics vary to some degree based on location, context, and form. Females make up a disproportionately large percentage of those trapped in forced labor in the private economy, which includes domestic work, forced marriage, and the sex industry. Women and girls account for about 61 percent of those ensnared in domestic servitude and about 84 percent of the world's victims of forced marriage. Current figures suggest that women and adolescent girls represent upward of 99 percent of victims of forced sexual exploitation. This figure, however, leads to the common misperception that sex traffickers only target females. As a result, male victims often go unnoticed, and governments frequently arrest and prosecute male trafficking victims for engaging in illicit sexual activities, instead of offering them support of protective services (U.S. Department of State 2019). Nevertheless, men and boys are also at high risk for sex trafficking and exploitation. Several organizations and government entities have contended that official figures tend to grossly underestimate the number of male victims (Swarens 2018).

Males are also disproportionately victims of state-imposed forced labor and forced labor in sectors of the private economy that traditionally involve manual labor. Men make up nearly 60 percent of victims of state-imposed forced labor, 100 percent of victims in mining and quarrying, 90 percent of victims forced to beg, 82 percent of victims in construction and manufacturing, and 68 percent of those in commercial agriculture and fishing.

Contributing Factors

As stated previously, slavery is illegal everywhere, but in reality, public corruption, incompetence, repressive government, conflict, political instability, discriminatory cultural practices, and social hierarchies often prevent the application of the law in the lives of the world's most vulnerable, making them further susceptible to exploitation. Slavery predominantly thrives in neighborhoods, countries, and regions with oppressive, arbitrary, or nonexistent systems of law and order. But even in countries with tough legal framework and functioning judicial systems—such as the United States, the United Kingdom, and Germany—victims can easily slip through the cracks because of social isolation, gaps in the law, inadequate resources to detect and protect the vulnerable, or poorly written laws, such as those that inadvertently punish victims of illicit sexual exploitation rather than their traffickers. Furthermore, those who live under the protection of the law to some extent facilitate exploitation by providing a market for goods produced by forced labor in countries where the rule of law and human rights are openly flouted.

Incompetent and Corrupt Systems of Public Justice

Public corruption and incompetence are chief contributors to the persistence of modern slavery. In an exposé of the chronic violence and oppression that plague the everyday lives of most of the world's poor, International Justice Mission CEO Gary Haugen and federal prosecutor Victor Boutros (2014) contend that while "the developing world is full of struggling systems—food systems, health systems, education systems, sanitation systems, water systems, etc.—the most fundamental *and the most broken* system is the public justice system." "It is the most fundamental," they argue, "because it provides the platform of stability and safety upon which every other system depends" (128). Sadly, however, as the Commission on Legal Empowerment of the Poor (2008) has revealed, "Most poor people do not live under the shelter of the law, but far from the law's protection and the opportunities it affords . . . and where they are not excluded from the legal system, they are often oppressed by it" (2). This is particularly true of victims of modern slavery.

The eradication of modern slavery depends first and foremost on the ability of victims to seek protection and redress through the investigation, prosecution, punishment, and restraint of perpetrators—but gross incompetence and rampant corruption in public justice systems throughout much of the developing world enable exploiters to operate with impunity. Haugen and Boutros (2014) point out that a large percentage of police forces deployed in rural villages, slums, and poverty-stricken city neighborhoods throughout the developing world have virtually no specialized training, are substantially undermanned, and lack the most rudimentary supplies, including means of transportation, phones, computers for keeping records, or forms and paper for filing criminal complaints. To the extent that well-trained, well-equipped forces do exist, they are generally deployed to protect the politically connected and elite or to participate in international law enforcement programs aimed at combating terrorism or narcotics and weapons trafficking. The lack of training, personnel, and equipment in poor communities contributes to the failure to gather or properly process evidence, the misapplication of the law, falsified reports, the inability to apprehend or retain suspects, and so on. Furthermore, because police in vulnerable areas often face political pressure to show reduced crime rates, they may attempt to make it look like there is less crime by ignoring crime reports altogether. In India, for example, special laws have been enacted to protect the Dalits or "untouchables," but local NGOs report that the police frequently refuse to register complaints or investigate crimes committed against them (Human Rights Watch 2009).

Another major problem hindering basic enforcement of laws against modern slavery is the prevailing culture of corruption that dominates police forces throughout the developing world. The efforts of numerous underpaid and overworked officers—who nevertheless work with courage and integrity to protect the vulnerable—should not be dismissed, yet extortion and bribery are typically expected norms for interactions with the police. Traffickers are able to pay off immigration officers, police, courts, and other public sector officials, in exchange for them turning a blind eye to instances of lawlessness, exploitation, and abuse. In places where impunity can easily be "bought," the profits of exploitation far outweigh the risks, and many traffickers take few efforts to conceal their crimes. What's worse, the police themselves often perpetuate exploitation. Siddharth Kara (2017) has highlighted the testimony of multiple victims explaining that when they do attempt to seek justice, police frequently rape or arrest them and return them to their slave owners. Even worse, police sometimes use the shroud of "law enforcement" to operate their own trafficking operations. In the rare instances when law enforcement officials do crack down on human trafficking—such as in the recent arrest of hundreds of traffickers in refugee camps along the Bangladesh border—securing a conviction is highly unlikely (Uttom and Rozario 2019). The massive caseloads that exist in regions with high levels of exploitation and violence are often compounded by a shortage of prosecutors, dysfunctional courts, and a lack of any kind of witness protection programs. Securing a judgment is consequently dangerous and financially and psychologically taxing and often takes years.

Repressive Government

Worldwide there is a strong correlation between elevated rates of modern slavery and highly repressive systems. As discussed in the previous overview of state-sponsored slavery in North Korea, slavery can be used to generate revenue for a repressive government or as a means of maintaining political control and stifling dissent. It is also frequently used as a method to control or eliminate ethnic or religious minorities. Forced labor has long been a tool of the Burmese military to suppress the indigenous Rohingya Muslims, and over the past few years, evidence has emerged showing that state-imposed forced labor has become an integral part of China's efforts to "reeducate" the largely Muslim minorities in its western Xinjiang region.

Since 2017, Chinese officials have imprisoned more than 1 million Uighurs, Kazakhs, Kyrgyz, and other religious and ethnic minorities in internment camps, where they are forced to undergo political indoctrination and engage in Chinese language study as part of a campaign to eliminate their culture and religion and make them loyal to the Communist Party (Zenz 2018). Many of these individuals are forced to labor on-site or in adjacent factories producing garments, carpets, cleaning supplies, and other goods for domestic and international distribution (U.S. Department of State 2019). Chinese companies, attracted by government subsidies and the cheap labor supply from internment camp networks, have been increasingly setting up production in Xinjiang. While most of the goods produced by forced labor in the region end up in domestic and Central Asian markets, clothes and other textile goods have been bought and sold by major apparel brands in the United States, Europe, and Japan (Buckley and Ramzy 2018; Mistreanu 2019).

Under some repressive regimes, forced marriage is used to grow the citizenry and the workforce. In Cambodia, under the Khmer Rouge, for example, several hundred thousand men and women were forced to marry strangers chosen by the regime. Couples who refused to consummate their marriage would be executed (Carmichael 2011). Some scholars have suggested that in addition to increasing the population, the practice was implemented to strengthen the regime's totalitarian control by weakening the bonds of family, community, and religion (Giry 2016). Complaints of a similar practice have come out of Burma (Myanmar), where Refugees International has reported soldiers using rape to impregnate women so they will bear "Burman" babies as part of the overall "Burmanization" campaign aimed at stamping out the heritage and identity of ethnic minority groups (Paterson 2013). In China, the state's one-child policy in combination with Chinese parents' general preference for sons has contributed to an unprecedented gender imbalance, which has created a huge market for trafficked girls from the border regions of surrounding countries. These girls, usually aged 13 to 16, are lured to China with false promises of economic opportunity and education only to be sold to Chinese men for sex and child bearing. After these girls have stayed with a man for three years and delivered a child, they may be sold to other men for the same purpose (McQuade 2018).

War and Conflict

The instability and breakdown of law and order produced by war and violent conflict places already vulnerable communities at much higher risk of exploitation and forced labor. Organized criminal syndicates take advantage of the lawlessness caused by the collapse of state institutions, and members of military or fighting groups use slavery as a means of controlling and suppressing local populations, annihilating opposition, financing war operations, and providing labor for fighting efforts or sexual services for soldiers. Rampant slavery has been one of the most enduring consequences of decades of ethnic and political conflict and civil war in places such as the Congo and Sudan, and over the past decade, it has provided a significant source of labor as well as a recruitment draw for Islamist terrorist groups such as Boko Haram and the Islamist State (Tyler 2017). Since Boko Haram began its insurgency in 2009, its militants have abducted thousands of girls and women in northeast Nigeria to be used as cooks, sex slaves, and suicide bombers. Leaders parcel out captured women to reward foot soldiers for their support and to attract new recruits. Similarly, the Islamic State, after capturing large areas of territory in Iraq and Syria, displaced and executed hundreds of thousands of ethnoreligious minorities, including Yazidi, Christians, and Kurds—while subjecting tens of thousands of women and girls to sexual slavery. Kidnappings and abductions have additionally generated upward of $30 million in ransom payments to the group (Tyler 2017).

Notably disconcerting is the fact that peacekeeping forces sent to provide international assistance and stabilize and rebuild regions torn apart by conflict frequently contribute to the problem of human trafficking. In 1999, Kathryn Bolknovac, an American contractor working for a company contracted to conduct police work during the Bosnia peacekeeping mission, won a wrongful termination lawsuit after being fired for exposing UN personnel involved in sex trafficking rings outside the gates of UN compounds. Since then, studies have demonstrated that peacekeeping forces, including military and civilian contractors, increase the demand for sex workers and that UN peacekeepers' presence specifically contributes to greater trafficking flows into a country (Bell et al. 2018). Over the past several years, the Associated Press has uncovered more than 150 allegations of abuse and exploitation by UN peacekeepers and other personnel in Haiti alone, and more than 2,000 cases worldwide (Dodds 2017).

Poverty and Discriminatory Social Hierarchies

Impoverished communities lacking basic necessities and opportunities for education, property ownership, and upward mobility are prime targets for exploitation. When individuals are unable to feed, clothe, educate, or provide for their family and have little chance of improving their economic situation through work, education, entrepreneurship, and so forth, they become more vulnerable to human predators and are easily lured by sham job offers, marriages, and other promises of opportunity. They also tend to lack the means or understanding to advocate effectively for themselves in work and contract negotiations. Consequently, they are prime targets for debt bondage and other forms of exploitive or forced labor. The economically destitute former Soviet Republic of Moldova, for instance, is a hotbed for human trafficking and a major source of sex slaves for Europe, Russia, and the Middle East (Ferrell 2016; Quinn 2014). During the era of the Union of Soviet Socialist Republics (USSR), human trafficking occurred on a massive scale at the hands of the state. Over 200,000 Moldovans were deported to labor camps in Siberia or to serve as prostitutes in Russia. Following the social and economic collapse of the USSR, human trafficking became an increasingly profitable enterprise and moved into the hands of organized criminal syndicates aided by corrupt government officials, police, border guards, and judges. With lives plagued by violence, poverty, and few domestic opportunities, Moldovans are desperate to leave their country and are uniquely susceptible to traffickers who make false promises of opportunity and prosperity elsewhere.

In many places around the globe, extreme poverty is compounded by cultural practices and discriminatory social hierarchies that work to increase the likelihood of exploitation. Individuals from indigenous and marginalized groups that experience social, political, and legal disenfranchisement are much more likely to be victims of modern slavery. Hereditary slavery continues to thrive in Mauritania where the country's history and very structure of society reinforces it (U.S. Department of State 2018). In the eighth century, Muslim Arabs conquered western North Africa and colonized the areas inhabited by black Africans and Berber nomads. After several failed uprisings, the Berbers decided to Arabize and adopt Islam. Most black tribes were forced into the more arid south and did not accept Islam until nearly a thousand years after the Arab conquest. All blacks who remained in the northern territories were forced into slavery. Over the centuries, a class system has developed in which the lighter-skinned Arabs (the Beydanes) and Arabized Berbers rule over former slaves who have been Arabized (the Haratin) and the black chattel slave class (Abid). Though Mauritania is now nearly completely Muslim, and though Islam in theory forbids Muslims from enslaving fellow Muslims, the severity of Arab racism and the entrenched class system transcends adherence to Islamic law (the Sharia).

Throughout South Asia, but particularly in India and Nepal, forced and bonded labors are interlinked with widespread caste-based discrimination. The more than 3,000 years old caste system divides Hindus into rigid hierarchical social classes based on their karma (work) and dharma (duty). Hindus are considered born into their caste and may not move up in social hierarchy without dying and going through the process of reincarnation. The Dalits, or "untouchables," who make up the bottom class of the Hindu caste system, and the tribal communities, who live completely outside of the caste system, have been socially and legally marginalized and discriminated against for decades. Limited access to justice, education, property rights, jobs, and other resources makes it virtually impossible for members of these groups to climb out of extreme poverty or acquire assets of any kind. Consequently, they frequently find themselves victims of forced or bonded labor from which they and their children cannot escape. Although both India and Nepal legally abolished their caste and bonded labor systems decades ago, legislation is poorly implemented, and social stratification remains severe and pervasive.

Migration

The unstable political, social, and economic conditions that cause slavery to flourish in particular areas also contribute to high levels of migration, as individuals seek safety, freedom, and social and economic opportunity elsewhere. Migration, which can occur from rural to urban areas within a country or across national borders, places individuals at unique risk for trafficking and enslavement.

Migrants, particularly those entering into a country illegally, are often disconnected from their family and any kind of legal or social support structure. This places them at a much higher risk of being detained and exploited by traffickers. This is especially true in regions serving as major transit hubs where the state and society are either unwilling or lack the capacity to protect them. Recently, the International Organization for Migration reported rampant slave market conditions endangering migrants in North Africa (IOM 2017). Abuse is particularly rife in Algeria and Libya, which are gateway countries for migrants traveling from sub-Saharan Africa to Europe. Tens of thousands of migrants from Nigeria, Burkina Faso, Egypt, Eritrea, Niger, Sudan, and elsewhere have been captured and subjected to torture and enslavement before reaching the Mediterranean.

Even when they are able to arrive safely at their intended destination, migrants may be at high risk due to social isolation, inability to speak the language, and a lack of resources. This is the case whether they have legal documentation or not. A 2014 study by the Urban Institute found that victims in agricultural work are less likely to have lawful immigration status upon entering the United States, but a majority of victims of forced labor across all sectors enter the United States on a lawful temporary visa (Owens et al. 2014).

Migrant workers are also highly vulnerable to discrimination, which puts them at greater risk for exploitation. Over the past decade, Qatar has come under particular fire for discrimination against and enslavement of migrant workers commissioned to help construct stadiums in preparation for the 2022 World Cup (Liew 2017). In advance of this global event, the Gulf monarchy experienced an influx of non-Muslim migrant workers—mainly from India, Nepal, Sri Lanka, and the Philippines—resulting in a population that is 90 percent non-Qatari. Growing fear of foreign influence has contributed to an increase of systematic and overt racial discrimination, which was already a vestige of Qatar's recent history of legal slavery. In an effort to protect the religious and cultural identity of the massively outnumbered local population, Qatar has implemented de facto systems of segregation and has opposed any form of organized labor. Consequently, tens of thousands of migrants who find themselves brutally oppressed in debt bondage and other slave-like conditions have little to no opportunity for recourse.

Social Isolation and Homelessness

While corruption, repressive government, conflict, political instability, cultural and legal stratification, multigenerational poverty, and migration greatly increase individuals' vulnerability, many victims of modern slavery are legal citizens of stable, high-GDP countries with low levels of corruption. A large percentage of victims in the United States, for example, are American citizens, foreign and natural born, who are recruited at homeless shelters, rehab facilities, jails, malls, and alternative high schools, online, and in foster or group homes (Withers 2017). These victims' susceptibility to trafficking often stems from the fact that they have become socially isolated for a variety of reasons.

Often having a history of abuse and lacking strong familial and social support networks, children in foster care are disproportionately victimized by human trafficking. Statistics vary by report, state, and city, but overwhelming evidence suggests that a large majority of all child sex trafficking victims nationwide have a history in the child welfare system (Lillie 2016). Traffickers sometimes recruit foster youth directly from group homes with false promises of money and a family structure, but most often homelessness is the primary factor in their susceptibility to trafficking. Foster youth who have runaway or aged out of the system and find themselves living on the streets are prime targets because they lack access to shelter, food, and personal connections and can be easily ensnared in forced labor or the commercial sex industry in exchange for basic necessities. A 2015 survey conducted by the National Network for Youth found that door-to-door trafficking sales rings had lured runaway and homeless youth by promising them housing, employment, and food. Recruited youth instead found themselves living in overcrowded motel rooms with other labor-trafficked youth, receiving little or no pay, and given unreasonable sales quotas (Walts 2017).

Global Supply Chains

Many trapped in forced labor today—whether in carpet factories, farms, brick kilns, mines, fishing boats, textile mills, and so on—are enslaved by governments, businesses, and individuals seeking to maximize profits by minimizing the cost of labor.

In today's global economy, customers unwittingly create perverse incentives for those at the bottom of the supply chain to exploit workers through their increasing demand for cheap goods. According to Katharine Bryant, the manager of global research for the Walk Free Foundation, some 16 million victims of slavery work within poorly monitored supply chains (Merelli 2019). While certain industries, including fashion, agriculture, and tech, are marred by the use of forced labor, most countries do not have laws in place that prevent businesses from buying products that may have relied on slave labor somewhere along the line of production. Even the ones that do have laws typically fail to enforce them effectively (Merelli 2019).

Unfortunately, the global circulation of goods and complexity in the supply chain sometimes makes it difficult to trace a product back to its source and determine whether or not it has been produced using slavery. Typically, final products pass through a long chain of producers, manufacturers, distributors, and retailers who have all participated in its production, delivery, and sale to the consumer. Take cobalt, for instance. The market for cobalt has exploded in recent years because it is a critical component of rechargeable lithium-ion batteries used in electric vehicles, mobile phones, and laptop computers. Most of the world's cobalt is extracted in artisanal mines in the Democratic Republic of Congo (DRC), commonly by means of child or other form of exploited labor (Felter 2018). It is then traded and sent abroad, often to China, for refinement before heading to Asian component producers and electronic manufacturers for assembly. The final products are then sold in the United States, Europe, and across Asia, making it easy to overlook the slavery involved in their origins.

Conclusion

Although slavery has been outlawed in every country and is frequently spoken about as a relic of the past, it has metastasized into a variety of forms and remains pandemic across the globe. Today, slavery thrives in war-torn, corrupt, and repressive regimes, but it also exists in wealthy countries with strong systems of the rule of law. Modern slavery remains a vicious assault on the value, dignity, and humanity of its victims. Regrettably, however, decades of antislavery activism, dozens of universal conventions, and hundreds of laws and treaties have done little to slow its reach and growth. As one author laments, "Words condemning slavery are far more common than vigorous steps eliminating it" (Welch Jr. 2009, 77). In a large percentage of cases, traffickers continue to operate with impunity, and victims face insurmountable barriers to protection and redress. If further progress is to be made, efforts to identify and rehabilitate victims, arrest and prosecute perpetrators, and address the driving factors must expand and increase.

References

Bales, Kevin. 2005. *Understanding Global Slavery: A Reader.* Berkeley, CA: University of California Press.

Bales, Kevin. 2007. *Ending Slavery: How We Free Today's Slaves.* Berkeley, CA: University of California Press.

Bales, Kevin. 2012. *Disposable People: New Slavery in the Global Economy.* 3rd edition. Berkeley, CA: University of California Press.

Bales, Kevin, and Ron Soodalter. 2009. *The Slave Next Door: Human Trafficking and Slavery in America Today.* 2nd edition. Berkeley, CA: University of California Press.

Batstone, David. 2010. *Not for Sale: The Return of the Global Slave Trade—And How We Can Fight It.* Revised and Updated Edition. New York: HarperCollins.

Bell, Sam R., Michael E. Flynn, and Carla Martinez Machain. 2018. "U.N. Peacekeeping Forces and the Demand for Sex Trafficking." *International Studies Quarterly* 62: 643–655.

Buckley, Chris, and Austin Ramzy. 2018. "China's Detention Camps for Muslims Turn to Forced Labor." *New York Times*. December 16. Accessed January 3, 2020. https://www.nytimes.com/2018/12/16/world/asia/xinjiang-china-forced-labor-camps-uighurs.html

Carmichael, Robert. 2011. "Cambodia Coming to Terms with Thousands of Forced Marriages under Pol Pot." *Deutsche Welle*. June 13. Accessed January 2, 2020. https://www.dw.com/en/cambodia-coming-to-terms-with-thousands-of-forced-marriages-under-pol-pot/a-6547301

Cohen, Lisa. 2019. "Thousands of Boys Forced to Beg by Religious Schools in Senegal." *CNN Freedom Project*. November. Accessed December 15, 2019. https://www.cnn.com/2019/11/08/africa/forced-child-begging-senegal-intl/index.html

Commission on the Legal Empowerment of the Poor. 2008. *Making the Law Work for Everyone: Report of the Commission on Legal Empowerment of the Poor*. Vol. 1. New York: United Nations Development Programme (UNDP). Accessed January 2, 2020. https://www.un.org/ruleoflaw/files/Making_the_Law_Work_for_Everyone.pdf

Counter-Trafficking Data Collaborative (CTDC). n.d. "Family Members Are Involved in Nearly Half of Child Trafficking Cases." Accessed December 1, 2019. https://www.iom.int/sites/default/files/our_work/DMM/MAD/Counter-trafficking%20Data%20Brief%2008081217.pdf

Dodds, Paisley. 2017. "UN Child Sex Ring Left Victims But No Arrests." Associated Press. April 12. Accessed January 10, 2020. https://apnews.com/e6ebc331460345c5abd4f57d77f535c1/AP-Exclusive:-UN-child-sex-ring-left-victims-but-no-arrests

Elbagir, Nima, Raja Razek, Alex Platt, and Bryony Jones. 2017. "People for Sale." *CNN*. November 14. Accessed October 15, 2019. https://www.cnn.com/2017/11/14/africa/libya-migrant-auctions/index.html

Felter, Claire. 2018. "The Cobalt Boom." *Council on Foreign Relations.* June 15. Accessed January 23, 2020. https://www.cfr.org/backgrounder/cobalt-boom

Ferrell, Kelsey Hoie. 2016. "History of Sex Trafficking in Moldova." *End Slavery Now.* Accessed January 16, 2020. https://www.endslaverynow.org/blog/articles/history-of-sex-trafficking-in-moldova

Frank, Michael J., and G. Zachary Terwilliger. 2015. "Gang-Controlled Sex Trafficking." *Virginia Journal of Criminal Law* 3: 342–352.

Ghafour, Hamida. 2013. "Syria's Refugee Brides: My Daughter Is Willing to Sacrifice Herself for Her Family." *The Star.* Accessed December 16, 2019. https://www.thestar.com/news/world/2013/03/22/young_brides_displaced_by_syria_conflict_sought_by_older_grooms.html

Giry, Stéphanie. 2016. "Married Off by the Khmer Rouge, and 'Nobody Could Help Me.'" *New York Times.* September 10. Accessed January 2, 2020. https://www.nytimes.com/2016/09/11/world/asia/married-off-by-the-khmer-rouge-and-nobody-could-help-me.html

Haugen, Gary A., and Victor Boutros. 2014. *The Locust Effect: Why the End of Poverty Requires the End of Violence.* New York: Oxford University Press.

Hawke, Angela, and Alison Raphael. 2016. "Offenders on the Move: Global Study on Sexual Exploitation of Children in Travel and Tourism." *ECPAT International and Defense for Children-ECPAT Netherlands.* May. Accessed December 20, 2019. https://www.ecpat.org/wp-content/uploads/2016/05/Offenders-on-the-Move-Final.pdf

Human Rights Watch. 2009. "Broken System: Dysfunction, Abuse, and Impunity in the Indian Police." Accessed January 2, 2020. https://www.hrw.org/report/2009/08/04/broken-system/dysfunction-abuse-and-impunity-indian-police

Hume, Tim, Lisa Cohen, and Mira Sorvino. 2013. "The Women Who Sold Their Daughters into Sex Slavery." *CNN Freedom Project*. December. Accessed December 1, 2019. https://www.cnn.com/interactive/2013/12/world /cambodia-child-sex-trade/

International Labour Organization (ILO). 1930. "Forced Labour Convention, 1930 (No. 29)." Accessed December 15, 2019. https://www.ilo.org/dyn/normlex/en/f?p=NOR MLEXPUB:12100:0::NO::P12100_ILO_CODE:C029

International Labour Organization (ILO). 1957. "Abolition of Forced Labour Convention, 1957 (No. 105)." Accessed December 15, 2019. https://www.ilo.org /dyn/normlex/en/f?p=NORMLEXPUB:12100:0::NO ::P12100_ILO_CODE:C105

International Labour Organization (ILO) and Walk Free Foundation. 2017. "Global Estimates of Modern Slavery: Forced Labour and Forced Marriage." Geneva. Accessed November 15, 2019. https://www.ilo.org/global /publications/books/WCMS_575479/lang--en/index.htm

International Organization for Migration (IOM). 2017. "IOM Learns of 'Slave Market' Conditions Endangering Migrants in North Africa." April 11. Accessed March 23, 2020. https://www.iom.int/news/iom-learns-slave-market -conditions-endangering-migrants-north-africa

Issara Institute and International Justice Mission. 2017. "Not in the Same Boat: Prevalence & Patterns of Labour Abuse Across Thailand's Diverse Fishing Industry." January. Accessed March 23, 2020. http://www.respect .international/not-in-the-same-boat-prevalence-patterns-of -labor-abuse-across-thailands-diverse-fishing-industry/

Kara, Siddharth. 2017. *Sex Trafficking: Inside the Business of Modern Slavery.* New York: Columbia University Press.

Liew, Jonathan. 2017. "World Cup 2022: Qatar's Workers Are Not Workers, They Are Slaves, and They Are Building

Mausoleums, Not Stadiums." *The Independent.* October 3. Accessed January 16, 2020. https://www.independent .co.uk/sport/football/international/world-cup-2022-qatars -workers-slaves-building-mausoleums-stadiums-modern -slavery-kafala-a7980816.html

Lillie, Michelle. 2016. "An Unholy Alliance: The Connection between Foster Care and Human Trafficking." *Human Trafficking Search.* Accessed January 20, 2020. https:// humantraffickingsearch.org/wp-content/uploads/2017/09 /Copy-of-An-Unholy-Alliance_The-Connection-Between -Foster-Care-and-Human-Trafficking.pdf

McQuade, Aidan. 2018. "How China's One-Child Policy Led to Forced Marriages in Myanmar." *Thomson Reuters Foundation.* November 1. Accessed January 2, 2020. http:// news.trust.org/item/20181101123457-9f4h6/

Mendoza, Martha. 2018. "US Warns of North Korea's Global Outsourcing of Forced Labor." Associated Press. July 26. Accessed December 1, 2019. https://apnews.com/42f4b6e6 58964fcb83305e7cb19faa47

Merelli, Annalisa. 2019. "There Are 16 Million Slaves Around the World Making Our Stuff." *Quartz.* July 17. Accessed January 20, 2020. https://qz.com/1667463/the-global -business-supply-chain-employs-16-million-slaves/

Miers, Suzanne. 2003. *Slavery in the Twentieth Century: The Evolution of a Global Problem.* Lanham, MD: AltaMira Press.

Mistreanu, Simina. 2019. "Foreign Companies in China Forced to Reckon with Xinjiang Camps." *Forbes.* Accessed January 3, 2020. https://www.forbes.com/sites /siminamistreanu/2019/12/14/foreign-companies-in-china -forced-to-reckon-with-xinjiang-camps/#63a0f5003b51

Office of the United Nations High Commissioner for Human Rights (OHCHR). 1926. "Slavery Convention of 1926." Accessed November 1, 2019. https://www.ohchr.org/EN /ProfessionalInterest/Pages/SlaveryConvention.aspx

Owen, Colleen, Meredith Dank, Justin Breaux, Isela
Bañuelos, Amy Farrell, Rebecca Pfeffer, Katie
Bright, Ryan Heitsmith, and Jack McDevitt. 2014.
"Understanding the Organization, Operation, and
Victimization Process of Labor Trafficking in the
United States." *The Urban Institute.* October. Accessed
January 20, 2020. https://www.urban.org/sites/default
/files/publication/33821/413249-Understanding-the
-Organization-Operation-and-Victimization-Process-of
-Labor-Trafficking-in-the-United-States.PDF

Paterson, Kerry K. 2013. "Mali Conflict Is the Latest to
Employ Forced Marriage as a Tool of War." *Women's Media
Center.* June 4. Accessed December 15, 2019. https://
www.womensmediacenter.com/women-under-siege/mali
-conflict-is-latest-to-employ-forced-marriage-as-tool-of-war

Polaris. 2018. "Human Trafficking in Illicit Massage
Businesses." January. Accessed December 1,
2019. https://polarisproject.org/resources
/human-trafficking-in-illicit-massage-businesses/

Quinn, Allison. 2014. "Modern-Day Slave Trade Snares
Moldovans." *Kyiv Post.* May 1. Accessed January 17, 2020.
https://www.kyivpost.com/article/content/russia/modern
-day-slave-trade-snares-moldovans-345856.html

Sadulski, Jarrod. 2019. "Gang Involvement in Human
Trafficking in Central America." *In Public Safety.*
September 6. Accessed December 1, 2019. https://
inpublicsafety.com/2019/09/gang-involvement-in-human
-trafficking-in-central-america/

Skinner, E. Benjamin. 2008. *A Crime So Monstrous: Face-to-
Face with Modern-Day Slavery.* New York: Free Press.

Skinner, E. Benjamin. 2009. "The Fight to End Global
Slavery." *World Policy Journal* (Summer 2009). Accessed
December 1, 2019. https://www.brandeis.edu/investigate
/selectedwork/docs/skinner/skinner-final-wpj.pdf

Skrivankova, Klara. 2015. "Why You Could Be Wearing Cotton Picked by Forced Labor." *CNN Freedom Project.* October 2. Accessed December 15, 2019. https://www .cnn.com/2015/10/02/opinions/uzbekistan-turkmenistan -cotton/index.html

Sullivan, Tim. 2017. "NKorean Workers Prep Seafood Going to US Stores, Restaurants." Associated Press. October 4. Accessed December 1, 2019. https://apnews.com/8b493 b7df6e147e98d19f3abb5ca090a/NKorean-workers-prep -seafood-going-to-US-stores,-restaurants

Sutter, John D. 2012. "Slavery's Last Stronghold." *CNN.* March. Accessed November 1, 2019. https://www.cnn .com/interactive/2012/03/world/mauritania.slaverys.last .stronghold/index.html

Swarens, Tim. 2018. "Boys—The Silent Victims of Sex Trafficking." *USA Today.* February 18. Accessed December 1, 2019. https://www.usatoday .com/story/opinion/nation-now/2018/02/08 /boys-silent-victims-sex-trafficking/1073799001/

Taylor, Lin. 2017. "From Boko Haram to Islamic State, Sex Slavery and Trafficking Fund Extremism." *Reuters.* October 9. Accessed January 15, 2020. https://www.reuters.com /article/us-global-slavery-extremists/from-boko-haram-to -islamic-state-sex-slavery-and-trafficking-fund-extremism -report-idUSKBN1CE1I3

Unknown. 2005. "Still With Us." *The Economist.* March 9. Accessed December 1, 2019. https://www.economist.com /unknown/2005/03/09/still-with-us

U.S. Department of State. 2018. "Country Report on Human Rights Practices: Mauritania." Accessed January 16, 2020. https://www.state.gov/reports/2018-country -reports-on-human-rights-practices/mauritania/

U.S. Department of State. 2019. "Trafficking in Persons Report." June. Accessed August 1, 2019. https://www.state

.gov/wp-content/uploads/2019/06/2019-Trafficking-in
-Persons-Report.pdf

U.S. Department of State. n.d. "What Is Modern Slavery?"
Office to Monitor and Combat Trafficking in Persons.
Accessed December 15, 2019. https://www.state.gov
/what-is-modern-slavery/

Uttom, Stephan, and Rock Rozario. 2019. "Justice Fails
to Protect Bangladesh Trafficking Victims." *UCA News.*
March 22. Accessed January 2, 2020. https://www
.ucanews.org/news/justice-fails-to-protect-bangladesh
-trafficking-victims/84756

Vogelstein, Rachel B. 2018. "Human Trafficking in the 21st
Century." *Council on Foreign Relations (CFR).* January 22.
Accessed on December 20, 2019. https://www.cfr.org/blog
/human-trafficking-and-slavery-21st-century

Walk Free Foundation. 2018. "Global Slavery
Index." Accessed October 12, 2019. https://www
.globalslaveryindex.org/resources/downloads/

Walk Free Foundation. 2019. "Measurement Action Freedom:
An Independent Assessment of Government Progress
towards Achieving UN Sustainable Development Goal
8.7." Accessed December 15, 2019. https://reliefweb.int
/report/world/measurement-action-freedom-independent
-assessment-government-progress-towards-achieving

Walts, Katherine Kaufka. 2017. "Child Labor Trafficking in
the United States: A Hidden Crime." *Social Inclusion* 5,
no. 2: 59–68.

Welch, Claude E., Jr. 2009. "Defining Contemporary Forms
of Slavery: Updating a Venerable NGO." *Human Rights
Quarterly* 31, no.1: 70–128.

Withers, Melissa. 2017. "Untangling Myths about
Human Trafficking." *Psychology Today.* July 26. Accessed
January 18, 2020. https://www.psychologytoday

.com/us/blog/modern-day-slavery/201707
/untangling-myths-about-human-trafficking

Zenz, Adrian. 2018. "New Evidence for China's Political
Re-education Campaign in Xinjiang." *China Brief* 18,
no. 10. *The Jamestown Foundation.* Accessed January 3,
2020. https://jamestown.org/program/evidence-for-chinas
-political-re-education-campaign-in-xinjiang/

HUMAN TRAFFICKING IN AMERICA
MODERN DAY SLAVER
ORCED LABOR | SEX TRAFFICKING | DOMESTIC SERVITUD

T'S HAPPENING IN OUR COMMUNIT
GET INFORMED
DHS.GOV/BLUECAMPAIGN

BLUE CAMPAIG
One Voice. One Mission. End Human Traffic

Introduction

Over the past two decades, the world has witnessed enhanced efforts to combat modern slavery through the passage of international and national legislation, expanded research and reporting, and extensive antislavery NGO activity. Such efforts have contributed to a substantial increase in awareness of the problem and an upward trend in the number of victims identified and traffickers convicted. These numbers are, nevertheless, miniscule compared to the estimated number of individuals enslaved. Despite all the recent attention given to the issue, modern slavery remains a high-profit, low-risk crime and continues to flourish globally, nationally, and in our own local communities.

This chapter explores some of the major barriers to the eradication of modern slavery, identifies key controversies surrounding the issue, and surveys efforts to address the root causes, to bring perpetrators to justice, and to restore and empower survivors. It additionally highlights ways in which the United States can provide global leadership in the fight against modern slavery and the specific need for collaboration

---

A poster depicting the U.S. Department of Homeland Security's Blue Campaign. The Blue Campaign is a national public awareness campaign designed to educate the public, law enforcement, and other industry partners to recognize and appropriately respond to indicators of modern slavery. (Department of Homeland Security)

51

between individuals, nonprofits, and government entities at the local level.

Quantifying and Identifying Victims

Estimates by governments and NGOs of the prevalence of slavery and the exact number of victims have varied widely and continue to be a matter of ongoing debate. In 2017, the International Labour Office (ILO) and Walk Free Foundation, together with the International Organization for Migration (IOM), published the *Global Estimates of Modern Slavery*. According to the report, which is widely considered to include the best available data and information about the scale and regional distribution of slavery, 25 million people were victims of forced labor (including sex trafficking and private and government-imposed forced labor), and 15 million were victims of forced marriage in 2016. These estimates were based on a new methodology derived from multiple data sources, including survey research involving face-to-face interviews with more than 71,000 people in 53 local languages, probabilistic modeling, administrative data on victims collected by IOM and ILO supervisory bodies, and analytic review of secondary sources. The report acknowledged several methodical limitations in compiling the numbers, including a lack of data due to underreporting, particularly in conflict zones. Estimates of child soldiers, for instance, were not included even though the practice is globally recognized as a form of modern slavery, and available evidence suggests that the use of children in armed conflict by government forces and nonstate armed groups is prolific. Although data collection has improved over the years, some scholars still criticize the numbers promulgated by the ILO and Walk Free Foundation as inaccurate (Gallagher 2017; Mügge 2017). Unfortunately, the clandestine nature of modern slavery makes it almost impossible to acquire a complete accounting of the number of victims, and significant gaps and blind spots remain a barrier to accuracy even in the most authoritative estimates.

Barriers to Identification

Among the greatest obstacles to the collection of empirical data on modern slavery is the fact that victims almost universally come from vulnerable, socially excluded groups and tend not to self-identify. Victims commonly refuse to cooperate with authorities because they fear violence against themselves or their family members or deportation if they are in a country illegally. Some victims may even blame themselves for their situation. Others develop a harmful attachment to their exploiter, resulting from what is referred to as trauma bonding, a form of psychological manipulation that traffickers use to control and obtain obedience from their victims by making them believe they are completely dependent on them. As a result of such manipulation, individuals who have undergone horrific exploitation and physical abuse may still feel affection toward and an attachment to their trafficker (Young 2019). This lack of self-identification is compounded by the fact that those who directly encounter victims are not always equipped to identify them as such. Comprehensive training in victim identification for those likely to come in contact with victims of modern slavery—such as law enforcement officers, health care providers, child welfare officials, educators, labor inspectors, and others—is becoming more common in places such as the United States, but such training is still in need of improvement and is not yet widespread.

A variety of additional factors make identification of certain classes of victims even more precarious. Male victims, for example, are far more likely than women and girls to remain undetected (U.S. Department of State 2017). Authorities, such as immigration officers, labor inspectors, and police, regularly fail to recognize male victims due to a widespread tendency to view men as less vulnerable or to view women and girls as the sole victims of sex trafficking. Furthermore, cases involving male victims receive less media coverage, and feelings of shame and humiliation often make male victims more unlikely to report their own exploitation (Lillie 2014).

Victims working in illicit sectors, who are forced to beg, steal, sell drugs, prostitute themselves, and so on, are at times mistakenly identified as criminals rather than victims because of the crimes they are forced to commit. Nevertheless, they are easier to identify than victims of other forms of forced labor because they interact with a variety of clients on a daily basis and are more likely to capture the attention of law enforcement and service providers. Victims of forced labor in domestic settings or legitimate businesses, on the other hand, are typically isolated and have less personal interaction with outsiders. In contrast to sex trafficking, labor trafficking is usually carried out in formal economies and industries, which makes it difficult to distinguish between legitimate and forced workers. This is particularly true in cases of child labor trafficking. In a study on child labor trafficking in the United States, Katherine Walts (2017) points out, for example, that children who are forced to work as domestic servants, in factories, restaurants, farms, or peddling candy or other goods, are much less likely to attract the suspicion of outside observers than children who are providing sexual services for money. Furthermore, in comparison to the commercial sexual exploitation of minors, few efforts have been made to understand, quantify, and respond to labor trafficking of children.

Another issue that arises in compiling correct numbers is the degree to which victims have or have not been formally identified by relevant authorities. As previously noted, relying on victims to recognize or admit their own victim status is not always feasible, so the way victims are counted usually depends on whether they have been identified by third parties such as governments, law enforcement, service providers, and other NGOs and whether they have cooperated with authorities. The various degrees of victim identification and outcomes can be classified in a pyramid form (Aronowitz 2017). At the very bottom and the largest part of the pyramid are victims who remain completely unidentified because they have not come to the attention of service providers, hospitals, educators, police, and so on. The next level includes those who have not identified themselves as victims but who are "presumed" or "possible" victims because they have been identified by third-party service providers, such as NGOs, police, medical staff, social workers, and labor inspectors, as living in situations tantamount to exploitation and slavery. The third level consists of those who have been identified by service providers and admit that they are victims but refuse to cooperate with police investigations or refuse the services of shelters. The fourth level includes those who accept services and cooperate with police investigations but refuse to testify at trial. Finally, the smallest top portion of the pyramid is made up of victims who accept services and agree to testify against their traffickers and either remain in the country or are repatriated. Typically, NGOs are more inclined to classify as victims all those who have been identified in an exploitative situation, whereas law enforcement or prosecutors view victims as those who have been identified in a police investigation and have cooperated in a criminal prosecution. This is a major reason why nongovernmental and governmental agencies produce vastly different figures on the number of victims of modern slavery.

Identifying the Hidden Victims of Modern Slavery

Providing a clear evidence-driven picture of modern slavery and its victims is essential for the creation of a well-balanced and tailored response. Available evidence suggests that eradication efforts lag where less is known about the actual conditions and scale of slavery (U.S. Department of State 2019a). In the United States, for example, there have been an increasing number of promising bills and initiatives geared toward protecting youth trafficked for commercial sexual exploitation, but due to a dearth of research and measures to identify victims of child labor trafficking, the plight of such children has largely been ignored (Walts 2017). Effectively responding to all forms of modern slavery thus requires reliable estimates not only of victims who have been officially identified in different capacities but also of those who remain completely hidden from public view. To raise awareness of the many victims living in the shadows, a growing number of NGOs now offer training on victim identification to professionals and private individuals alike, and some states in the United States have begun to change their laws to require such training of law enforcement personnel and social service and health care providers.

In 2017, the Dutch National Rapporteur on Trafficking in Human Beings worked with the United Nations Office on Drugs and Crime (UNODC) to develop a Multiple Systems Estimation (MSE) method, which enlists the help of private and local organizations to determine the number of nondetected victims in a given country. The method was designed to provide a reliable estimate of the number of victims that had previously remained out of the sight of authorities and support agencies. Applied in the Netherlands, the MSE method revealed that the number of actual victims is about five times higher than the number of victims officially registered by authorities or support agencies (U.S. Department of State 2019a). The data also revealed that persons of non-Dutch origin and Dutch girls between the ages of 12 and 17 are most at risk (Dutch National Rapporteur 2017). This example has been used to highlight the importance of expanding and improving microlevel data collection throughout the world for a more accurate picture of what slavery looks like on the ground.

Competing Legal Approaches to Prostitution

Even when there are agreed-upon methods for counting official and presumed victims, controversies may arise over who classifies as such a victim. The most contentious issue regarding quantification lies in the realm of commercial sexual exploitation. Those in the anti-trafficking field unanimously agree that the kidnapping and fraudulent recruitment of adults and minors for prostitution is a violation of human rights, and nearly all agree that prostitution tends to be exploitive, but there is widespread disagreement over how many prostitutes should be considered slaves and the appropriate legal response. The main line of division arises between those who believe that all prostitution is a form of slavery and should be criminalized as such and those who maintain that consensual prostitution among adults should be tolerated because it is a matter of free choice, an inevitable fact of life, and impossible to do away with (George et al. 2010). Advocates of the first view argue that those individuals who are not coerced into prostitution through threats of violence or fraud, which are normally associated with modern slavery, often have a history of sexual abuse and may be "forced" by other constraints such as a lack of money or opportunity. On the other side of the argument are those who admit that prostitution can occur in instances of extreme exploitation, even slavery, but maintain that it can also occur in instances where prostitutes or "sex workers" exercise informed choice. These competing views have contributed to three distinct legal approaches to prostitution: decriminalization/legalization, criminalization, and the Nordic or Swedish model.

Decriminalization has been the norm in places such as the Netherlands, Germany, and Switzerland for over two decades. In 2000, the Netherlands fully legalized brothels in addition to street prostitution. Advocates of this approach have argued that legal regulation and oversight of the sex trade would improve the health, well-being, and social status of voluntary sex workers and would curb trafficking leading to a reduction in the number of minors, migrants, and citizens forced into prostitution. Opponents have posited that legalized prostitution has done little to curb trafficking or reduce the criminality associated with prostitution. On the contrary, they point out that by normalizing the sex industry, legalization increases demand and spurs traffickers to recruit and enslave marginalized women, girls, boys, and transgender youth to meet that demand (Lloyd 2015). In fact, in the years following full legalization, the Netherlands saw an increase in underage and adult sex trafficking and trafficking of undocumented immigrants (Raymond 2003).

In 2013, researchers from Germany, Switzerland, and the United Kingdom released a quantitative study analyzing how the legal status of prostitution affects the incidence of human trafficking inflows to countries by testing two competing theories on the effect of legalization: scale and substitution (Cho et al. 2013). The scale effect theory contends that legalizing prostitution leads to an expansion of the prostitution market and thus increases human trafficking, while the substitution effect holds that legalization reduces the demand for trafficked prostitutes because buyers favor prostitutes with legal status. The study concluded that the scale effect dominates the substitution effect and that on average countries with legalized prostitution experience a larger degree of human trafficking inflows. Other studies have confirmed this conclusion on the effects of legalization. Amsterdam, for example, has become a sex tourism destination, incentivizing criminal syndicates to traffic women from Africa, Eastern Europe, and Asia to meet the demand. It is also common for grooming gangs to seek out young vulnerable girls who can be marketed as virgins (Bindel 2013). Full legalization in Amsterdam has led to further unintended consequences, including the fact that support for prostituted women diminished, and trafficked individuals, unable to register with the government because they are illegal in the country, are driven further underground with less access to resources for help (Palimiotto 2015).

Even those who acknowledge the association between increased trafficking and legalized prostitution do not always advocate full criminalization as a viable solution. Under full criminalization, prostitutes run the risk of being treated as criminals or delinquents rather than victims and are more likely than their pimps and traffickers to be targeted for arrest and prosecution, effectively making victims fearful of criminalization reluctant to come forward. Although prostitution is criminalized throughout most of the United States, federal law now provides that "victims of trafficking should not be inappropriately incarcerated, fined, or otherwise penalized solely for unlawful acts committed as a direct result of being trafficked" (TVPA 2000, sec. 102[a][19]). Many states also have gender-neutral "soliciting" laws that can be utilized to arrest the men soliciting sex. Nevertheless, the laws are rarely applied in a gender-neutral fashion. Women and minors forced into prostitution are typically arrested for soliciting, while the buyers are allowed to go free (Lederer 2011). In an effort to protect victims from criminalization, many states have begun to implement safe harbor laws that prevent minor victims of commercial sexual exploitation from being held as juvenile delinquents and prosecuted for prostitution. While the intentions behind safe harbor laws are good, opponents argue that such laws make it difficult to prosecute pimps or johns because victims who are not cooperative with the criminal justice process cannot be detained. Proponents contend that the states could still exercise their right to hold witnesses, even when the witness is a victim (Palimiotto 2015).

Because sex trafficking is a market-driven criminal industry based on the principle of supply and demand, many scholars and activists have begun to call for a greater attention on the buyers of commercial sex who are driving the demand (Lederer 2011). In 1999, Sweden became the first country to pass legislation focusing criminal justice resources solely on traffickers and buyers. This approach, known as the Nordic or Swedish model, criminalizes pimping and the purchase, but not the sale of sex. Under this model, pimps and those who buy sexual services can be prosecuted and face fines and prison time, but prostitutes are offered services to help them leave prostitution.

In contrast to Norway and Denmark, which saw a dramatic increase in street prostitution following legalization, Sweden saw a 50 percent decrease in street prostitution in the decade following implementation of the Nordic model (Palimiotto 2015). There is also no evidence that the reduction in street prostitution has led to an increase in prostitution elsewhere, whether indoors or on the internet. Sweden has witnessed other positive results as well, including women reporting increased services that enable them to exit prostitution, fewer men purchasing sexual services, and a reduction in traffickers who now find Sweden an unfriendly market (Lederer 2011). In the wake of Sweden's success, several other countries, including Norway, have begun to adopt similar laws.

Given that the commercial sex industry tends to prey on society's most vulnerable individuals and that the demand for prostitution is frequently met with women, men, and children who have been trafficked and enslaved through fraud, violence, or other forms of coercion, there is clearly a need for comprehensive, ongoing efforts to identify, assist, and bring victims to justice under all levels of legality.

Enhancing Criminal Accountability

Although international pressure has led most nations to enact comprehensive anti-trafficking laws, a lack of effort on behalf of legal authorities to identify victims combined with extremely low global prosecution and conviction rates indicates that such laws have little meaning for individuals suffering under the various forms of modern slavery throughout much of the world. According to the State Department's 2019 *Trafficking in Persons Report* (TIP Report), in 2018 only 85,613 victims were identified, and only 11,096 traffickers were prosecuted. Of those prosecuted, a meager 7,481 were convicted. The vast majority of those convictions were for sex trafficking, with a mere 259 perpetrators convicted for labor slavery. This means that out of the estimated 40 million victims of modern slavery, only 2 percent were identified by authorities and far fewer were brought to justice. These numbers suggest that existing laws against trafficking are of minimal deterrence to perpetrators for whom the financial rewards for engaging in modern slavery far outweigh the risks of prosecution and conviction.

Need for Renewed Attention on Developing Effective Public Justice Systems

According to CEO of the International Justice Mission Gary Haugen and federal prosecutor Victor Boutros (2014), the most significant issue affecting the poor and marginalized throughout the developing world is their chronic vulnerability to predatory violence, including rape, forced labor, illegal detention, land theft, police abuse, and other brutality. Lacking the protection of basic systems of criminal justice, they live in a state of de facto lawlessness with little to no recourse for abuses committed against them. In testimony before the U.S. Senate (2015), Haugen contended that the legal impunity of perpetrators in such situations is the primary reason why slavery exists on a massive scale in the world today. To stress this point Haugen illustrated that "in South Asia, if you enslave a poor person, you are more likely to be struck by lightening than you are to actually go to prison for that crime."

Haugen and Boutros (2014) maintain that there are three main reasons for the atrophy and decay of public justice. First, law enforcement systems in the developing world tend to be products of oppressive governments or colonial relics that were set up to protect the regime from the poor, rather than to protect the poor from violence. Sadly, these systems have never been restructured to serve the common people. Second, the wealthy, well connected, and powerful have largely abandoned the dysfunctional, corrupt, and clogged systems of public policing and have set up private security forces to protect them from violence and to resolve disputes in their favor. Third, the massive global movement to alleviate poverty in the developing world over the last half century has, tragically, made no meaningful effort to address the problem of failing justice systems. In spite of the trillions of dollars that have been spent on movements and institutions dedicated to addressing poverty, scandalously little attention, investment, or assistance has been directed toward providing a reasonable degree of security for the poor against oppression and violence through the construction of functioning criminal justice systems. Although a small percentage of overall investment aid from international donors and agencies has been allocated to promoting "rule of law," Haugen and Boutros point out that such investments focus on three separate efforts that have very little to do with ensuring that the common poor person is protected from violence and oppression: rebuilding a small handful of postconflict countries (such as Iraq and Afghanistan); addressing transnational crimes of terrorism and narcotics and arms trafficking; and building attractive and stable conditions for business, commercial activity, and capital investment. In fact, due to substantial risks and difficulties in working with law enforcement systems, significant development agencies such as the World Bank and the U.S. government's primary foreign aid agency USAID (U.S. Agency for International Development) have been prohibited by their own policies from making investments in criminal justice sectors in the developing world.

In spite of the tragic and unique neglect of public justice systems, Haugen and Boutros contend that unless the poor are protected from the devastation of daily violence, none of the other goodwill efforts, such as providing food, health care, education, and microloans, will ultimately matter. This is particularly true when it comes to victims of modern slavery. Inadequate legal protections and penalties, poorly trained and under-equipped law enforcement, and dysfunctional, arbitrary, and corrupt judicial systems are a major source of the problem. Thus, eradicating modern slavery depends in large part on renewed attention and effort to build basic public justice systems that work to protect the poor and vulnerable rather than to extort them.

Common Challenges

In 2017, the U.S. State Department opened its annual TIP Report by focusing on the distinct responsibility of sovereign governments under the Palermo Protocol to criminalize human trafficking in all its forms and to prosecute and hold offenders accountable for their crimes. The report identified some of the major challenges that governments must overcome in their efforts to establish an effective criminal justice response to human trafficking.

First and foremost, effective prosecution depends on laws that clearly define an illegal action and impose penalties commensurate with the serious nature of the crime. Such penalties must be strict enough to serve as a strong deterrent for perpetrators. Consistent with the Palermo Protocol, such laws should also authorize court-ordered restitution or compensation to victims in conjunction with successful convictions. Unfortunately, many governments do not impose clear sentencing guidelines that include adequate jail time. Consequently, judges are able to impose suspended sentences, easily paid fines, or other administrative penalties with little deterrent effect in lieu of incarceration and have the flexibility to apply penalties in a discriminatory manner based on socioeconomic considerations. Furthermore, in numerous countries, including several with functioning justice systems, courts do not award restitution to victims during criminal sentencing, and in some cases, prosecutors will fail to even request such restitution.

A second major challenge impeding effective enforcement of anti-trafficking laws is that local police forces frequently do not have the resources, training, or capacity to investigate instances of trafficking properly and to build a strong case against perpetrators. Gathering enough evidence to restrain violent criminals and prove their guilt is nearly impossible without specialized knowledge and training on how to properly carry out a criminal investigation. Patrol officers must be taught where to look and how to identify victims of trafficking, particularly in areas outside the commercial sex industry. Even when they are able to identify victims, building a strong case can be difficult when victims are reluctant to cooperate. In such instances, local officials must be given the authority, the training, and the resources to engage in sophisticated evidence-collection techniques, including undercover investigations, wiretaps, managing informants, and the ability to seek search warrants.

While specialized, well-resourced forces do exist in some larger cities, the average local police officer throughout much of the developing world has received almost no specialized or formal training in basic policing and criminal investigations (Haugen and Boutros 2014). Many lack even a rudimentary understanding of the criminal law. A dearth of basic equipment can also obstruct effective police work. For example, in testimony before the U.S. Senate (2015), Gary Haugen observed that although the fishing industry on Lake Volta in Ghana is rife with forced labor, and at least 60 percent of children fishing on the lake are clearly slaves, Ghana's anti-trafficking police force does not even own a boat with which to patrol the lake. In some places, the police forces lack not only the qualitative ability to address trafficking cases but also the quantitative capacity. Regions with the high levels of violence and modern slavery tend to spend very little on law enforcement personnel, particularly for service in the lowest income areas. Some districts in Bangladesh, for example, have only one police officer for every 8,000 citizens, and the Kibera slum in Nairobi, Kenya, with its 1 million residents has no regular police post or station (Haugen and Boutros 2014).

Official corruption and complicity is another major barrier to the successful delivery of justice. In many places, those charged with enforcing the law actually work to reinforce abuse and exploitation. Law enforcement officials may ignore clear signs of exploitation or work to obstruct investigations in exchange for bribes, or they may actively participate in human trafficking. As reported in the 2017 TIP Report, some off-duty police officials work as security guards at brothels or other establishments where victims are exploited, making themselves complicit and reducing the likelihood that victims will trust the police enough to come forward. Other officials use their positions to directly facilitate or commit trafficking crimes for their own financial gain.

Even when police do successfully investigate and apprehend perpetrators, in many countries a gross shortage of judges, lawyers, and prosecutors, irregular and inconsistent convening of courts, and complicit and corrupt officials contribute to court backlogs and obstruct prosecution. Criminal investigations and trials are generally time sensitive. Lengthy judicial processes taint evidence and cause survivors with limited time and financial resources to seek out-of-court mediation rather than a criminal investigation. Significant delays in prosecution enable traffickers to continue exploiting, threatening, or intimidating current victims and survivors whose testimony is necessary to achieve a conviction, and sometimes individuals called to testify may have already left the country. Efforts to expedite prosecutions are essential to improving overall conviction rates. The Philippines provides a useful model (U.S. Department of State 2017). In 2013, prosecuting a human trafficking case in the Philippines took an average of three-and-a-half to five years to complete. In 2014, the Supreme Court of the Philippines instituted a continuous trial system pilot project to expedite prosecutions. During its first year of operation, the court successfully completed seven trafficking cases in less than a year.

Usefulness of Task Forces and Partnerships

In every society, there are people, groups, and institutions that deliberately seek to make justice systems fail so they can advance their own personal, economic, and political interests by exploiting the weak. Reforming criminal justice systems so that they serve the marginalized victims of modern slavery thus requires an extraordinary degree of intentionality and commitment. Some countries have made great strides in this regard through the establishment of national task forces and dedicated prosecution units. These units are able to provide specialized expertise in detecting trafficking indicators, stabilizing and protecting victims, and investigating conduct that often spans domestic jurisdictions and international borders. They consequently play a key role in navigating the complexities that arise in the process and coordinating the various stakeholders needed to successfully prosecute and convict perpetrators.

Several countries have unilaterally begun to apply promising practices to improve the prosecution of human trafficking cases through dedicated task forces and units. In Guatemala, for example, the Attorney General's Office (commonly referred to as the public ministry [MP]) expanded its anti-trafficking prosecutor's office and opened up a new specialized regional office to address cases arising in areas where there has previously been little MP coverage of human trafficking prosecutions. The new specialized office focuses on aiding the National Police Force in carrying out large-scale raids on human trafficking networks (U.S. Department of State 2017). Brazil also became a world leader in the fight against modern slavery with the establishment of the National Commission for the Eradication of Slave Labor (CONATRAE), which helps coordinate the anti-trafficking efforts of governmental agencies, law enforcement, judges, prosecutors, businesses, NGOs, and civil society groups, and the launch of Special Mobile Inspection Groups (GEFMs) consisting of labor inspectors, federal police, and labor prosecutors, which conduct surprise inspections and raids on estates suspected of using forced labor. These mobile units are responsible for successfully identifying and freeing thousands of victims each year, but low prosecution and conviction rates of perpetrators suggest that there is still a need for stronger collaboration between labor prosecutors (who can only apply civil penalties) and public ministry prosecutors (who have the ability to initiate criminal cases) (Haugen and Boutros 2014).

In many countries, partnerships with outside entities are necessary to further strengthen the ability of local governments to respond to the highly contextualized failures of their public justice systems. The International Justice Mission (IJM) has been one of the most successful NGOs in terms of establishing plans of action and building effective partnerships with local investigators, law enforcers, prosecutors, and judges. In 2006, with the help of a generous grant from the Bill and Melinda Gates Foundation, IJM launched Project Lantern in Cebu City, the Philippines' second largest metropolitan area (IJM 2010). The goal of the project was to build a Filipino team and mobilize counter-trafficking stakeholders to accomplish two objectives within four years. The objectives were to transform the performance of local law enforcement in fighting the sex trafficking of minors and to demonstrate to outside auditors a measurable 20 percent reduction in the availability of children in the commercial sex trade. Among many strategies applied during implementation of the program, IJM worked to build the capacity of local and national law enforcement to investigate trafficking in persons and rescue victims through intense and specialized training. IJM then advocated for the establishment of a dedicated police task force composed of personnel who had received such training and worked with members of the task force to build actual cases. To reduce the possibility of corruption and ensure safety for victims, IJM required that lawyers and caseworkers accompany local law enforcement on all trafficking raids.

Throughout the project, IJM additionally worked to improve the integrity and capacity of the prosecution and court system to secure successful convictions. IJM hosted trainings for prosecutors and judges and published a guidebook consisting of legal briefs addressing common legal issues along with an overview of anti-trafficking laws and practice tips that could be used by prosecutors and judges preparing for trial. In 2008, IJM discovered that during inquest proceedings, courts were requiring the victims and the accused to wait in the same room. As a result, victim witnesses were often harassed and intimated by defendants and their supporters while they were waiting to testify. IJM and the Regional State Prosecutor thus worked together with the Cebu City Prosecutor's Office to designate and renovate a separate holding area for vulnerable witnesses in all types of cases, including human trafficking cases (IJM 2010).

Lastly, the project incorporated victim aftercare and rehabilitation. After each successful operation, IJM social workers worked closely with the regional Department of Social Welfare and Development and locally based NGOs to ensure that victims were provided with medical care, counseling, and case management and that they had access to halfway houses and rehabilitation centers.

By all accounts, the model successfully exceeded the program's initial objectives. Three years after the project was initiated, a team of independent criminologists found a 79 percent reduction in the availability of minors for sex in commercial establishments (Burkhalter 2012). An IJM-commissioned external review of Project Lantern concluded that the program had contributed significantly to enhanced police operations, services to rescued victims, and prosecution of criminals as well as to a public justice system that is increasingly capable and mobilized to crack down on and deter sex traffickers (Jones et al. 2010). Due to the success of the model, the Philippines government began to establish additional anti-trafficking task forces throughout the country and decided to work directly with IJM to replicate the model in two other locations.

IJM has achieved success in other countries, such as Cambodia, using similar intervention strategies. In recent years, a growing number of NGOs, following the IJM approach, have stepped up on the ground efforts to provide critical specialized training, personnel, accountability, and resources to local forces within and outside of the United States. Organizations such as DeliverFund recruit former elite intelligence operators from the CIA, NSA, FBI, and Navy Seals who use their experience in special operations and counterterrorism to equip, train, and advise law enforcement officers and help them obtain the information they need to dismantle trafficking rings and arrest and prosecute traffickers. Others, such as the Human Trafficking Institute, focus on establishing and equipping specialized Human Trafficking Units and fast-track courts that understand local law and how to apply it in different scenarios.

Reducing Slavery in Supply Chains

Related to the issue of supply and demand is the ethical dilemma that with the rise of globalization and complex supply networks, consumers, companies, and governments are inadvertently supporting and profiting from various forms of modern slavery. Global corporate supply chains offer many benefits—they help deliver a diverse array of low-cost products to consumers, while providing an influx of capital and economic opportunity into developing nations. But such supply chains also provide fertile ground for forced labor. As goods and services from dozens of industries rife with exploited and forced labor flow into the global market, eliminating slavery from supply chains presents an enormous challenge for the modern abolitionist movement.

Voluntary Corporate Action

In response to growing awareness of slavery in supply chains, many companies have begun to adopt voluntary, self-regulating policies or codes of conduct. A 2014 report released by the American Bar Association and Arizona State University's McCain Institute and School of Politics and Global Studies indicated that 54 percent of Fortune 500 companies have policies targeting human trafficking and 68 percent have committed to external and internal supply chain monitoring. In fact, a vanguard of companies, including Walmart, Target, GE, and others, have launched pilot projects with their suppliers to eliminate forced labor and improve working conditions. Industry associations such as the Responsible Business Alliance, the Consumer Goods Forum, Better Cotton Initiative, and Ethical Trading Initiative are also working to coordinate industry and cross-industry responses and actions. One of the largest coalitions, the Global Business Coalition against Human Trafficking (gBCAT), whose current members include the Coca-Cola Company, Microsoft, Google, LexisNexis, Delta, and others, provides training on trafficking and helps design effective and pragmatic solutions to identify and combat traffickers (gBCAT 2017).

Some organizations have developed tools to encourage ethically minded consumers to pressure companies to eliminate slave labor from their supply chains. For example, using funding from the U.S. Department of State, the nonprofit Made in a Free World (MIAFW) developed a model similar to carbon footprinting that would educate consumers on their connection to modern slavery. In 2011, MIAFW launched the website SlaveryFootprint.org that asks visitors the question "How many slaves work for you?" The site provides an online lifestyle survey in which consumers can enter in details about the food they eat, the products they use, and the hobbies they engage in to find out approximately how many forced laborers are involved in their everyday lives. The goal is to enlighten consumers so that they pressure the companies and brands they love to eradicate slave practices in their supply chains. The "Free World" Mobile App also enables users to send an open letter to their personal Facebook and Twitter networks and to company executives asking them to provide products made without slave labor.

Another market-based incentive approach that NGOs have adopted to encourage corporate self-regulation has been to establish industry standards and then to credential good actors with the aim of driving business toward them and away from tainted supply chains. For example, Goodweave, an NGO working to eradicate child labor in the handmade rug industry, monitors, credentials, labels, and markets adult-made rugs from Nepal, Afghanistan, and India (IJM 2018).

Regulatory Mechanisms

In addition to the active role many corporations have voluntarily adopted, national and regional governments have slowly started enacting regulatory mechanisms to prevent corporations within their territories from contributing to forced labor violations abroad. In 2012, California enacted the California Transparency in Supply Chains Act (CTSCA), the first-in-the-world effort to combat forced labor through corporate supply chain disclosure requirements. The CTSCA requires that any retailers or manufacturers operating in California that generate at least $100 million a year must make annual disclosures of their efforts to eradicate slavery and human trafficking from their direct supply chains. Following implementation of the CTSCA, other jurisdictions, including the U.S. federal government, the British Parliament, and the European Union, soon followed suit with similar public reporting and disclosure requirements (Baker & McKenzie 2014).

Despite such legal mandates and the considerable efforts of NGOs and multinational corporations to protect supply networks from human trafficking and forced labor, corporate leaders report that significant challenges remain (Baker & McKenzie 2014). These challenges include difficulty uncovering less visible forms of forced labor and trafficking, obfuscation of trafficking victims by the sheer magnitude of the network of suppliers that results from globalization in so many industries, inability to exercise control over third-party contractors and sub-suppliers, the difficulty of mapping and policing complex supply webs, and a lack of regulatory oversight and enforcement in many source countries.

Reforming Labor Recruitment Practices

The conditions that lead to modern slavery in global supply chains often occur in the labor recruitment process. The labor recruitment industry has grown in scope and importance in recent decades as globalization has driven markets toward temporary or seasonal contract workers who are mobile and flexible. It is thus common for employers to subcontract hiring and human resources management to labor brokers. Each year, millions of workers either seek out or are recruited by these agents who facilitate the movement of labor within countries and across borders to satisfy global labor demands (U.S. Department of State 2019b). In many cases, labor recruiters offer legitimate guidance and assistance in connecting workers with jobs and helping workers acquire necessary travel and other documentation. Workers' dependence on these intermediaries, however, also increases their risk of falling victim to trafficking and forced labor. Some recruiters take advantage of workers' desperate economic situation in their home, village, or country to traffic and exploit them under the guise of fraudulent job offers, only to destroy or confiscate their identity documents so they are unable to leave exploitive situations. Others may require potential workers to pay exorbitant recruitment fees, leaving them subject to debt bondage, often in harsh and inhumane conditions.

In response to fraudulent and exploitive recruitment practices, migrant rights activists and antislavery NGOs have openly called for global labor recruitment reform as a means of reducing slavery in the global supply chain. Over the past several years, there has been an exponential growth in initiatives focused on eradicating exploitive labor recruitment practices, developing models for fair recruitment, and changing industry standards in hiring practices. The U.S. Department of State's 2019 TIP Report provides several examples of such promising initiatives. In 2014, for example, the ILO launched the Fair Recruitment Initiative, a multistakeholder collaboration that focuses, among other objectives, on enhancing knowledge of national and international recruitment practices and improving laws, policies, and enforcement mechanisms for fair recruitment. That same year, the IOM brought together a coalition of stakeholders to develop the International Recruitment Integrity System (IRIS) initiative, a "social compliance scheme" designed to promote fair labor recruitment by prohibiting worker-paid recruitment fees and identifying and supporting ethical labor recruiters. In 2017, the Responsible Business Alliance (RBA) launched the Responsible Labor Initiative (RLI), a multi-industry initiative to reduce the risk of forced labor in global supply chains by transforming recruitment markets.

Government Responsibility

While consumers, NGOs, labor recruiters, and corporations, including multinational textile companies, global seafood exporters, and electronic manufacturers, play an important role in eradicating slavery from supply chains, often missing from the conversation is the distinct responsibility of sovereign nations to protect exploited individuals within their borders. In fact, one of the unintended consequences of relying too much on proactive business practices and corporate regulation is that such reliance takes the pressure off governments and thereby actually weakens the political will of states and public justice systems to address exploitive and criminal labor practices (IJM 2018). The criminals who recruit, exploit, and directly profit from child labor and forced labor with impunity lay at the heart of slavery in global supply chains, and they must be prosecuted. Consequently, demands for corporate responsibility and regulation should not overshadow the fact that sovereign governments bear ultimate responsibility and should accordingly be held to account. They are the ones with the authority and obligation to enforce national laws against forced labor, and they—not distant corporate executives and consumers—are the ones with the capacity to investigate, prosecute, and punish perpetrators.

Empowering the Poor

Second to a shortage of well-functioning public justice systems, extreme poverty with no opportunity for upward mobility is one of the most determinative factors contributing to individual vulnerability to slavery, child labor, and other forms of exploitation. Nearly all slaves lack a viable source of income, access to effective education, or a reasonable alternative to their condition of servitude. Thus, government groups, UN agencies, and NGOs generally emphasize preventative antipoverty initiatives as a part of their overall abolition efforts. Agencies seeking to alleviate the crushing poverty that renders individuals vulnerable to slavery typically focus on providing access to financial and medical resources, basic education, job training, and income-generating projects. Such actions, while highly important, are only effective when the poor have the legal ability to take full advantage of the opportunities afforded by them. Development initiatives tend to assume that the contract and property rights necessary for the poor to participate in the formal economy are in place, but most poor people do not live under the shelter of the law. In many countries, the laws, institutions, and policies governing economic, social, and political affairs deny a large part of society, including indigenous communities, the chance to participate on equal terms. So long as the poor and marginalized are excluded from the full rights and protection of the legal system, antipoverty initiatives will have little long-term value for them.

In 2008, the Commission on the Legal Empowerment of the Poor, a group of distinguished scholars, former heads of state, and senior policymakers, came together to explore the issue of the legal empowerment of the poor. In the course of its deliberations, the commission concluded that although the sources of legal exclusion are numerous and vary to some degree by country, four common threads stand out. First, legal empowerment is impossible when poor people are denied access to a well-functioning judicial system. Second, most of the world's poor lack effective property rights, and the intrinsic economic power of their property remains untapped. Third, poor people, in particular women and children, suffer in unsafe working conditions because their employers often operate outside the formal legal system. Fourth, poor people are denied economic opportunities as their property and businesses are not legally recognized. Consequently, they cannot access credit, investment, or global and local markets. The commission resolved that if state laws are reformed to appropriately recognize the marginalized, then those who were previously excluded will be able to transcend their current circumstances and contribute to the solution of otherwise chronic economic and social problems. The commission thus recommended that international and national development initiatives aimed at alleviating global poverty should include not only investment in education, public services, and infrastructure but also a focus on unlocking the civic and economic potential of the poor through social and legal transformation. In particular, efforts that focus on securing access to justice and the rule of law, property rights, labor rights, and business rights will complement more traditional initiatives, multiplying their impact by creating the conditions for success.

Rehabilitating Survivors

Available evidence suggest that victims of modern slavery are highly vulnerable to being re-enslaved, particularly within the first two years of being rescued (IOM 2010). Although it is difficult to separate the causes of re-trafficking from the wider causes of modern slavery generally, several causal factors directly relate to a victims' previous experience of trafficking or to their experience with assistance organizations. The IOM found, for example, that young victims, ages 15–25 years old, and victims with drug or alcohol dependence are more susceptible to re-trafficking. Those at greatest risk include formerly trafficked persons who are members of ethnic minority groups and who would continue to be subject to discrimination in their country of origin, female victims who face significant gender inequali-ties in their country of origin, victims from countries that have experienced ongoing or recent conflict, and victims who are also refugees or displaced persons. Other organizations, such as the U.S. Department of State (2019a), have likewise attributed high levels of revictimization to ongoing conflict and instabil-ity, to a lack of transitional housing and effective reintegra-tion resources, and to government officials returning victims to high-risk environments. Due to the many potential causes of revictimization, it is clear that efforts to equip vulnerable populations, rescue victims, and convict perpetrators must also include significant endeavors to aid and mentor survivors so they are able to transition successfully from slavery to freedom. Governments, antislavery and humanitarian NGOs, and civil society in general play a crucial role in providing the various aftercare services required to reduce victims' vulnerability to being re-enslaved and equipping them with the tools necessary to thrive.

Proper aftercare, first and foremost, requires measures to provide for physical, psychological, and social recovery. Upon being rescued, victims have numerous and immediate needs, including housing, food and clothing, security, counseling, medical care, and legal support. Governments sometimes pro-vide emergency food and housing immediately after a rescue, but victims also require longer-term transitional housing to provide them time to heal and consider their options. Long-term secure housing is particularly vital for those who have decided to cooperate with law enforcement in building a case against their trafficker.

During this first phase of aftercare, victims should be assessed to determine whether it would be beneficial and safe to repatriate them to their home country or community. In many cases, victims—especially those of commercial sexual exploitation—are unable to return to their homes because of the stigma they will face due to discriminatory cultural practices and norms. Governments should thus have laws in place that offer foreign victims asylum when it is not feasible to repatriate them. The United States' T visa program, for example, allows foreign victims of trafficking to remain in the country legally. Sometimes, in extreme cases in which victims are in danger of retaliation for testifying against their trafficker, they and their families may require asylum in a third unaffiliated country. In the case that victims are repatriated, coordination between aftercare providers is essential to ensure that victims continue to receive follow-up care in the destination country.

Support for survivors of modern slavery often focuses on meeting their immediate needs, but investments in their future are necessary as well. Because extreme poverty with no opportunity for upward mobility is one of the most decisive factors contributing to individual vulnerability, empowering and equipping survivors with a sense of purpose and an ability to provide for themselves and their families is an essential component of preventing revictimization. According to the U.S.-based nonprofit End Slavery Now (2020), empowerment activities fall under three main categories: job training, employment, and survivor advocacy. Many NGOs provide basic and advanced job training to equip survivors to access jobs and earn an income to provide for their families. Other organizations provide survivors directly with employment opportunities whether through survivor-based enterprises or businesses that commit to hiring survivors. Finally, some organizations equip survivors to become antislavery advocates and to use their stories to educate others and to influence policy. The Survivor Alliance, for example, was launched in 2018 to unite survivors of human trafficking and provide them with a professional network of their peers, a platform to connect across time zones and geographies, and opportunities to consult in the antislavery movement (Dang 2018).

The Role of U.S. Leadership

The passage of the Trafficking Victims Protection Act of 2000 (TVPA) and its reauthorizations, along with the establishment of the State Department's Office to Monitor and Combat Trafficking in Persons (commonly referred to as J/TIP), have helped make the issue of slavery a top concern of U.S. foreign policy. To date, the United States has been a leading watchdog in the worldwide fight against slavery and can continue to expand and improve on this role. One of the most useful tools in this regard is the State Department's annual TIP Report, which provides the latest information on the status of human trafficking around the world and a comprehensive assessment of what governments are doing to combat it. As mandated by the TVPA, the TIP Office places each country in the report onto one of four tiers based on the extent of the governments' efforts to meet the TVPA's minimum standards for the elimination of human trafficking. A Tier 1 ranking indicates that a country's government fully meets the TVPA's standards for elimination of trafficking. To maintain a Tier 1 ranking, governments must demonstrate each year that they are not only maintaining but also increasing their efforts to combat trafficking. A Tier 2 ranking indicates that a country is making significant efforts to bring itself into compliance with TVPA standards. Tier 3 rankings are assigned to countries that are not making significant efforts to comply with the TVPA's minimum standards. Pursuant to the TVPA, a Tier 3 ranking can trigger sanctions limiting access to nonhumanitarian aid from the United States, the International Monetary Fund, and the World Bank.

The annual TIP Report—which not only names and shames but also offers specific recommendations for improvement— is a critical diplomatic instrument for the United States and has been the catalyst for positive changes by governments on every continent (Enos and Lagon 2018). Studies indicate that using rankings is a powerful foreign policy tool for encouraging countries motivated by a concern for their own reputation and desire to avoid sanctions to address a public problem. Judith Kelley (2017), the dean of Duke University's Sanford School of Public Policy, quantitatively documents how the tier rankings issued through the U.S. State Department's TIP Report have contributed to the improvement of various laws and governmental conduct.

The use of rankings in the TIP Report, however, has not been without flaws. In 2015, the report came under fire after the upgraded rankings for several countries were disputed on the ground that they had been altered for political reasons. A Reuters investigation revealed that although human rights experts working for J/TIP concluded that trafficking conditions had not improved in Malaysia and Cuba and had even grown worse in China, senior political staff at the State Department and regional U.S. diplomatic bureaus overruled J/TIP analysts and upgraded the ranking of all three countries for political purposes (Szep and Spetalnick 2015). Human rights groups were particularly critical of the Malaysian upgrade from the Tier 3 blacklist to the Tier 2 watch list the same year in which authorities discovered in Malaysia dozens of suspected mass migrant graves and human rights activists reported a drop in human trafficking convictions and continued widespread forced labor in the nation's palm oil, construction, and electronic industries. Many speculated that the improved ranking was motivated by the Obama administration's desire to smooth the way for the Trans-Pacific Partnership, an ambitious U.S.-led free-trade deal with Malaysia and 11 other countries. Congress had approved legislation giving the president expanding trade negotiating powers but had prohibited trade deals with Tier 3 countries, such as Malaysia. Cuba's upgrade to Tier 2 after 12 years on the blacklist also came at a time when the United States was seeking to reopen an embassy in the country. Human rights groups widely criticized these unearned upgrades, arguing that they undermined the integrity and effectiveness of the TIP Report. To prevent the politicization and maintain the credibility of the report, TIP rankings should not be used as a tool for advancing diplomatic goals; rather they should solely reflect the facts on the ground, specifically the extent to which countries are complying with time-tested best practices for reducing the number of victims of modern slavery, prosecuting traffickers, and assisting survivors.

In addition, to its annual rankings, the TIP Office manages a wide range of foreign assistance programs and grants to NGOs, public international organizations, institutions of higher learning, and for-profit organizations dedicated to combating all forms of human trafficking around the world. In 2017, the TIP Office launched the Program to End Modern Slavery (PEMS), a ground-breaking foreign assistance program authorized and funded by Congress. The PEMS, which has received a total of over $75 million to date, aims to support transformational programs and projects that seek to achieve a measurable and substantial reduction of the prevalence of modern slavery in targeted populations in specific countries or regions (U.S. Department of State 2019b).

The TIP Office works closely with the USAID to manage projects and ensure that aid is disseminated to countries that have the political will to address human trafficking and a great need for assistance. During fiscal year 2017 alone, the Department of State, the Department of Labor (DOL), and USAID—through agreements with implementing partners—managed 120 international counter-trafficking in persons projects. However, a 2018 Government Accountability Office (GAO) review of these projects found that the Department of State did not have monitoring plans or complete progress reports for one-third of its projects and often lacked targets for performance in its final progress reports. The GAO also found that the Department of State and USAID used inconsistent and incomplete performance information. The GOA review concluded that without implementing such controls, State and USAID officials cannot fully or accurately understand what projects are, or are not, achieving and how their efforts might be improved. A similar earlier Inspector General audit of USAID programming against human trafficking found several deficiencies in the agency's implementation of programs and application of best practices (USAID and Office of Inspector General 2013).

In spite of the many worthy projects funded through the Department of State and USAID, it is evident that more needs to be done to ensure that anti-trafficking funding is used to support known successful programs and to aid countries that are most in need and most willing to combat trafficking. Without clearly defined objectives and strong performance evaluation, aid could end up funding bad actors or corrupt officials rather than providing justice and much-needed assistance to victims. Policy analysts Lisa Curtis and Olivia Enos (2015) have suggested that the TIP Office and USAID apply Millennium Challenge Corporation (MCC)–type criteria to U.S. anti-human trafficking assistance to ensure that funds are used in the most effective and efficient ways. The MCC is a foreign assistance agency created by Congress in 2004 to provide time-limited grants to developing countries committed to good governance, economic freedom, and poverty reduction (MCC 2019). To qualify for MCC assistance, countries must meet predetermined benchmarks that measure the economic and political climate of the country, focusing specifically on measurable indicators such as free trade, corruption, political freedom, and public health data. The MCC additionally measures the prevalence of human trafficking and how the government is addressing the problem as a component of eligibility. The MCC assessment model has been deemed a highly effective instrument for encouraging developing countries to achieve reasonable policy and institutional reform (Parks and Rice 2013). Furthermore, the MCC's attention to human trafficking as part of its selection criteria ensures that it is not rewarding countries that willfully traffic their own citizens and that aid workers and contractors administering MCC aid are not intentionally or unintentionally facilitating trafficking through their programs. In addition to developing more solid criterion for aid eligibility such as that modeled by the MCC, the U.S. government could also further collaborate with academic institutions and NGOs to carry out empirical analysis and to track the implementation, successes, failures, and long-term impacts of U.S. funded anti-trafficking programs.

Combating Slavery Locally

Slavery is a global crime that often defies borders and, in that regard, requires a comprehensive international response, but actual instances of slavery take place locally—in nail salons, massage parlors, hotels, businesses, factories, farms, and restaurants, on the street, and in homes. Furthermore, the dynamics that facilitate slavery vary greatly by local context. Numerous factors unique to particular communities, including cultural beliefs and practices, legal and social structures, conflict and migration levels, and political and economic situations, contribute to the prevalence of slavery in different ways. In 2018, the TIP Report recognized this reality by suggesting that governments and communities work together to address trafficking where it starts—in their own neighborhoods (U.S. Department of State 2018). Highlighting the need for "local solutions to a global problem," the report identifies four chief elements of an effective community-based approach and the specific ways that national governments can facilitate each of these elements.

The first element of an effective community-based approach is the building of strong partnerships and areas of cooperation between multiple stakeholders. These partnerships should exist vertically between national, regional, and local governments and horizontally between law enforcement, service providers, and other key actors within and across individual communities. At every level, the expertise, time, and resources of a wide range of stakeholders are essential to preventing and responding to instances of modern slavery and providing comprehensive care to victims. For example, law enforcement officers can arrest and prosecute traffickers, but they do so more effectively when they work in tandem with care providers who are able to coordinate support services for victims. Effective enforcement also depends on a public that is well trained in the indicators of human trafficking and is willing to report suspicious activity. Victims need the support of law enforcement, and a variety of public and private philanthropic and faith-based service providers that can likewise benefit from the subject matter expertise and input of victims turned survivors. And while local leaders are well-situated to understand their communities and to effectively implement and adapt policies, they may necessarily depend on national governments and NGOs for funding, training, and expertise. To facilitate effective partnership and coordination between multiple stakeholders, national governments can support the establishment of human trafficking task forces and encourage collaboration with NGOs, provide access to experts to help build local capacity, and foster the sharing of best practices across jurisdictions.

The second element of an effective community-based approach includes assessing communities to better understand which groups or individuals are most vulnerable to victimization and the particular dynamics contributing to their vulnerability, the range of services victims may need, and the current resources that exist to address those needs. It is additionally important to assess the general level of awareness of local trafficking-related issues among those most likely to come into contact with victims and the current processes in place for law enforcement response and victim care. Such information gathering on the current landscape of victim identification, service provision, and law enforcement action provides a helpful baseline from which to build improved community action plans. National governments can assist in this information gathering by developing national and local diagnostic tools to help with the identification of at-risk populations, by conducting assessments of slavery at the national level, by encouraging and supporting monitoring and reporting from local-level stakeholders, by providing a national platform for information sharing and data collection, and by funding studies designed to better understand successful anti-trafficking models.

Even the best laws and policies are ineffective without proper knowledge of how to identify and assist victims. Thus, the third element of an effective community-based approach requires raising awareness and providing training on victim identification and the appropriate response to those most likely to come in contact with situations of slavery, such as law enforcement officers, health care professionals, school administrators and teachers, labor inspectors, transportation providers, and others. Community leaders can also promote general awareness among the public at large to help them recognize indicators of trafficking and to encourage them to alert authorities when they recognize indicators of trafficking. National governments can promote the effectiveness of training and community awareness efforts by developing victim-centered training for public servants, by sharing information about the common indicators of human trafficking and typical methods of recruitment with local officials and community stakeholders, and by publicizing the various avenues for reporting human trafficking and seeking assistance.

Finally, an effective community response is dependent on the development of strong response processes and protocols to coordinate the various identification, short- and long-term care, and prevention efforts of relevant stakeholders. National governments can aid in the development of protocols and processes by setting up and funding a national anti-trafficking hotline and a national referral mechanism and by making sure that relevant officials, professionals, and community groups are aware of these resources, by creating a central point for operational coordination and the development of law enforcement and judicial expertise, and by collaborating with local stakeholders to develop long-term sustainable care programs based on proven best practices.

Conclusion

Because modern slavery is complex, clandestine, and nuanced in nature, developing effective counter strategies and policies can be extremely difficult. As in so many other aspects of human rights, the political will and ability to enforce change remain far weaker than the multiplicity of national laws and international agreements would suggest. Furthermore, although it is apparent that slavery is prolific across the globe, quantifying the magnitude remains challenging, and significant gaps in identifying vulnerable populations persist. Modern slavery is often referred to as a crime that is "hidden in plain sight" because victims are unlikely to self-identify, and service providers and members of the community who encounter or interact with them are not always equipped to perceive their victimhood. Continued efforts to improve micro-level data collection and uncover and identify the hidden victims of the crime are thus essential to developing a well-tailored response.

Ultimately, countering the multiple and various manifestations of modern slavery requires a multifaceted approach focused first and foremost on building strong systems of law enforcement. In most places throughout the world, existing laws against slavery have no meaning for the millions of slaves who find themselves with no avenue to justice. Without addressing the state of de facto lawlessness that plagues the lives of most of the world's poor and vulnerable—as a result of dysfunctional, underresourced, corrupt, and clogged systems of public justice—all other goodwill efforts to prevent and eradicate slavery will be in vain. Responding to this problem will require robust efforts on behalf of sovereign governments to clearly define illegal action and impose tough penalties and sentencing guidelines. NGOs also play an essential role in aid-ing willing governments in their efforts to improve the integrity and capacity of their criminal justice systems by providing spe-cialized expertise and training, financial and human resources, and accountability.

With the rise of globalization and complex supply networks that provide fertile ground for forced labor, uncovering and fighting slavery has become even more difficult. Sovereign gov-ernments bear primary responsibility for addressing exploitive and criminal labor practices within their borders and for legally empowering the poor and vulnerable through well-defined property, labor, and business rights, but consumers, businesses, labor recruiters, and multinational corporations also have a duty to make sure that they aren't purposefully or unintention-ally profiting off the backs of slaves.

Powerful, developed countries such as the United States should not only seek to more effectively address their own issues with domestic slavery but also continue to strive to spur other governments to improve their laws and conduct, both by pub-licly shaming countries that participate in or tolerate slavery and by supporting through precise objectives those countries that have exhibited a strong political will for positive change.

Along with the efforts of international and national organi-zations and sovereign governments, partnerships between law enforcement, public service providers, businesses, and private philanthropic and faith-based organizations are essential to combating and responding to slavery where it germinates in local neighborhoods. Such networks are vital not only for tailoring successful responses to slavery based on the unique contexts of particular communities but also for securing effec-tive short- and long-term care for survivors. With continued and improved concerted efforts on behalf of multiple dedi-cated stakeholders, progress can be made toward restoring the freedom and dignity of the millions oppressed by modern slavery.

References

American Bar Association and Arizona State University. 2014. "How Do Fortune 100 Corporations Address Potential Links to Human Rights Violations in a Globally Integrated Economy?" June 2. Accessed February 10, 2020. https://www.americanbar.org/content/dam/aba/administrative/human_rights/fortune_100_report_on_trafficking.authcheckdam.pdf

Aronowitz, Alexis A. 2017. *Contemporary World Issues: Human Trafficking.* Santa Barbara, CA: ABC-CLIO.

Baker & McKenzie. 2014. "Managing Corporate Supply Chains: Challenges and Successes in the Fight to Combat Forced Labour and Human Trafficking." Accessed February 10, 2020. https://www.bakermckenzie.com/-/media/files/newsroom/2016/04/brochure_csb37264_amiller_gsc_1118_v2.pdf?la=en

Bindel, Julie. 2013. "Why Even Amsterdam Doesn't Want Legal Brothels." *The Spectator.* February 2. Accessed February 4, 2020. https://www.spectator.co.uk/2013/02/flesh-for-sale/

Burkhalter, Holly. 2012. "Sex Trafficking, Law Enforcement and Perpetrator Accountability." *Anti-Trafficking Review* 1 (June). Accessed February 13, 2020. https://www.ijm.org/documents/studies/Sex-Trafficking-Law-Enforcment-and-Perpetrator-Accountability2.pdf

Cho, Seo-Young, Axel Dreher, and Eric Neumayer. 2013. "Does Legalized Prostitution Increase Human Trafficking?" *World Development* 41: 67–82. Accessed February 4, 2020. http://eprints.lse.ac.uk/45198/1/Neumayer_Legalized_Prostitution_Increase_2012.pdf

Commission on Legal Empowerment of the Poor. 2008. "Making the Law Work for Everyone: Volume I Report of the Commission on Legal Empowerment of the Poor."

Commission on Legal Empowerment of the Poor and United Nations Development Programme. Accessed February 15, 2020. https://www.un.org/ruleoflaw/files/Making_the _Law_Work_for_Everyone.pdf

Curtis, Lisa, and Olivia Enos. 2015. "Combatting Trafficking in Asia Requires U.S. Leadership." *The Heritage Foundation.* February 26. Accessed February 16, 2020. https://www.heritage.org/asia/report /combating-human-trafficking-asia-requires-us-leadership

Dang, Minh. 2018. "Survivors of Modern Slavery as Anti-Slavery Leaders." *Freedom Fund.* May 2. Accessed February 18, 2020. https://freedomfund.org/blog /survivors-of-modern-slavery-as-anti-slavery-leaders/

Dutch National Rapporteur on Trafficking in Human Beings. 2017. "Reliable Estimate Reflects True Numbers of Victims of Human Trafficking." September 28. Accessed February 2, 2020. https://www.dutchrapporteur.nl/current/news /reliable-estimate-reflects-true-numbers-of-victims-of -human-trafficking.aspx

End Slavery Now. 2020. "Empowerment." Accessed February 18, 2020. http://www.endslaverynow.org/learn /abolition-today/empowerment

Enos, Olivia, and Mark Lagon. 2018. "The Fight against Trafficking Is Too Important for Trump and Pompeo to Ignore." *Foreign Policy.* May 30. Accessed February 16, 2020. https://foreignpolicy.com/2018/05/30/human -trafficking-report-ambassador-at-large-state-department -trump-pompeo-2/

Gallagher, Anne T. 2017. "What's Wrong with the Global Slavery Index?" *Anti-Trafficking Review* 8: 90–112.

George, Annie, U. Vindhya, and Sawmya Ray. 2010. "Sex Trafficking and Sex Work: Definitions, Debates and Dynamics—A Review of Literature." *Economic and Political Weekly* Vol. 45, No. 17 (April 24–30): 64–73.

Global Business Coalition against Human Trafficking (gBCAT).
2017. "Global Business Coalition against Human Trafficking
Expands Scope and Steps Up Efforts to End Trafficking."
July 26. Accessed February 10, 2020. https://www.3blmedia
.com/News/Global-Business-Coalition-Against-Human
-Trafficking-Expands-Scope-and-Steps-Efforts-End

Government Accountability Office (GAO). 2018. "Human
Trafficking: State and USAID Should Improve Their
Monitoring of International Counter-Trafficking Projects."
December 4. Accessed February 16, 2020. https://www
.gao.gov/products/gao-19-77

Haugen, Gary A., and Victor Boutros. 2014. *The Locust Effect:
Why the End of Poverty Requires the End of Violence.* New
York: Oxford University Press.

International Justice Mission (IJM). 2010. "Project Lantern
Results Summary." Accessed February 13, 2020. https://
www.ijm.org/documents/studies/Cebu-Project-Lantern
-Results-Summary.pdf

International Justice Mission (IJM). 2018. "Justice Review: A
Journal on Protection and Justice for the Poor." Accessed
January 15, 2020. https://www.ijm.org/documents/studies
/IJM-Justice-Review.pdf

International Labour Organization (ILO) and Walk
Free Foundation. 2017. "Global Estimates of Modern
Slavery: Forced Labour and Forced Marriage." Geneva.
Accessed November 15, 2019. https://www.ilo.org/global
/publications/books/WCMS_575479/lang--en/index.htm

International Organization for Migration (IOM). 2010. "The
Causes and Consequences of Re-trafficking: Evidence from
the IOM Human Trafficking Database." Geneva. Accessed
February 18, 2020. https://publications.iom.int/system
/files/pdf/causes_of_retrafficking.pdf

Jones, Andrew, Rhonda Schlangen, and Rhodora Bucoy.
2010. "An Evaluation of the International Justice Mission's

Project Lantern: Assessment of Five-year Impact and Change in the Public Justice System." October 21. Accessed February 13, 2020. https://www.ijm.org/studies/evaluation-of-project-lantern/

Kelley, Judith G. 2017. *Scorecard Diplomacy: Grading States to Influence Their Reputation and Behavior*. Cambridge, United Kingdom: Cambridge University Press.

Lederer, Laura J. 2011. "Addressing Demand: Why and How Policymakers Should Utilize Law and Law Enforcement to Target Customers of Commercial Sexual Exploitation." *Regent University Law Review* 23: 297–310.

Lillie, Michelle. 2014. "Invisible Men: Male Victims of Sex-Trafficking." *Human Trafficking Search*. Accessed January 30, 2020. https://humantraffickingsearch.org/invisible-men-male-victims-of-sex-trafficking/

Loyd, Rachel. 2015. "Legalizing Prostitution Leads to More Trafficking." *New York Times*. August 24. Accessed February 4, 2020. https://www.nytimes.com/roomfordebate/2012/04/19/is-legalized-prostitution-safer/legalizing-prostitution-leads-to-more-trafficking

Millennium Challenge Corporation (MCC). 2019. "About MCC." Accessed February 16, 2020. https://www.mcc.gov/about

Mügge, Daniel. 2017. "40.3 Million Slaves? Four Reasons to Question the New Global Estimates of Modern Slavery." Beyond Trafficking and Slavery (BTS) Policy Brief No. 1. *Open Democracy*. Accessed January 15, 2020. https://cdn-prod.opendemocracy.net/media/documents/Mugge_4_reasons_to_question_GEMS.pdf

Palmiotto, Michael J. 2015. *Combatting Human Trafficking: A Multidisciplinary Approach*. Boca Raton, FL: Taylor & Francis Group.

Parks, Bradley C., and Zachary J. Rice. 2013. "Measuring the Policy Influence of the Millenium Challenge Corporation:

A Survey-Based Approach." *College of William and Mary, Institute for the Theory and Practice of International Relations.* February. Accessed February 17, 2020. https://www.wm.edu/offices/global-research/_documents/reform-incentives-report-mcc.pdf

Raymond, Janice G. 2003. "Ten Reasons for *Not* Legalizing Prostitution and a Legal Response to the Demand for Prostitution." *Journal of Trauma Practice* 2: 315–332.

Szep, Jason, and Matt Spetalnick. 2015. "Special Report: State Department Watered Down Human Trafficking Report." Reuters. August 3. Accessed February 16, 2020. https://www.reuters.com/article/us-usa-humantrafficking-disputes-special/special-report-state-department-watered-down-human-trafficking-report-idUSKCN0Q821Y20150803

U.S. Agency for International Development (USAID) and Office of Inspector General. 2013. "Review of USAID's New Counter-Trafficking in Persons Program." November 27. Accessed February 16, 2020. https://oig.usaid.gov/sites/default/files/2018-06/9-000-14-001-s.pdf

U.S. Department of State. 2017. "Trafficking in Persons Report." June. Accessed January 30, 2020. https://www.state.gov/wp-content/uploads/2019/02/271339.pdf

U.S. Department of State. 2018. "Trafficking in Persons Report." June. Accessed January 30, 2020. https://www.state.gov/wp-content/uploads/2019/01/282798.pdf

U.S. Department of State. 2019a. "Trafficking in Persons Report." June. Accessed August 1, 2019. https://www.state.gov/wp-content/uploads/2019/06/2019-Trafficking-in-Persons-Report.pdf

U.S. Department of State. 2019b. "International Programs: Office to Monitor and Combat Trafficking in Persons." Accessed February 16, 2020. https://www.state.gov/international-programs/

U.S. Senate. 2015. Committee on Foreign Relations. *Ending Modern Slavery*. 114th Cong., 1st sess., February 4 and February 11. Accessed February 10, 2020. https://www.govinfo.gov/content/pkg/CHRG-114shrg96256/html/CHRG-114shrg96256.htm

Victim of Trafficking and Violence Prevention Act of 2000 (TVPA). 2000. Accessed February 4, 2020. https://www.govinfo.gov/content/pkg/PLAW-106publ386/html/PLAW-106publ386.htm

Walts, Katherine Kaufka. 2017. "Child Labor Trafficking in the United States: A Hidden Crime." *Social Inclusion* Vol. 5, No. 2: 59–68.

Young, Yvette. 2019. "The Bond That Harms: The Impact of Trauma Bonding on Human Trafficking Victims." *Forbes*. November 6. Accessed January 30, 2020. https://www.forbes.com/sites/civicnation/2019/11/06/the-bond-that-harms-the-impact-of-trauma-bonding-on-human-trafficking-victims/#2cb34af852c3

3 Perspectives

Introduction

This chapter includes seven essays written by authors from a variety of perspectives and professional backgrounds on a range of topics related to the issue of modern slavery. The chapter opens with an essay by Joseph W. Bergee, a PhD student in political theory and international relations, who argues that revisiting the famous Lincoln-Douglas debates provides a useful reminder of why appeals to objective morality are necessary for combating slavery in all its forms. The second and third essays explore the connection between the nation state and modern slavery. Steven Childs, an assistant professor of international relations and national security, makes the case that foreign aid should be directed toward helping nations strengthen their authority, capacity, and legitimacy as a means of combating both terrorism and modern slavery. Kevork Kazanjian, a political science instructor, defends strong borders as a deterrent to forced human trafficking. The next two essays examine different facets of policy. Vicki Alger, a research and policy analyst, highlights the overlooked problem of child labor in the United States, and Autumn Burris, an exited sex trafficking survivor and legislative advocate, makes the case for an Equality

---

Burmese laborers looking to better their life by working in Thailand's commercial fishing industry. A large percentage of migrants working on fishing vessels in South Asia have become trapped in debt bondage and are forced to work in extreme conditions by greedy captains and exploiters. (Kay Chernush for the U.S. State Department)

Model approach to prostitution, which includes providing exit funding and services for prostitutes while criminalizing traffickers and penalizing johns. The final two essays each make an argument for prevention and eradication. Peter C. Hodgson, an antislavery advocate, argues that the Christian Church and Christians in general are obligated by the tenets of their faith to assume an active role in the prevention and eradication of modern slavery. Finally, Carl Ralston, the founder and president of Remember Nhu, highlights research demonstrating that preventative efforts like those adopted by Remember Nhu are the most effective means of eradicating child sex trafficking.

The Slavery Question in the Age of Moral Relativism: An American Perspective from the Lincoln-Douglas Debates
Joseph W. Bergee

Today, especially in the Western world, moral relativism—the belief that objective morality is a farce and that moral judgments are merely a product of time, place, and culture—predominates the thought and speech of many intellectuals, politicians, and, oxymoronically, religious leaders. This belief is best summed up in the statement by American philosopher Richard Rorty (1999): "I do not have much use for notions like 'objective value' and 'objective truth'" (2). Yet, while many, including Rorty, would unequivocally denounce slavery, in any form or time period, as objectively wrong, their adherence to moral relativism prohibits them from having an intellectual or philosophical foundation from which to base this moral judgment. The consequence of rejecting the possibility or need of objective truth as a foundation for unequivocally denouncing the institution of slavery was first exemplified in one of the greatest political showdowns in American history fought between Stephen Douglas, who claimed that objective morality had no place in deciding whether slavery is right or wrong, and Abraham Lincoln, who claimed that we could not answer this important question without guidance from such morality. Revisiting the Lincoln-Douglas debates provides a useful reminder of why appeals to objective morality are necessary for combating slavery in all of its forms.

While the issue of the morality of slavery does not predominate political/policy discussions in America today, it was at one time the focal point of the most consequential crisis of American history. The crisis of how to approach the institution of slavery dates back to the Constitutional Convention of 1787 and culminated in a bloody civil war. While the crisis was eventually resolved with the complete abolition of chattel slavery in America, this outcome was in no way inevitable. Prior to the outbreak of the American Civil War (1861–1865), debates concerning whether slavery should be prohibited or permitted to expand into newly acquired territories as they became new states dominated the politics of the entire country. Hostile political parties on both sides, proslavery and antislavery, showed no willingness to compromise as tensions over the fate of slavery worsened.

The most significant of the debates concerning the proper fate of American chattel slavery were fought during the U.S. Senate race of 1858 in Illinois between political heavyweight Stephen Douglas of the Democratic Party and the relatively unknown Abraham Lincoln of the newly formed Republican Party. While the two managed their own separate political campaigns in the typical fashion, that is, traveling throughout the congressional districts of Illinois delivering speeches at their own respective events, they incorporated within their campaigns a series of seven joint debates, each in a different district, between August 21 and October 15, 1858. Historian James G. Randall (1945) notes that during these debates, "those two candidates for the Senate talked as if there were only one issue," that concerning slavery (121–122). Although only a local race for U.S. Senate, the seven debates between Lincoln and Douglas gained national attention and had an immense impact on the worsening crisis.

Even prior to their official campaign debates, Lincoln and Douglas had exchanged critiques of each other's positions on the Supreme Court's decision in *Dred Scott v. Sandford* (1857). This decision, which declared that the federal government, and therefore Congress, could not prohibit slavery in the territories, was met with approbation by Douglas and harsh indignation by Lincoln.

Douglas supported the decision because it further affirmed the doctrine of which he had become a famous advocate: popular sovereignty. According to Douglas, "The great principle is the right of every community [i.e. a state] to judge and decide for itself, whether a thing is right or wrong, whether it would be good or evil for them to adopt it" (Johansenn 1968, 27). Thus, the allowance or prohibition of slavery in a state could only be determined by the states themselves, "without interference from any other State or power whatsoever" (73); for Douglas, this question would be best answered through the local democratic process without judgments or federal actions based on objective claims to right and wrong. According to American political theorist Harry V. Jaffa (2009), Douglas believed that "the only way out [of the obstacle of the slavery question in America] was an agreement to disagree and a concentration of all loyalties upon that Constitution which safeguarded this very precious right—the right to disagree" (51). Lincoln, on the other hand, vehemently opposed popular sovereignty believing that slavery was a moral evil that deprived "our republican example of its just influence in the world—[it] enables the enemies of free institutions, with plausibility, to taunt us as hypocrites" (Johansenn 1968, 50). For Lincoln, popular sovereignty was based on "no right principle of action but *self-interest*" (51), and therefore, it was a threat to America's great republican example. For this principle, based solely on self-interest, allowed no room for amorality to guide political decisions and would consequently prove fatal to the ideals of liberty and equality.

At the core of the Lincoln-Douglas debates was their disagreement over the immortal words from the Declaration of

Independence: "all men are created equal." Men like Douglas, and John C. Calhoun before him, argued that the Founders either did not seriously mean these words or did not believe that blacks were true men. Either way, according to these views, the Founders never believed blacks to be naturally equal to whites in any capacity, and thus, white men were justified in enslaving them. While Douglas may have held private animosities toward the institution of slavery, his adherence to the principle of popular sovereignty forbade him from publicly denouncing slavery as a moral evil. For Douglas, no moral judgments could be made by others outside the deciding state because the right thing for each state was simply whatever was in the interest of the majority residing in each state at a given time, even if such decisions resulted in completely contradictory decisions regarding the institution of slavery.

This is an illogical position: the choice of one state voting to prohibit slavery and another's choice voting to allow it cannot both be the "right" choice. Similarly, modern moral relativists exercise the same beliefs that two opposite things can both be right. If the cultures of many African and Middle Eastern countries today believe that slavery *is not* morally evil, how can moral relativists objectively maintain, which they certainly will, that slavery *is* morally evil? They are required by their rejection of objective morality to follow in Douglas' footsteps in being unable to seriously condemn slavery as morally evil.

Conversely, Lincoln maintained that the Declaration's statement of equality "contemplated the progressive improvement in the condition of all men everywhere" (Basler 1990, 362); it is a maxim for all posterity to strive toward removing slavery from the earth. Lincoln's antislavery position, unlike Douglas's, is founded on a philosophical interpretation of the Declaration that supported the claim that slavery was, and will always remain, an objective moral evil.

The age of moral relativism allows for shallow, and often contradictory, platitudes dictating what is right and wrong that lack any meaningful foundation. If we adhere to this school of thought regarding the issue of slavery, we cannot hope to combat this crime against humanity with any serious vigor. The fight to end slavery in our times rests on our ability to argue for the objective truth that slavery is morally evil, regardless of time or place. Our actions in combating it should be guided by firm convictions based on our claims to universal truth. For, without such truth, there is no argument preventing those that enslave today from being enslaved tomorrow.

Joseph W. Bergee is pursuing a PhD in political science with an emphasis in political theory and international relations at the University of California, Riverside.

References

Basler, Roy P. 1990. *Abraham Lincoln: His Speeches and Writings*. New York: Da Capo Press.

Jaffa, Harry V. 2009. *Crisis of the House Divided: An Interpretation of the Issues in the Lincoln-Douglas Debates.* 50th Anniversary Edition. Chicago, IL: University of Chicago Press.

Johannsen, Robert W. 1968. *The Lincoln-Douglas Debates.* New York: Oxford University Press.

Randall, James G. 1945. *Lincoln the President*. Vol. 1. New York: Dodd, Mead & Company.

Rorty, Richard. 1999. "Trotsky and the Wild Orchids." Reprinted from *Philosophy and Social Hope*. New York: Penguin Books.

A Single Medicine for Two Diseases? State Capacity as the Bulwark against Terrorism and Human Trafficking
Steven Childs

The factors that aid and encourage both terrorism and human trafficking are significant security threats, and the solutions to these factors rest in helping national governments around the world strengthen their authority, capacity, and legitimacy. Ever mindful of local challenges, the United States and other developed nations should pursue an active foreign policy of providing assistance to encourage state building.

The region of sub-Saharan Africa has become the newest front in the global fight against terrorism. Salafi-Jihadi terror groups such as al Qaeda and its various offshoots such as the Islamic State have spread their influence, expanding their operations from Central Asia, the Middle East, and North Africa into West and East Africa (Jones et al. 2018, 11). The effects of these groups on the security of the continent have been significant. From 2002 to 2017, researchers estimate that sub-Saharan Africa suffered an average of 4.35 fatalities per terrorist attack, the highest death-per-attack measure out of all regions surveyed, including the Middle East and North Africa, at 2.76 (Institute for Economics & Peace 2018, 34). In fact, the deadliest act of terrorism in all of 2017 was a coordinated suicide attack by the group al-Shabaab in Mogadishu, Somalia, on October 14, 2017. This attack in east Africa killed 587 people and wounded another 316, with a further 62 people unaccounted for (Sullivan 2017). In 2015, these same researchers noted that the West African group Boko Haram had surpassed the Islamic State as the world's deadliest terror group in the period of their assessment. Furthermore, terrorism in this region is shifting to new countries. In October 2017, a team of U.S. Special Forces were ambushed and killed in the West African nation of Niger by the Islamic State of the Greater Sahara. More recently, that group has undertaken additional attacks against the individuals and forces of neighboring countries, such as Burkina Faso, Chad, and Mali (Meservey 2019).

As devastating as these acts of terrorism are, their overall impact is worsened by the fact that the groups that perpetrate them are connected to modern slavery and human trafficking. A direct example of the intersection of the two is evident in the case of the girls from Chibok, Nigeria. In April 2014, Boko Haram kidnapped 276 girls from that town's government school, and many of the girls were trafficked out of the region and forced to marry Boko Haram militants against their will, effectively becoming sex slaves. Although some were fortunately able to escape, over 100 of the girls remain missing to date. While it is the best known case of trafficking, sadly this incident is not the only one. The United Nations Children Fund estimates that over 1,000 children have been abducted by the group since 2013 (Tidey and Hinds 2018). Moreover, the entire region of West Africa remains afflicted by human trafficking. In April 2019, International Police and national law enforcement officials rescued over 200 children who were forced into labor and prostitution (Interpol 2019). While their rescue is clearly a case of success to be celebrated, the trafficking issue in Africa remains a significant challenge. As of the 2019 Trafficking in Persons report by the U.S. State Department, no African country meets the minimum standards of the Trafficking Victims Protection Act (TVPA), which include prohibiting trafficking, punishing traffickers, and demonstrating results in eliminating the practice. Human trafficking remains a lucrative enterprise in Africa, yielding as much as $13.1 billion in profit each year to traffickers (May 2017, 21).

How are the two practices of terrorism and human trafficking related, and what can be done?

Simply stated, the countries in which terror groups and traffickers operate suffer from limited, poor, and weak governance. Persistent state weakness in Somalia and Nigeria enables the rise of terror groups such as al Shabaab and Boko Haram, and unfortunately, such weakness is not exclusive to these two countries on the continent. National governments that fail to govern their legal territories provide effective safe havens for groups to flourish. Research by political scientist James Piazza notes that "states experiencing governability challenges are more prone to terrorism" and that this terrorism is transnational (Piazza 2008, 483).

Piazza's research findings fit within the broader contention of political scientist Samuel Huntington, who famously argued that "the most important political distinction among countries concerns not their form of government but their degree of government" (1968, 1). For Huntington, "The primary problem is not liberty but the creation of a legitimate public order. Men may, of course, have order without liberty, but they cannot have liberty without order" (1968, 7–8). Huntington outlined the need for governance in providing order within a state's boundaries, as the absence of it leads to the viciousness of anarchy where "might makes right" rather than a rule of law. Only after providing for effective governance can liberty be pursued.

Although not a cure-all solution, an important tool in the battle against both terrorism and human trafficking is building the capacity of national governments to provide this order internally. It stands to reason that the same conditions that allow for the unregulated trafficking and exploitation of persons across international borders also allow for the movement of weapons, materials, and combatants (Lounnas 2018, 4). This approach is nested within the concept of sovereignty, a hallmark principle in international relations that a recognized state government is responsible for managing the affairs within its defined boundaries.

Scholars disagree on the primary means of tackling these challenges. Critics contend that efforts toward state building are ineffective and counterproductive. In the case of Africa, Ian Spears argues that many regimes are interested in remaining in power, not in exerting control over the full territory of the state. He notes that because of this, some regimes even have an incentive to keep their countries divided (Spears 2018, 120–121). In lieu of state building, Spears suggests the need for alternate sovereignty models within the state. Examples of this might include relying on tribal leaders, warlords, or militias. Others, such as Robert Malley and Jon Finer, assert that U.S. assistance and involvement in counterterrorism efforts effectively does more harm than good (2018, 65). Citing the case of Egypt, the authors argue that working with its authoritarian government encourages the human rights abuses of the regime, while others see the need to work with that government to go after the Islamic State in the Sinai Peninsula as outweighing those concerns.

These critiques are important, and there are rarely easy answers in foreign policy. Frequently, policymakers search for the "least worst" option in pursuit of the "lesser of the evils." Although national government leaders in Africa and the Middle East regularly commit human rights abuses to stay in power, the empowerment of rival groups within the state frequently encourages anarchy rather than alleviating it. Arguably, the prize of democracy by itself is not a stable form of government unless an effective government has first been cultivated and institutionalized such that it is mature for liberal democracy and capable of providing civil liberty protections for minority groups. Thus, initially good governance should be prized over democratization. Following Huntington's framework provides useful guidance. Encouraging a government to assert control over its territory to counter violent groups and trafficking would be preferred to insisting on reform efforts that undercut those efforts. The Sinai Bedouin who helped the insurgency launch have long maintained grievances against the central government of Egypt owing to marginalization and a lack of effective state capacity in that region of the country. In fact, the U.S. withdrawal from Iraq in 2011 was a key development that allowed for the nearly defeated militants who created the Islamic State to rebound and grow into a regional menace in 2014. Moreover, much like Boko Haram does in Nigeria, the group leveraged its expansion to engage in a plethora of human rights abuses, including the abduction and forced slavery of more than 6,000 Iraqi Yazidi women and children, most of whom were sold at slaver's auctions and sexually assaulted (Whyte 2016). It was Iraq's governmental weakness coupled with a U.S. policy of going "hands-off" that ultimately produced the security and slavery problems made apparent in 2014.

Patrick Henry's famous admonition to "Give me liberty or give me death" may well be amended to "Give me order to avoid death before giving me liberty" in the developing world. Policies to counter terrorism and reduce the tragic impact of human trafficking will require an active foreign policy posture couched in strengthening the capacity of nation-states.

Steven Childs is an assistant professor of political science at California State University, San Bernardino. He teaches undergraduate courses in international relations and graduate courses in national security studies.

References

Huntington, Samuel. 1968. "Political Order in Changing Societies." Accessed March 23, 2020. https://projects.iq .harvard.edu/gov2126/files/huntington_political_order _changing_soc.pdf

Institute for Economics and Peace. 2018. "Global Terrorism Index 2018: Measuring the Impact of Terrorism." November. Accessed March 23, 2020. http:// visionofhumanity.org/app/uploads/2018/12/Global -Terrorism-Index-2018-1.pdf

Interpol. 2019. "Human Trafficking: Hundreds Rescued in West Africa." Accessed March 23, 2020. https:// www.interpol.int/en/News-and-Events/News/2019 /Human-trafficking-hundreds-rescued-in-West-Africa

Jones, Seth G., Charles Vallee, Danika Newlee, Nicholas Harrington, Clayton Sharb, and Hannah Byrne. 2018. "The Evolution of the Salafi-Jihadist Threat: Current and Future Challenges from the Islamic State, Al-Qaeda, and Other Groups." *Center for Strategic and International Studies*. November. Accessed March 23, 2020. https://csis -prod.s3.amazonaws.com/s3fs-public/publication/Jones _EvolvingTerroristThreat_FULL_WEB.pdf

Lounnas, Djallil. 2018. "The Links between Jihadi
    Organizations and Illegal Trafficking in the Sahel." *Middle
    East and North Africa Regional Architecture Working Paper
    25*. November. Accessed March 23, 2020. https://www.iai
    .it/sites/default/files/menara_wp_25.pdf

Malley, Robert, and Jon Finer. 2018. "The Long Shadow of
    9/11: How Counterterrorism Warps U.S. Foreign Policy."
    Foreign Affairs 97, no. 4: 58–69.

May, Channing. 2017. "Transnational Crime and the
    Developing World." *Global Financial Integrity*. March.
    Accessed March 23, 2020. https://secureservercdn
    .net/45.40.149.159/34n.8bd.myftpupload.com/wp
    -content/uploads/2017/03/Transnational_Crime-final.pdf

Meservey, Joshua. 2019. "Africa's Sahel Region Grows as
    Breeding Ground for Terror, Posing Critical Danger
    to U.S. and Allies." *The Heritage Foundation*. May 8.
    Accessed March 23, 2020. https://www.heritage.org/africa
    /commentary/africas-sahel-region-grows-breeding-ground
    -terror-posing-critical-danger-us-and

Piazza, James A. 2008. "Incubators of Terror: Do Failed
    and Failing States Promote Transnational Terrorism?"
    International Studies Quarterly 52, no. 3: 469–488.

Spears, Ian. 2018. "The State System and Africa's Permanent
    Instability." In *Routledge Handbook of African Security*,
    edited by James Hentz. Oxfordshire, United Kingdom:
    Taylor & Francis.

Sullivan, Emily. 2017. "Mogadishu Truck Bomb's
    Death Toll Now Tops 500, Probe Committee Says."
    National Public Radio. December 2. Accessed March
    23, 2020. https://www.npr.org/sections/thetwo
    -way/2017/12/02/567985077/mogadishu-truck-bombs
    -death-toll-now-tops-500-probe-committee-says

Tidey, Christopher, and Eva Hinds. 2018. "More Than 1,000
    Children in Northeastern Nigeria Abducted by Boko
    Haram Since 2013." *United Nations Children Fund*. April

13. Accessed March 23, 2020. https://www.unicef.org/wca
/press-releases/more-1000-children-northeastern-nigeria
-abducted-boko-haram-2013

Whyte, Lara. 2016. "Germany Opens Its Doors to Yazidi
Women and Children Enslaved by Isis." *The Guardian.*
March 2. Accessed March 23, 2020. https://www.theguardian
.com/global-development/2016/mar/02/germany-opens
-doors-yazidi-women-children-northern-iraq-enslaved-isis

Modern Slavery and Open Borders
Kevork Kazanjian

Although much of the controversy over President Donald
Trump's 2016 campaign promise to secure the United States'
border with Mexico has focused on the proper approach to
immigrants pursuing a better life, safety, and economic opportunity, very little attention has been paid to how open borders contribute to modern slavery and how building a stronger
barrier might help reduce forced human trafficking (Gorman
2018).

The United States shares nearly 2,000 miles of border-
land with Mexico, and only 1,100 miles have a fence or wall.
According to the U.S. Customs and Border Patrol (CBP),
in fiscal year (FY) 2018, 683,000 people were apprehended
while trying to illegally enter the country. In the first eight
months of FY 2019, CBP apprehended more than 1 million
persons. In 2018, the Global Slavery Index (GSI) estimated
that, based on 2016 numbers, 403,000 people lived as slaves
in the United States, with roughly 17,000–19,000 having
been trafficked per year through the border and other ports
of entry. Worldwide, the GSI estimated that in 2016, 40.3
million people lived in some sort of modern slavery, which
involves the exploitation of a person through force, fraud, or
coercion, such as forced and early marriages and forced labor.

In October 2018, President Trump appeared before an
interagency task force on trafficking and has several times

since argued that securing the border is necessary to combat forced human trafficking, but the argument that a secure border reduces human trafficking was also made by presidents before Trump. In 2010, President Obama and the Department of Homeland Security (DHS) created the Blue Campaign to coordinate the various anti-trafficking efforts within DHS in an effort to fight human trafficking and modern slavery. According to DHS, as part of a "united effort" under the Blue Campaign, the CBP is "uniquely situated to deter and disrupt human trafficking" (Wyllie N.D.). Porous borders make the jobs of trained border patrol agents seeking to identify victims of forced human trafficking more difficult. The United Nations Office of Drugs and Crime (UNODC) Toolkit to Combat Trafficking in Persons (2006), for instance, specifically cites a link between porous borders and human trafficking: "The permeability of borders aids criminal organizations in the trafficking of persons." In the same article, the UNODC recommends that states increase their border infrastructure to reduce trafficking.

The European Union (EU) is a prominent example of the consequences of unsecured borders. The Schengen Agreement, which was signed in 1985, enacted in 1995, and is signed by any country joining the EU, allows its citizens passport-free movement across borders of other member-states. Without a barrier to force traffickers to bring their victims through controlled entry points, crossing the border with victims is not complicated. According to the European Parliament (EP), between 2013 and 2014, nearly 16,000 victims of trafficking were detected. Between 2012 and 2014, the EP also detected 63,000 victims of human trafficking, and 21 million are estimated to be involved in some sort of forced labor, 54 percent of whom are sexually exploited. The top five countries of origin for victims are the Netherlands, Poland, Hungary, Romania, and Bulgaria, which has caused many to question whether the benefits of the Schengen Agreement are worth the risks. According to the Migration Policy Institute, Romania and

Bulgaria suspended their participation in the agreement over security concerns due to the permeability of borders created by the agreement.

In opposition to those who maintain that a border wall or barrier along the United States southern border would help reduce human trafficking, Bradley Myles (2019), the CEO of Polaris, contends, "A wall along the southern border is not an effective tool to prevent or disrupt human trafficking." According to Myles, many who are subjected to human trafficking have entered the United States through some legal means, and thus, human traffickers are not always caught even when they enter through legal ports of entry. Such claims, however, are notoriously difficult to substantiate, given the extremely hidden nature of the crime. Assuming Myles is correct, the fact remains that victims who are brought into the United States illegally are a particularly vulnerable group. Many of them are lured by the promise of legitimate jobs, and once here, their abusers use deportation as an effective means of deterring victims from seeking help. While there is cause for continued debate over the appropriate approach to immigration policy generally, making illegal entry more difficult effectively reduces the number of the vulnerable migrants residing in the United States.

Israel's human smuggling crisis from Africa between 2010 and 2012 is an excellent example of how a border wall hinders and stops illegal immigration and smuggling. According to the Organization of Economic Cooperation and Development's (OECD) 2015 Migration Policy Debates report, Israel's desert border with Egypt was not fenced, and its permeability was a haven for smugglers who brought in nearly 10,000 victims annually. Once a fence was erected and the country instituted restrictive immigration policies, Israel saw its illegal border crossings "plummet" (OECD 2015). One adopted policy allows victims to reside in temporary facilities until further processing is complete. If the victims' home country is safe, they are sent back. If their home countries are not safe, those seeking asylum are relocated to Canada, Italy, or Germany. This policy is based on a deal made with the United Nations.

Every nation has the right and a duty to protect its borders. This right has been internationally recognized and codified through the Westphalian Treaty (1648), the Montevideo Convention (1933), and the Universal Declaration of Human Rights (UDHR; 1948). Without building a barrier at its unprotected southwest border, the United States will continue to struggle to solve not only its illegal immigration problem but also its modern slavery problem. Congress must reform the immigration process and build the wall at the unsecured portion of the border if they truly seek to combat slavery in the United States. The government has a basic duty to protect its borders in order to secure the rights and liberties of its citizens, while doing what it reasonably can to protect others. A wall to the south will not only help secure the border to protect its citizens but also help protect future victims from being enslaved.

Kevork Kazanjian has a master's degree in national security studies and is a political science instructor at Victor Valley College.

References

Bruxvoort, Dana. 2004."Immigration Controls: Protecting Borders to End Trafficking?" *Human Trafficking Center*. May 15. Accessed September 18, 2019. https://humantraffickingcenter.org /immigration-controls-protecting-borders-end-trafficking/

European Parliament. 2017."Human Trafficking: Nearly 16,000 Victims in the EU." *News*. October 17. Accessed September 18, 2019. http://www.europarl.europa .eu/news/en/headlines/society/20171012STO85932 /human-trafficking-nearly-16-000-victims-in-the-eu

Gorman, Robert F. 2018. "Open Border Advocates Downplay Human Trafficking." *Crisis Magazine*.

November 14. Accessed September 18, 2019. https://www.crisismagazine.com/2018 /open-border-advocates-downplay-human-trafficking

Hyldgaard, Philip. 2015. "Human Trafficking, Migration and Refugees." *End Slavery Now.* April 21. Accessed September 18, 2019. https://www.endslaverynow.org/blog/articles /human-trafficking-migration-and-refugees

Koikkalainen, Saara. 2011. "Free Movement in Europe: Past and Present." *Migration Policy Institute.* April 11. Accessed September 18, 2019. https://www.migrationpolicy.org /article/free-movement-europe-past-and-present

Myles, Bradley. 2019. "Polaris Statement on a Border Wall and Human Trafficking." *Polaris.* February 1. Accessed September 18, 2019. https://polarisproject.org/news/press-releases /polaris-statement-border-wall-and-human-trafficking

Organisation for Economic Cooperation and Development. 2015. "Can We Put an End to Human Smuggling?" *Migration Policy Debates.* November 9. Accessed September 18, 2019. https://www.oecd.org/migration/Can%20 we%20put%20an%20end%20to%20human%20 smuggling.pdf

United Nations Office on Drug and Crime. 2006. "Tool 5.11 Border Control Measures." *Toolkit to Combat Trafficking in Persons.* Accessed September 18, 2019. https://www.unodc .org/documents/human-trafficking/Toolkit-files/08-58296 _tool_5-11.pdf

U.S. Customs and Border Patrol. 2019. "Southwest Border Migration FY 2019." Accessed September 18, 2019. https://www.cbp.gov/newsroom/stats/sw-border-migration

Wyllie, James-Denton. n.d. "Ending Modern Slavery: CBP Fights Human Trafficking through DHS Blue Campaign." *U.S. Customs and Border Protection.* Accessed September 18, 2019. https://www.cbp.gov/frontline /frontline-january-ending-modern-day-slavery

Child Labor Trafficking in the United States: A Hidden Form of Modern Slavery
Vicki Alger

Understanding Child Labor Trafficking

Modern efforts to combat a wider array of forms of human trafficking have intensified over the past two decades. In October 2000, Congress passed the Trafficking Victims Protection Act of 2000 (TVPA), which has been reauthorized several times since, most recently in January 2019 (Enos et al. 2019). In November 2000, the United Nations adopted the Protocol to Prevent, Suppress and Punish Trafficking in Persons, Especially Women and Children, often referred to as the Palermo Protocol, to supplement the UN Convention against Transnational Organized Crime (DOS 2019, 4).

While these measures are intended to promote international cooperation in combating modern slavery, the term "trafficking" suggests that it is largely a transnational problem involving organized crime networks in far-away places (DOS 2019, 6). That notion has impacted public opinion. Most Americans think that human trafficking requires movement across state or international borders (59 percent), while more than 9 out of 10 Americans believe most human trafficking victims are female (92 percent) and illegal immigrants (62 percent) (Bouche et al. 2015, 30). Most Americans acknowledge that labor trafficking happens in the United States (69 percent), but they are less likely to say it is happening in their own states (50 percent) and local communities (20 percent) (Bouche et al. 2015, 31).The reality is quite different.

The defining characteristics of human trafficking today are the actions taken by the traffickers, the means they use, especially force, fraud, or coercion, and the purpose of their exploitation. Importantly, people do not have to be transported from one location to another to be considered human trafficking victims (DOS 2019, 5). Available evidence suggests that more than three-fourths of all trafficking victims globally (77 percent) are exploited in their countries of residence, and that most traffick-ers are also citizens of the countries where they are convicted. The U.S. Department of State reports that "victims of sex traf-ficking more likely faced transnational human trafficking while victims of forced labor typically experienced exploitation in their country of residence" (DOS 2019, 3).

According to the TVPA, child trafficking involves people who are younger than 18 years old. Any minor involved in a commercial sex act is considered a child sex trafficking victim. In contrast, to be considered a victim of child labor traffick-ing, there must be use of force, fraud, and/or coercion (DSGI 2016, 1). Thus, for child labor exploitation to be considered trafficking, those elements must be present (Owens et al. 2014, 5). Child labor trafficking includes both work performed by them as a result of coercion by a third party (other than their parents) either to the children or their parents, and work per-formed by children as a direct consequence of their parents having to perform forced labor (DOL and ILAB 2018; ILO 2012, 16–19; ILO and WFF 2017, 16).

Yet quantifying the extent of human trafficking, child labor trafficking in particular remains challenging and controversial.

Challenges to Identifying the Magnitude of Child Labor Trafficking

The consensus holds that scientifically credible estimates of child labor trafficking in the United States simply do not exist, and the estimates that do exist focus on adults or sex traffick-ing victims (DSGI 2016, 2; Gibbs et al. 2015, 1–1; Hepburn and Simon 2010, 4; KaufkaWalts 2017, 60, 62–63). Reasons include the covert nature of trafficking, which makes it diffi-cult to identify victims, as well as victims' fear about identify-ing themselves. Moreover, child labor and sex trafficking often overlap (DSGI 2016, 1–2). Compounding these challenges are inconsistent definitions and interpretations of child labor traf-ficking (DSGI 2016, 2).

Both the TVPA and the UN Palermo Protocol describe child labor trafficking in terms of compelled service using a variety of terms, "including involuntary servitude, slavery or practices similar to slavery, debt bondage, and forced labor" (DOS 2019, 3). The United States now considers "trafficking in persons," "human trafficking," and "modern slavery" to be "interchangeable umbrella terms" encompassing both sex and labor trafficking (DOS 2019, 3). Moreover, the UN Palermo Protocol does not define key terms such as trafficking, slavery, forced labor, servitude, or exploitation (DOS 2019, 4; Gallagher 2017, 987, 1004).

The failure to define foundational terms, apply them consistently, and the prevailing tendency to conflate slavery and trafficking has complicated efforts to obtain reliable statistics on the scope of child labor trafficking in the United States. There are also notable disparities among estimates reported by international organizations, as well as American government and non-government organizations (Chuang 2014, 623–26; GAO 2006, 1–2, 2018, 1–2; KaufkaWalts 2017, 60; Weitzer 2014, 7–10).

For example, according to the International Labour Organization, the number of forced labor victims worldwide has essentially doubled from 12.3 million victims in 2005 to 25 million in 2017 (DOS 2012, 7, 45; Gallagher 2017, 93; ILO 2017a, 13; Weitzer 2014, 10). The ILO adds that approximately 4.3 million children are in forced labor, representing 18 percent of nearly 25 million forced labor victims worldwide (ILO 2017a, 13). Estimates published in the Walk Free Foundation's *Global Slavery Index* are much higher at 40.3 million people worldwide living in modern slavery (WFF 2018, i–ii, 2, 9, 16, 20, 21, 27; cf. ILO 2017b). Turning to the United States, the Walk Free Foundation estimates that 403,000 people are modern slavery victims, which is a sixfold increase from its upper-bound estimate of 63,000 victims in 2013 (WFF 2013, 121, 123, 2018, 78, 180).

Scholars and journalists alike question—and criticize—such large estimates, especially given the far lower statistics reported by various government agencies (Enos 2017, 3; Gallagher 2017, 93; Kessler 2015; Weitzer 2014, 14). Initial estimates cited in the 2000 TVPA suggested that approximately 50,000 individuals were trafficked into the United States annually. This estimate was subsequently reduced to between 18,000 and 20,000 in the State Department's June 2003 Trafficking in Persons Report and lowered again in its 2005 and 2006 reports to between 14,500 and 17,500 individuals trafficked annually into the United States (Hepburn and Simon 2010, 4).

Ultimately, the State Department's estimation methodology drew such heavy criticism from the U.S. Government Accountability Office, among others, that it no longer offers global or national estimates (Enos 2017, 3; Gallagher 2017, 93; GAO 2006, 1–2, 2018, 2). Meanwhile, the U.S. Bureau of Justice Statistics estimates that between 2008 and 2011 nearly 14 percent of trafficking investigations in the United States involved labor trafficking, based on state and local law enforcement data. Of these cases, 257 involved child trafficking, including 5 labor trafficking cases and 248 sex trafficking cases (DSGI 2016, 3).

Other estimates come from non-government agencies. The Polaris Project, for example, manages the National Human Trafficking Resource Center Hotline (NHTRC) in partnership with the United States government. It estimates that there were 1,090 cases of labor trafficking involving at least one minor in the United States between December 2008 and March 2017, roughly 20 percent of all labor trafficking cases reported to the NHTRC (DSGI 2016, 3; KaufkaWalts 2017, 60).

In spite of the lack of uniform definitions and methodologies for identifying human trafficking victims, federal and state legislative efforts have intensified in recent years. In fact, today every state now has laws criminalizing human trafficking (NCSL n.d.; Tiegen 2018, 1–2). Recent research also indicates that since 2003 state penalties for child labor trafficking have become more severe, increasing from an average of 2 years to 20 years (DSGI 2016, 7).

Still, most state laws largely focus on combating sex trafficking of children (Bouche et al. 2015, 12–13; Enos et al. 2019;

KaufkaWalts 2017, 63–64; Tiegen 2018, 2–3). Such efforts must continue, but the plight of children victimized by labor trafficking in the United States must not be overshadowed.

Scholars worry that the lack of credible data about child labor trafficking in the United States could be underrepresenting the magnitude of the problem, as well as efforts to eliminate it (DSGI 2016, 3; KaufkaWalts 2017, 60). Research also suggests that despite the growing number of laws criminalizing child labor trafficking, they are rarely applied. Some researchers believe that state and county prosecutors need more education about applying the laws to protect child labor trafficking victims (Bouche et al. 2015, 1–3; DSGI 2016, 7; KaufkaWalts 2017, 65). Moreover, even though a variety of human trafficking screening tools exist for social service providers, none have been validated for identifying child labor trafficking victims (DSGI 2016, 8).

Children at Greatest Risk for Labor Trafficking

Despite the data limitations, sufficient evidence exists that several populations of children are vulnerable to labor trafficking in the United States. Foreign-born and undocumented children are one vulnerable population. Unaccompanied children who are smuggled into the United States often become labor trafficking victims when they are forced to pay off the costs of bringing them across the border. Forms of forced labor they endure include domestic servitude as nannies or housekeepers, agriculture, work in restaurants and factories, or even criminal work for drug cartels and gangs (DSGI 2016, 3–4; KaufkaWalts 2017, 61–62; NHTRC 2015, 2–5). Under the TVPA, the Secretary of the U.S. Department of Health and Human Services may issue Letters of Eligibility to child trafficking victims, which make them eligible to receive the same benefits and services as refugees (Attorney General 2018, 5t6; HHS 2019b). The U.S. Department of Health and Human Services (HHS) has issued 2,383 Eligibility Letters to children from 2001 through 2018 (HHS 2019a). Foreign-born children lured to the United States through competitive sports are also vulnerable, falling prey to promises of a high school education and college scholarships (KaufkaWalts 2017, 62).

Contrary to popular belief, several populations of American-born children are also at risk for labor trafficking. Homeless and runaway youth are vulnerable to promises of paid employment, food, shelter, and clothing. Often these children become part of traveling sales crews forced to sell magazines, candy, or other items door to door or outside of gas stations. They live in cramped motel rooms, are driven around in crowded vans to unfamiliar neighborhoods, and forced to sell items. Often, they are given unreasonable sales quotas, and their food is rationed (KaufkaWalts 2017, 61). Although precise estimates of homeless youth who are victims of labor trafficking are not available, the U.S. Department of Housing and Urban Development reports that each night approximately 111,592 children experience homelessness (Henry et al. 2018, 11).

More disturbing still is that fact that children who are connected with social service and justice systems are also at greater risk for labor trafficking. These include minors in the child welfare, juvenile justice, and foster-care systems (DOS 2019, 492; Gibbs et al. 2015, 1–2). Few social-service programs exist that focus exclusively on child labor victims, and those that do have not been rigorously evaluated (DSGI 2016, 8–9). Emerging research finds that child labor trafficking victims often encounter more than one social service system that fails to identify them as victims. One analysis of the state of Illinois, for example, found that suspected child trafficking victims had at least four encounters with the child welfare system (KaufkaWalts 2017, 65).

Conclusion

The recent reauthorization of the TVPA is an important step in the right direction. It encourages private-sector support to strengthen federal enforcement efforts to combat human trafficking, including child labor trafficking, as well as enhanced training in victim protection for law enforcement, service providers, and school officials. It also provides direct services for victims and requires improved data collection (Public Law No [PL] 115-392 2018; PL 115-393 2018; PL 115-425 2019; PL 115-427 2019). Yet efforts to combat child trafficking must not be limited to the federal government.

Child labor trafficking is happening in the communities where we live. Supporting strong networks of private, philanthropic, and faith-based organizations in our neighborhoods to help combat child labor trafficking is something we can all do. Coordinating information sharing, volunteer efforts, and lessons learned could make a significant difference in the lives of children who are or who may become child victims. Child labor trafficking is a hidden form of modern slavery, but it does not have to be. The next time we see a young person begging, or children who seem too young to be peddling cheap goods, we should talk to them. Ask them where their parents are, if they are hungry, or whether they would like help. If anything seems amiss, we should call the local authorities and share our concern that they may be a child labor trafficking victim. Those simple first steps just may be the lifeline a trafficked child needs.

Vicki Alger, PhD, is a research fellow at the Independent Institute in Oakland, California, and author of Failure: The Federal Misedukation of America's Children. *She is also a Senior Fellow at the Independent Women's Forum in Winchester, Virginia.*

References

Attorney General. 2018. "Attorney General's Annual Report to Congress on U.S. Government Activities to Combat Trafficking in Human Persons: Fiscal Year 2017." *Department of Justice.* Accessed November 13,

2019. https://www.justice.gov/humantrafficking/page/file/1103081/download

Bouche, Vanessa, Amy Farrell, and Dana Wittmer. 2015. "Identifying Effective Counter-Trafficking Programs and Practices in the U.S.: Legislative, Legal, and Public Opinion Strategies That Work." *Prepared for the U.S. Department of Justice.* Accessed October 13, 2019. https://www.ncjrs.gov/pdffiles1/nij/grants/249670.pdf

Chuang, Janie A. 2014. "Exploitation Creep and the Unmaking of Human Trafficking Law." *American Journal of International Law* 108, no. 4: 609–649.

Development Services Group. 2016. "Child Labor Trafficking. Literature Review." *Prepared for the U.S. Office of Juvenile Justice and Delinquency Prevention.* Accessed October 13, 2019. https://www.ojjdp.gov/mpg/litreviews/child-labor-trafficking.pdf

Enos, Olivia. 2017. "The Case for Reforming the Trafficking in Persons Report." Issue Brief. No. 4727. *The Heritage Foundation.* June 30. Accessed October 13, 2019. https://www.heritage.org/sites/default/files/2017-06/IB4727.pdf

Enos, Olivia, Michelle Kim, Yeondoo Kim, and Emma Childs. 2019. "These New Laws Will Strengthen US Efforts to Combat Human Trafficking." *Daily Signal. The Heritage Foundation.* March 25. Accessed August 3, 2019. https://www.dailysignal.com/2019/03/25/these-new-laws-will-strengthen-us-efforts-to-combat-human-trafficking/

Gallagher, Anne T. 2017. "What's Wrong with the Global Slavery Index?" *Anti-Trafficking Review* No. 8 (April): 90–102.

Gibbs, Deborah, Jennifer L. Hardison Walters, Alexandra Lutnick, Shari Miller, and Marianne Kluckman. 2015. "Evaluation of Services for Domestic Minor Victims of

Human Trafficking." *U.S. Department of Justice.* Accessed October 13, 2019. https://www.ncjrs.gov/pdffiles1/nij /grants/248578.pdf

Henry, Meghan, Anna Mahathey, Tyler Morrill, Anna Robinson, AzimShivji, and Rian Watt. 2018. "The 2018 Annual Homeless Assessment Report (AHAR) to Congress." *U.S. Department of Housing and Urban Development, Office of Community Planning and Development.* Accessed November 13, 2019. https://files .hudexchange.info/resources/documents/2018-AHAR -Part-1.pdf

Hepburn, Stephanie, and Rita J. Simon. 2010. "Hidden in Plain Sight: Human Trafficking in the United States." *Gender Issues* 27, no. 2: 1–26.

International Labour Office (ILO). 2012. "Hard to See, Harder to Count: Survey Guidelines to Estimate Forced Labour of Adults and Children." Accessed July 29, 2019. http://un-act.org/wp-content/uploads/2015/06/Harder-to -See-Harder-to-Count.pdf

International Labour Organization (ILO). 2017a. "Global Estimates of Child Labour: Results and Trends, 2012-2016." Accessed July 29, 2019. https://www.ilo.org /wcmsp5/groups/public/---dgreports/---dcomm /documents/publication/wcms_575499.pdf

International Labour Organization (ILO). 2017b. "40 Million in Modern Slavery and 152 Million in Child Labour Around the World." September 19. Accessed July 29, 2019. https://www.ilo.org/global/about-the-ilo /newsroom/news/WCMS_574717/lang--en/index.htm

International Labour Organization (ILO) and Walk Free Foundation (WFF). 2017. "Global Estimates of Modern Slavery: Forced Labour and Forced Marriage." Accessed July 29, 2019. https://www.ilo.org/wcmsp5/groups /public/@dgreports/@dcomm/documents/publication /wcms_575479.pdf

Kaufka Walts, Katherine. 2017. "Child Labor Trafficking in the United States: A Hidden Crime." *Social Inclusion* 5, no. 2: 59–68.

Kessler, Glenn. 2015. "Why You Should Be Wary of Statistics on 'Modern Slavery' and 'Trafficking.'" *Washington Post*. April 24. Accessed August 15, 2019. https://www.washingtonpost.com/news/fact-checker/wp/2015/04/24/why-you-should-be-wary-of-statistics-on-modern-slavery-and-trafficking/

National Conference of State Legislatures. n.d. "Human Trafficking State Laws." Accessed November 13, 2019. http://www.ncsl.org/research/civil-and-criminal-justice/human-trafficking-laws.aspx

National Human Trafficking Resource Center (NHTRC). 2015. "Child Labor Trafficking in the United States." *Polaris*. Accessed September 5, 2019. https://humantraffickinghotline.org/sites/default/files/Child%20Labor%20Trafficking%20Fact%20Sheet%20-%202015%20Update%20-%209.29.15.pdf

Office of the United Nations High Commissioner for Human Rights (OHCHR). 2000. "Protocol to Prevent, Suppress and Punish Trafficking in Persons Especially Women and Children, supplementing the United Nations Convention against Transnational Organized Crime. Adopted and opened for signature, ratification and accession by General Assembly resolution 55/25 of 15 November 2000." Accessed July 3, 2019. https://www.ohchr.org/EN/ProfessionalInterest/Pages/ProtocolTraffickingInPersons.aspx

Owens, Colleen, Meredith Dank, Justin Breaux, Isela Bañuelos, Amy Farrell, Rebecca Pfeffer, Katie Bright, Ryan Heitsmith, and Jack McDevitt. 2014. "Understanding the Organization, Operation, and Victimization Process of Labor Trafficking in the United States." *The Urban Institute*. Accessed October 13, 2019. https://www.rhyttac.net/

assets/docs/Research/research%20-%20understanding%20 the%20process%20of%20labor%20trafficking.pdf

Public Law No: 115-392. 2018. "Abolish Human Trafficking Act of 2017 (S. 1311)." Accessed July 25, 2019. https://www.congress.gov/115/plaws/publ392/PLAW -115publ392.pdf

Public Law No: 115-393. 2018. "Trafficking Victims Protection Act of 2017 (S.1312)." Accessed July 25, 2019. https://www.congress.gov/115/plaws/publ393/PLAW -115publ393.pdf

Public Law No: 115-425. 2019. "Frederick Douglass Trafficking Victims Prevention and Protection Reauthorization Act of 2018 (H.R.2200)." Accessed July 25, 2019. https://www.congress.gov/115/plaws/publ425 /PLAW-115publ425.pdf

Public Law No: 115-427. 2019. "Trafficking Victims Protection Reauthorization Act of 2017 (S. 1862)." Accessed July 25, 2019. https://www.congress.gov/115 /plaws/publ427/PLAW-115publ427.pdf

Tiegen, Anne. 2018. "Prosecuting Human Traffickers: Recent Legislative Enactments." *National Conference of State Legislatures.* Accessed November 13, 2019. http://www .ncsl.org/Portals/1/HTML_LargeReports/Prosecuting _Traffickers_091818_32767.pdf

United States Department of Health and Human Services, Office on Trafficking in Persons. 2019a. "Certification and Eligibility Letters Issued." July 15. Accessed November 13, 2019. https://www.acf.hhs.gov/otip/resource/lettersissued

United States Department of Health and Human Services, Office on Trafficking in Persons. 2019b. "Eligibility Letters." August 7. Accessed November 13, 2019. https:// www.acf.hhs.gov/otip/victim-assistance/eligibility-letters

United States Department of Labor (DOL), Bureau of International Labor Affairs (ILAB). 2018. "Child Labor,

Forced Labor & Human Trafficking." Accessed August 2, 2019. https://www.dol.gov/agencies/ilab/our-work /child-forced-labor-trafficking

United States Department of State (DOS). 2019. "Trafficking in Persons Report." Accessed July 29, 2019. https://www .state.gov/wp-content/uploads/2019/06/2019-Trafficking -in-Persons-Report.pdf

United States Department of State (DOS). 2012. "Trafficking in Persons Report." Accessed July 29, 2019. https://2009 -2017.state.gov/documents/organization/192587.pdf; https://2009-2017.state.gov/j/tip/rls/tiprpt/2012//index .htm

United States Government Accountability Office (GAO). 2006. "Human Trafficking: Better Data, Strategy, and Reporting Needed to Enhance U.S. Antitrafficking Efforts Abroad." *GAO-06–825*. Accessed July 29, 2019. https:// www.gao.gov/new.items/d06825.pdf

United States Government Accountability Office (GAO). 2018. "2018 Human Trafficking: State and USAID Should Improve Their Monitoring of International Counter- trafficking Projects." *GAO-19–77*. Accessed July 29, 2019. https://www.gao.gov/assets/700/695792.pdf

Walk Free Foundation (WFF). 2013. "Global Slavery Index 2013." *United States*. Accessed November 12, 2019. http://www.freedom.firm.in/wp-content/uploads/2014 /04/GlobalSlaveryIndex_2013_Download_WEB1 .pdf

Walk Free Foundation (WFF). 2018. "Global Slavery Index 2018." Accessed August 3, 2019. https://www .traffickingmatters.com/wp-content/uploads/2018/08/GSI -2018_FNL_180807_DigitalSmall_p.pdf

Weitzer, Ronald. 2014. "New Directions in Research on Human Trafficking." *Annals of the American Academy of Political and Social Science* 653, no. 1: 6–24.

Prostitution: Upholding Women's Rights as Human Rights with the Equality Model
Autumn Burris

> "It is a violation of human rights when women and girls are sold into the slavery of prostitution."
>
> —First Lady Hillary Rodham Clinton
> Remarks for the United Nations
> Fourth World Conference on Women,
> Beijing, China, September 5, 1995

Twenty-five years ago, former first lady Hillary Clinton declared before the United Nations Fourth World Conference on Women, "If there is one message that echoes forth from this conference, let it be that human rights are women's rights and women's rights are human rights, once and for all" (Clinton 1995). At that time, the exploitation and purchase of women and girls' bodies was widely acknowledged as a degradation of women's rights. Currently, however, public perception is being manipulated by well-funded individuals and organizations, many of whom promote and profit from the sex trade. Self-described "sex workers" and the pro-prostitution lobby loudly promulgate the myth that selling sex is a legitimate form of employment; some even argue that it is a symbol of women's empowerment. Certain large philanthropic non-governmental and international organizations echo these arguments. In fact, in 2008, an employee for Amnesty International, who had promoted the organization's pro-prostitution stance, was revealed to be a pimp (Bindel 2017).

In reality, the argument that prostitution is merely a freely chosen form of employment is erroneous. The sex trade in all of its forms perpetuates male entitlement to sexual gratification through violence and the sexual commodification of women and girls, particularly women of color and indigenous women. Thus, as world leaders meet at the United Nations headquarters in New York City for the Beijing +25 Commission on the

Status of Women, it is more important than ever that they acknowledge that all systems of prostitution are a violation of human rights—in particular women's right *not* to be bought and sold.

The argument over prostitution as a women's rights issue has caused a split within feminism. Like other feminists, abolitionist feminists—those who oppose prostitution as a violation of women's human rights—aim to promote full equality of males and females and staunchly oppose the prison industrial complex and racism, sexism, and patriarchy in all its forms. Feminists on both sides of the issue agree that exploited persons should not be arrested or criminalized in any manner and that amnesty should be granted to women who are arrested and prosecuted for engaging in prostitution. In contrast, to other feminists, however, abolitionist feminists (among which I am included) believe that prostitution itself violates equality and helps maintain patriarchy by enabling males to purchase and abuse female bodies for their own sexual gratification. Thus, abolitionist feminists depart from other feminists in that they support penalizing the purchasers of sexual access to women's bodies, who contribute to the demand for prostituted persons, and criminalizing traffickers, who profit at the expense of women and girls. In short, abolitionist feminists support the Equality Model.

The Equality Model, sometimes referred to as the Nordic, Swedish, or Abolitionist model, has been adopted in some form by eight countries. The Equality Model decriminalizes all prostituted persons, provides exit funding and services for women wishing to leave the sex trade, holds sex buyers accountable, and continues to criminalize traffickers. Importantly, the model also supports a public awareness and education campaign to counter the view that purchasing sex is an acceptable societal behavior.

The Equality Model is the only approach to the sex trade that is consistent with the current tenets of international and U.S. law. The United Nations' Protocol to Prevent, Suppress and Punish Trafficking in Persons Especially Women and Children, often referred to as the "Palermo Protocol," has been ratified by 190 State Parties since its introduction in 2000. The Palermo Protocol states that trafficking includes "the transportation, transfer, harboring or receipt of persons, by means of the threat or use of force or other forms of coercion, of abduction, of fraud, of deception, of the abuse of power or of a position of vulnerability or of the giving or receiving of payments or benefits to achieve the consent of a person having control over another person, for the purpose of exploitation. Exploitation shall include, at minimum, the exploitation of the prostitution of others or other forms of sexual exploitation." The Protocol further asserts that "States Parties shall adopt or strengthen legislative or other measures, such as educational, social or cultural measures, including through bilateral and multilateral cooperation, to discourage the demand that fosters all forms of exploitation of persons, especially women and children, that leads to trafficking." (OHCHR 2000, Articles 3 and 9.5). The Equality Model fully supports and is designed to achieve this mandate.

The Equality Model is likewise congruent with the U.S. Justice for Victims of Trafficking Act of 2015 (JVTA). The JVTA changed the landscape of U.S. law by amending the Trafficking Victims Protection Act to include U.S. citizens and permanent residents who are victims of severe forms of trafficking. Additionally important, the JVTA changed the definition of trafficking to include as perpetrators persons who obtain, patronize, or solicit commercial sex acts involving a person subject to severe forms of trafficking in persons (i.e., the buyers who fuel the demand for trafficked persons). Thus, the act mandates prosecution of individuals who patronize or solicit persons for a commercial sex act, making traffickers and buyers equally culpable for sex trafficking offenses.

In addition to its compatibility with international and U.S. law, the Equality Model is rooted in the lived experience and stories of exited survivors, rather than the narratives of those currently profiting from the sex trade. The vast majority of exited survivors worldwide do not view prostitution as just another form of employment and do not condone legal immunity for either pimps or buyers of sex no matter what the circumstance. On one international panel featuring the voices of survivors, for example, Jeanette Westbrook—a survivor from Louisville, Kentucky—criticized efforts in the United States to legally distinguish between prostitution and trafficking, arguing that such efforts ignore the fact that prostitution inherently involves violence and exploitation, and that for nearly all prostitutes "that continuum of violence began years ago in incest, child abuse, and poverty" (Murphy 2016). Ne'Cole Daniels, another survivor, testified that although criminalizing prostitutes further victimizes women, legalization would only lead to more victims. Nearly all of the women she sees in prostitution, Daniels pointed out, come from dysfunctional backgrounds, such as the foster care system, which make them extremely vulnerable to exploitation. The only solution for helping the exploited is the Nordic Model, which focuses on providing exit funding and services while still criminalizing traffickers and johns (Murphy 2016).

My own experience as an exited survivor of the sex trade supports these conclusions. In March of 1997, I exited the sex trade in all its various forms—from the stripping "industry" orchestrated by organized crime to street prostitution, high end, low end, and all points in between. The venue of paid sexual access to my body deeply affected my psyche and each encounter felt like a tax on my soul. I exited because I was sick and tired—physically, emotionally, psychologically, and spiritually—from the harms I endured in "the life" that is no life at all for a human being.

During my time spent in the sex trade, the term "sex trafficking" did not exist. Young women like me were not considered victims but criminals to be repeatedly arrested and stigmatized.

We were deemed "bad girls" and were offered no services or way out. It was clear that very few cared about our lives and well-being and that no one would "rescue" us. I often felt that dying would be easier than living. My soul and belief in my own humanity were undergoing death by prostitution. I myself, along with a majority of women in the trade, did not recognize how our pre-existing life conditions had contributed to our involvement in the trade. We minimized the multitude of harms, exploitation, violence, and near-death experiences we had on a daily basis. We continued to cope with the objectification of our bodies by laughing it off and telling ourselves that our lives were lucrative, a choice, empowering, and part of "work." It is impossible to be actively engaged in prostitution and fully acknowledge the exploitive reality of one's life—one must believe these myths and lies in order to continue in the exploitive environment. Only after I exited did the truth about the sex trade become clear to me. Hustling, as we called it—whether in a strip club, on a street corner, or in an upscale hotel—violated my human-ity and basic rights on the deepest level.

In the 1970s, the personal is political became the mantra of the feminist movement. This has been the mantra of my life as well. Since exiting, I have sought to use my personal experi-ence to influence the political. Within six months of exiting, I pursued employment at Standing Against Global Exploita-tion (SAGE), a San Francisco-based survivor-led program. This experience provided me with the training necessary to engage in policy advocacy and activism as a subject matter expert. In this capacity, I have proudly worked alongside others to ensure the enactment of laws and policies that penalize the demand, criminalize profiteers, and offer exit programming for those who wish to exit systems of prostitution.

My lifelong journey has shown me that pro-prostitution myths of empowerment and "choice" must be dismantled and that recovering from the sex trade is possible. To those still in systems of prostitution, there is hope, real empowerment, resiliency, and a life beyond exploitation. To the many women whose lives have been lost as a result of the violence and exploitation in the sex trade, I forever hold you in my heart. The past two decades of my efforts to end all systems of prostitution are for you, Sisters!

Autumn Burris holds a bachelor of arts in political science and public policy and a minor in human rights from the University of California, San Diego. As a subject matter and lived-experience expert, she has advocated for policy at the United Nations and British Parliament and has been involved in legislative advocacy internationally, in the United States at the federal level, and in multiple states and local jurisdictions.

References

Bindel, Julie. 2017. "A Union of Pimps and Johns." *Truthdig.* May 19. Accessed October 7, 2019. https://www.truthdig.com/articles/a-union-of-pimps-and-johns/

Clinton, Hillary R. 1995. "Remarks at the United Nations Fourth World Conference on Women, Beijing, China." September 5. Accessed October 7, 2019. https://www.un.org/esa/gopher-data/conf/fwcw/conf/gov/950905175653.txt

Murphy, Meghan. 2016. "Survivors Say the Nordic Model Is Our Only Hope." *Feminist Current.* March 15. Accessed October 7, 2019. https://www.feministcurrent.com/2016/03/15/survivors-say-the-nordic-model-is-our-only-hope/

Office of the United Nations High Commissioner for Human Rights (OHCHR). 2000. "Protocol to Prevent, Suppress and Punish Trafficking in Persons Especially Women and Children, Supplementing the United Nations Convention against Transnational Organized Crime." Accessed October 7, 2019. https://www.ohchr.org/Documents/ProfessionalInterest/ProtocolonTrafficking.pdf

The Role of the Church in Fighting Modern Slavery
Peter C. Hodgson

Of all the injustices plaguing the world today, human trafficking is the largest, most profitable, most heinous, and most difficult to eradicate (Federal Bureau of Investigation). It can be easy to believe that human trafficking is too entrenched to even be addressed by legislation and prosecution—that it can be fought, but not eradicated. While this sentiment might be justified, the fact remains that there continues to be hope in the fight against human trafficking—both globally and in the United States. Although this injustice is addressed by various non-governmental organizations and falls directly under the purview of legitimate governments, the Church should be the vanguard in this fight because Christians have an obligation to actively fight injustice and oppression in their nation and community.

Why the Church Should Fight Slavery

The Church's obligation to fight human trafficking is built upon three pillars—the culpability of the Church, the benefits to the Church, and God's will for His Church. On the whole, members of the Church do not tend to differ from the bulk of society in either sinfulness or buying habits, which leads to the inevitable conclusion that they unwittingly contribute to systems of slavery (Bales 2009; Somers 2014). More importantly, churches that are striving together in a shared mission will find their community grow closer, their faith strengthened, and their love for God deepened (Martin 2012). Finally, and most essentially, God primarily works His will on the earth through the Church. The Scriptures are clear that God is a God of justice, and since He regularly commands His people to seek justice, we can only conclude that His desire for the Church to seek justice is as universal as His desire of us to love one another, care for the vulnerable, or spread the Gospel (Haugen 2009, pp. 83, 111).

How the Church Should Fight Slavery

There are four key ways in which the Church is uniquely positioned to fight modern slavery. These include reducing the demand for illicit sex, changing buying habits, protecting the vulnerable from becoming future victims, and helping current victims. By holding its members accountable, extolling the dignity of all people, and refusing to turn a blind eye to the consumption of pornography, the Church can reduce demand for sexual services, and through increased awareness and education, the Church can encourage its members to purchase objects that are ethically sourced, reducing demand for labor trafficking. By building better families and creating safe havens for the vulnerable, the Church can help prevent future victims from being caught up in trafficking. Finally, by partnering with NGOs that are already fighting trafficking in their communities and across the world, the Church can help to rescue and restore current victims of trafficking.

The First Element: Reducing Demand for Illicit Sex

In modern Western society, personal desire—particularly in the realm of sexual autonomy—is often valued above all other freedoms. By placing their own desires above the needs and desires of those around them, individuals break the moral framework of what constitutes a decent, loving relationship. Instead of seeking the well-being of the other for their own sake, they internally rationalize, "I want what I want, and I don't care what it takes to get it." This attitude leads individuals to fulfill their desires through pornography and prostitution, where consent is implied to the consumer, and sometimes through rape and assault, where consent is ignored by the consumer.

How can the Church respond to this? The answer can only be found in Scripture—recognizing that each person is made in the Imago Dei (Image of God) and as such is due dignity and respect. When the needs and dignity of the other are constantly placed above our own, as Paul directs, there is no room for sex-seeking behavior that destroys that dignity. The only healthy foundation for all relationships is love, which always strives to lift the other up. This foundation must be stressed constantly by the Church, because the benefits that it reaps are innumerable. The mentality of putting others first leads to stronger marriages, homes, and communities—but it also eliminates the drive to gratify one's own desire at the expense of another.

The Second Element: Protecting the Vulnerable

The second distinct way that the church can combat human trafficking is by working to protect the vulnerable. Among the most vulnerable in America are children in the foster care system—roughly half a million youth (U.S. Department of Health and Human Services, 2015). If each of the nearly three hundred thousand churches in the United States found two members to adopt a child, orphans would disappear from the United States and criminals would be deprived of their most vulnerable targets (Stier, 2016).

The church can also work to protect those vulnerable to trafficking by working to eradicate sexual and physical abuse against children. The U.S. Department of Justice reports that as many as one in six boys and one in four girls are sexually abused before the age of 18 (n.d). Considering the equivalence in statistics between Christians and non-Christians when it comes to other sexual sins, there is no reason to suspect that this issue will be any less rampant inside the Church than outside of it. This horror needs to be addressed both in the Church and in the communities around them if the Church is going to have any impact on future victims. Church staff and children's ministry workers should understand mandatory reporting laws, know the signs of sexual abuse and trafficking, and be prepared to ask hard questions of individual members (Martin 2012, 159).

Instead of being a place of judgment and shame, the Church needs to be a safe haven for both victims and perpetrators of abuse to find the help they need and unconditional support. The church should strive to offer concrete services to victims in need (Martin 2012, 159–160). To discover resources latent within the church, Martin recommends that churches conduct a survey to find skills, talents, possessions, and passions that can be utilized in the fight for justice (Martin 2012, 162). Ideally, healthy communities will be able to intervene before their members fall into abusive behavior, but this can only be achieved through the careful development of open and honest small groups that prioritize accountability.

The Third Element: Changing Buying Habits

Labor trafficking is the most common form of trafficking in the world, and it typically manifests by infecting the supply chains of everyday products (Bales 2009, 141–142). By choosing to educate themselves about potentially dangerous products, churchgoers can make informed decisions about their buying habits. For example, one might choose to avoid clothing made in Bangladesh because of the high prevalence of sweatshops in that nation. Or one could choose to seek out brands that are Fair Trade Certified, especially for common products such as coffee and chocolate. Some items, such as diamonds or exotic fish, should be avoided altogether because of the risks associated with their supply chains. Also, churches should actively pressure corporations to investigate and clean up their supply chains.

In addition to attempting to avoid slave-made goods, individuals should seek out goods made by those who have been rescued from human trafficking. Numerous organizations train those they rescue to provide for themselves by making clothing, jewelry, and numerous other items. It is fairly simple to identify such organizations and pass the information on to an entire church or community. Larger churches may even wish to partner with local organizations in order to showcase the products made by local survivors, boosting the organizations while raising awareness within their congregation.

The Fourth Element: Helping Current Victims

The Church is uniquely equipped to help current victims of human trafficking, but not always in the way that laypeople first imagine. Martin and Haugen agree that, "the kind of engagement that actually serves the children and families who are suffering right now is often not what is pictured by a passionate leader anxious to get moving immediately" (Martin 2012, 101). In his work, Martin shares numerous examples of churches contributing to the work of justice in wonderful ways, which can be boiled down to a few major categories: partnering with active organizations to rescue victims, partnering with or creating new organizations to restore victims, pushing government officials to make trafficking and other justice issues a bigger priority in their jurisdiction, and making justice a more present theme in their regular teaching and activities.

While these methods may seem, at first glance, to be less impactful than "kicking down doors and rescuing people," the reality is that direct intervention is best left to the experts. Even the most well-meaning volunteers can easily find themselves running afoul of best practices in this field, simply because of the inherent complexities of the issue. Thus, church is best suited to adopt a supportive role—one that is crucial to the success of the work, both globally and in the United States.

Conclusion

When individuals hear of evil being perpetrated, often their initial desire is to immediately try to stop it. The sheer size and prevalence of modern slavery means that it cannot be dealt with through a single act or movement, but only through a long, concentrated fight to rework the systems that allow slavery to flourish. The Church is uniquely suited to provide crucial support to those on the frontline of that fight while simultaneously striving to change the very fabric of society, and the hearts of individuals, to make slavery untenable.

Peter C. Hodgson's heart broke when he learned about modern slavery as a high schooler. He has since devoted himself to studying modern slavery, raising awareness, and urging the local church to fulfill their obligation to fight for justice. He lives in Tennessee with his wife, who serves as a mentor and therapist for survivors of sex trafficking.

References

Bales, Kevin R. S. 2009. *The Slave Next Door: Human Trafficking and Slavery in America Today.* London, United Kingdom: University of California Press.

Federal Bureau of Investigation. n.d. "Human Trafficking." Accessed December 4, 2016. https://www.fbi.gov /investigate/civil-rights/human-trafficking

Haugen, G. 2009. *Good News About Injustice: A Witness of Courage in a Hurting World.* Nottingham, United Kingdom: InterVarsity Press.

Martin, J. 2012. *The Just Church.* Carol Stream, IL: Tyndale House Publishers.

Somers, M. 2014. "The Washington Times." August 24. Accessed October 2016. http:// www.washingtontimes.com/news/2014/aug/24 /more-than-half-of-christian-men-admit-to-watching-/

Stier, G. 2016. "The Christian Post." February 16. Accessed November 21, 2016. http://www.christianpost.com/news /church-planting-growth-pastors-evangelicals-ministry -america-157730/

U.S. Department of Health and Human Services. 2015. "Trends in Foster Care and Adoption: FY 2005 - FY 2014." Accessed March 23, 2020. http://www.acf.hhs.gov/sites /default/files/cb/trends_fostercare_adoption2014.pdf

U.S. Department of Justice. n.d. "Raising Awareness about Sexual Abuse: Facts and Statistics." Accessed December 4,

2016. https://www.nsopw.gov/en-US/Education/FactsStatis
tics?AspxAutoDetectCookieSupport=1

Ending Child Sex Trafficking through Prevention
Carl Ralston

The Problem: The Worldwide and Economic Scope of Child Sex Trafficking

UNICEF estimated that in 2017, 1,200,000 children entered the sex trade for the first time, a 20 percent increase from 2003 (UNICEF 2018). The contribution of increased demand to this rise in trafficking was made obvious by researchers who concluded that without male demand for commercial sex, the slave trade would not exist (Siddharth 2009, 33). The continuous drop in prices for sex enticed return customers and new clients. Researchers focused on the economic realities of trafficking have found that while poverty-stricken sections of the world provide the soil for this practice of child sex trafficking to thrive, the demand comes from even the most affluent corners of the world. One study found that of the 240 foreigners who abused children in Asia, 25 percent were from America (Rafferty 2013, 559–575). Additionally, researchers have found that persons from every state in America and most nations have engaged in or fostered the sexual trafficking of children (Campagna and Poffenberger 1988, 4).

Responses to the Worldwide, Economic Scope of Child Sex Trafficking

The two main responses to child sex trafficking are referred to as "Intervention" and "Prevention." Most of the work to overturn child sex trafficking has involved "intervention." Organizations and some governments engage in various heroic protocols to liberate children *after* they enter the sex trade. By a cruel irony, and without any inherent fault of interventionists, these efforts have not prevented child sex slavery from continuing and increasing by 20 percent between 2003 and 2018

(UNICEF 2018). Researchers have found that for each successful intervention, those benefitting from the sex trade simply recruit other children to replace those rescued. This cycle of rescue efforts has ended with perpetrators bringing even more children for the first time into the sex trade. Through research and 15 years of field work, the author discovered that many interventionist programs had recidivism rates greater than 70 percent and that intervention costs were often ten times that of prevention costs (Ralston 2004, 2009). Research also demonstrated that intervention organizations outnumber prevention organizations ten to one (Ralston 2004, 2009).

In contrast to intervention, the prevention approach identifies children at risk of being sold and prevents such sales by providing scholarships, village support, family care (eliminating at risk factors within a family), foster care and entire homes for children with house parents where their room, board, education, and medical care are provided free of charge.

Remember Nhu is one such organization engaged in prevention efforts. Because of the high recidivism rates and high costs of intervention efforts, Remember Nhu was built and operates on *prevention* as the most effective model for keeping children from entering the sex trade. From 2007 to 2019, Remember Nhu grew to care for more than 2,000 children in more than 100 homes in 16 countries with a $3,700,000 annual budget. Prior to the author's dissertation research cited below, no studies were located that included formal research results to show the success or failure of prevention programs such as Remember Nhu.

After Remember Nhu had worked in Thailand for 12 years, the author along with a team of Thai researchers conducted research on the success of Remember Nhu's prevention efforts for inclusion in the author's doctoral dissertation (Ralston 2019). The 63 villages Remember Nhu had served over the previous 12 years were invited to participate in this research. In February 2019, some 33 village leaders came to Chiang Mai, Thailand, to be interviewed, double the respondents needed for an adequate sample size of the total population. The participants included 4 teachers, 6 pastors and 23 village leaders and assistant leaders, and by gender 10 females and 23 males. The smallest village in this study consisted of 60 people, the largest over 6,000, and nine villages of more than 1,000. The median number of people living in the sampled villages was 444, and the mean was 860.

The major finding of the research was a 99 percent positive correlation between Remember Nhu's efforts during its 12-year presence in Thailand and a significant decrease of the numbers of children entering the sex trade (Ralston 2019). Villages where Remember Nhu offered and provided services saw a reduction from 6.5 children to 1.5 children entering the sex trade on a yearly basis.

A 21st-Century Approach to Ending Child Sex Trafficking

Despite the laudable and heroic efforts of interventionists, child sex trafficking increased by 20 percent from 2003 to 2018. Prevention programs during that time were barely 10 percent of the worldwide effort to eradicate this practice and their results were not formally reported. The one organization that has established an empirical record of successfully preventing child sex trafficking, Remember Nhu, should serve as a twenty-first century empirically grounded prevention model that could inspire others to work toward effectively ending child sex slavery through prevention.

As a nonprofit, Remember Nhu invested $20 million USD to prevent about 2,000 children from entering the sex trade in Thailand (2007–2019). By raising another $20 million and continuing our current strategy another 2,000 children may be prevented from entering the sex trade. This strategy alone will never end worldwide child sex trafficking. However, hope for *truly ending* child sex trafficking can be found in helping others start nonprofits with the goal of "Ending child sex slavery through prevention." Remember Nhu's record could be replicated around the world. Based on the past performance of Remember Nhu, at the investment cost of $100,000 each, 200 people could start 200 nonprofits similar to Remember Nhu for a total of $20 million. If the 200 new nonprofits taken as a cohort were able to merely average helping the same number of children as Remember Nhu, 400,000 children could be prevented from entering the sex trade. If 1,000 non-profits were started with the goal of ending child sex slavery through prevention and taken as a cohort were merely able to duplicate Remember Nhu's work in Thailand, 2 million children could be prevented from ever entering the sex trade!

Remember Nhu's Accelerated Vision is a manual that provides a comprehensive guide for others to use in starting a 501-c-3 nonprofit from inception. Remember Nhu also provides free-of-charge training that compliments the manual for those seeking to start such nonprofits. We have one goal: "Ending child sex slavery through prevention." We are hopeful that this vision will become a reality within the twenty-first century.

Carl Ralston sold two successful businesses to become the founder and president of Remember Nhu, a nonprofit dedicated to ending child sex slavery through prevention. From 2007 to 2019, Remember Nhu grew to care for over 2,000 children in more than 100 homes for children in 16 countries with a $3,700,000 budget. Carl completed his doctoral studies in global leadership in 2019 with a dissertation on ending child sex slavery through prevention.

References

Campagna, Daniel S., and Donald L. Poffenberger. 1988. *The Sexual Trafficking in Children: An Investigation of the Child Sex Trade*. Dover, MA: Auburn House Publishing Company.

Rafferty, Yvonne. 2013. "Child Trafficking and Commercial Sexual Exploitation: A Review of Promising Prevention Policies and Programs." *American Journal of Orthopsychiatry* 83, no. 4: 559–575.

Ralston, Carl. 2004. *The Creation of Effective Ministry Partnerships with Remember Nhu, A Nonprofit Corporation Dedicated to Eliminating the Use of Children in the Sex Trade Industry in South West Asia.* Master's Thesis. Chicago, IL: Trinity Evangelical Divinity School.

Ralston, Carl. 2009. "Contemporaneous Notes: Interviews of Those Who Either Started or Ran an Organization to Keep Children Out of the Sex Trade." Cambodia and Thailand, 2004–2009, TMs (photocopy).

Ralston, Carl. 2019. *How Remember Nhu Safe Houses Prevented Children from Entering the Sex Trade in Thailand (2007-2018).* Doctoral Dissertation. Nyack, NY: Alliance Theological Seminary.

Siddharth, Ashok Kara. 2009. *Sex Trafficking: Inside the Business of Modern Slavery.* New York: Columbia University Press.

UNICEF. 2018. "Annual Report 2017." Accessed September 18, 2019. https://www.unicef.org/publications/files /UNICEF_Annual_Report_2017.pdf

antislavery.org

Latest | Reports & resources

anti-
slavery

today's fight for tomorrow's freedom

Slavery Today   What we do   Our Impact   Take action

Our i
201

We di
affec

W

We use cookies on this site to enhance your user experience. By clicking any link on this page y

Introduction

Although not exhaustive, this chapter lists and describes many key governmental and nongovernmental organizations currently or previously involved in efforts to eradicate modern slavery through a wide array of awareness, prevention, eradication, and rehabilitation efforts.

A21

A21 is a global nonprofit working to fight modern slavery through a three-pronged goal to reach, rescue, and restore. The "Reach" approach includes efforts to reduce vulnerability by engaging people through events, student presentations, and educational programs. One such event, the Walk for Freedom, is an awareness and fundraising effort in which tens of thousands rally in cities all across the world. Through another campaign, "Can You See Me?" A21 aspires to equip people in countries across the world to report tips to national hotlines when they suspect trafficking.

Anti-Slavery International (ASI) is the world's oldest international human rights organization. Founded in 1839 by Thomas Clarkson and other British abolitionists, the organization has been involved in the development of the major international antislavery laws, including the 1926 and 1956 Slavery Conventions, the 1930 ILO Convention on Forced Labor, the 1990 ILO Convention on the Worst Forms of Child Labor, and the 2011 Convention on Domestic Work. (Piotr Trojanowski/Dreamstime.com)

A21's "Rescue" approach consists in working with law enforcement on the ground to support police operations, identifying victims through A21 hotlines, assisting in the prosecution of traffickers, representing survivors in court proceedings, and collaborating with governments and other NGOs in eradication efforts. A21 additionally trains first responders, hospital staff, and transportation authorities to identify and report slavery.

Finally, A21 seeks to "Restore" survivors by interacting with them on a personal basis and providing them with access to housing, medical treatment, counseling, education, and employment. Because victims of human trafficking are commonly transported from a source country to a destination country, A21's SAFE program further seeks to restore survivors by repatriating them to their home country. A21 then works to provide opportunities for survivors. A21 currently runs a social enterprise, called "Liberty," that hires survivors to knit scarves. Every purchase of a handmade Liberty scarf helps provide vocational skills and income for the survivors in A21's care.

A21 currently operates 14 offices in 12 different locations across the globe and is one of a few organizations drawing attention to the under-detected problem of modern slavery in Europe. Each office focuses on a unique aspect of antislavery work from intervention and reducing vulnerability in refugee camps to protecting and providing restorative care for survivors.

American Anti-Slavery Group

The American Anti-Slavery Group (AASG) is an abolitionist organization, cofounded in 1993 and headquartered in Boston, Massachusetts, that focuses primarily on raising awareness of and eradicating systems of black chattel slavery in North Africa. AASG's efforts in this regard are based on the three-part approach of awareness, advocacy, and activism. The AASG seeks first and foremost to educate the public of the continued existence of black chattel slavery through publications, school curricula, conferences, and a Speakers' Bureau consisting mainly of survivors of slavery. Secondly, the AASG engages in advocacy through government lobbying and online campaigns designed to put pressure on corporations that benefit from modern slavery and governments that turn a blind eye towards it. Finally, the AASG promotes abolitionist activism in the form of rallies, freedom marches, petitions, letter-writing campaigns, and partnerships with agencies working to free slaves.

The AASG maintains updated reports of ongoing black chattel slavery in several North African countries, including Algeria and Libya, where sub-Saharan African refugees fleeing violence and poverty for Europe are captured and enslaved by Algerian and Libyan Arabs as they try to cross the Mediterranean; in Mauritania, where the class structure of the society reinforces slavery and hundreds of thousands of black slaves are held as private property by the lighter-skinned Arabs (Beydanes) and Arabized Berbers; in Nigeria, where the recent rise of terrorist organizations like the ISIS-affiliated Boko Haram has been the main source of contemporary slave raids; and in Sudan, where slavery remains a painful vestige of the Second Sudanese Civil War (1983–2005) between the Arab Muslim government in the north and the Christian and animist blacks in the south.

Between 1995 and 2005, AASG cofounder Charles Jacobs helped bring international attention to the enslavement of tens of thousands of Africans by raiders sent by the Arab government in Khartoum. Jacobs built coalitions with black American clergy and politicians, staged protests, and even testified on Capitol Hill. Jacobs also played a pivotal role in ensuring that pensions for New York City public employees would no longer be invested in Sudanese oil. On September 18, 2000, Jacobs was presented with the inaugural Boston Freedom Award by Coretta Scott King and Boston mayor Thomas Menino, and on October 21, 2002, Jacobs was invited to the White House to witness President Bush's signing of the Sudan Peace Act. Jacobs and the AASG also played a highly influential role in convincing the Bush administration to enforce a North-South peace treaty negotiated in 2005, which ended the slave raids and eventually led to the creation of South Sudan in 2011.

Anti-Slavery International

Anti-Slavery International (ASI) is the world's oldest international human rights organization. Founded in 1839 by Thomas Clarkson and other British abolitionists, the organization has been involved in the development of all the major international antislavery laws, including the 1926 and 1956 Slavery Conventions, the 1930 ILO Convention on Forced Labor, the 1990 ILO Convention on the Worst Forms of Child Labor, and the 2011 Convention on Domestic Work.

ASI was the first organization to campaign against slavery in modern day Britain, and today it is the only British charity exclusively working to eliminate all forms of slavery in the world. Together with local partnerships, the organization works to investigate and expose causes, current cases, and potential solutions to various manifestations of slavery, to press for the effective implementation of antislavery laws, to support victims in their fight for freedom, and to identify and address slavery in global supply chains.

ASI hosts and chairs the Anti-Trafficking Monitoring Group (ATMG), a coalition organization that monitors how governments implement the antislavery policies suggested by the European Union Trafficking Directive and standards for protecting victims of slavery set by the Council of Europe Convention on Action against Trafficking in Human Beings. The group regularly publishes major reports and briefings scrutinizing current law and practice, which it incorporates into campaigns designed to influence the British government's response to modern slavery. Following one campaign, the UK Parliament introduced forced labor as a criminal offense under the Coroners and Justice Act 2009, which allowed forced labor to be treated as a separate offense to those connected to trafficking foreign nationals into the UK from abroad.

ASI was instrumental in pressing for the introduction of the UK Modern Slavery Act in 2015, and the inclusion of a Transparency in Supply Chains (TISC) clause in the act, which requires businesses with an annual turnover of £36 million to report on steps they are taking to eradicate modern slavery. Today, the organization continues to campaign to resolve weaknesses in identifying and protecting victims regardless of their immigration status and to strengthen the transparency in supply chains provision of the Modern Slavery Act by requiring that public sector industries also report on modern slavery.

ASI works to provide members of the Ethical Trading Initiative (an alliance of companies, trade unions, and voluntary organizations) with training and expert advice on the risks of modern slavery and is directly involved in projects designed to eliminate slavery from global supply chains. Under the banner of the Cotton Crimes campaign, ASI has worked to end state-sponsored forced labor in cotton production in Uzbekistan and Turkmenistan. Together with its partners from the Cotton Campaign coalition, ASI has convinced over 250 global brands to stop using Uzbek cotton in their products. In similar fashion, ASI has uncovered and worked to tackle child slavery in the West Africa's cocoa industry and the forced labor of migrant workers in Thailand's fishing industry.

ASI has ongoing projects to combat descent-based slavery in Mauritania and Niger, forced child begging and labor in Senegal and Tanzania, and bonded labor in Nepal. These projects involve raising awareness, lobbying governments, providing legal assistance to prosecute slave owners, and securing educational, economic, and other resources for former slaves.

California Against Slavery

In 2009, after watching *Dateline*'s "Sex Slaves in America" and learning of the injustices that trafficked victims suffer in the judicial system, financial analyst Daphne Fung determined that laws must be changed to reflect the atrocity of human trafficking and the reality of modern slavery. That same year, Fung founded California Against Slavery (CAS), as a grassroots organization aimed at putting a citizen initiative on the California ballot to strengthen the criminal penalties against traffickers. Fung and other like-minded supporters began organizing rallies, knocking on doors in Sacramento, and gathering signatures. After a three-year effort and one failed attempt to gather the requisite number of signatures, CAS partnered with the Safer California Foundation to sponsor Proposition 35 the "Californians against Sexual Exploitation Act." Chris Kelly, a 2010 candidate for California Attorney General and former chief of privacy at Facebook, helped draft the initiative and contributed over $2.3 million of the nearly $4 million raised for the campaign. The initiative proposed sweeping changes to California's laws on trafficking, including increasing prison terms for individuals who traffic teenagers, children, and immigrant laborers on the streets of California cities and over the internet; requiring convicted sex traffickers to register as sex offenders; requiring criminal fines from convicted human traffickers to pay for services to help victims; mandating law enforcement training on human trafficking; and requiring all registered sex offenders to disclose their internet accounts. In May 2012, California's Secretary of State announced that the initiative had qualified for the upcoming November ballot. The initiative faced some opposition from groups and individuals who claimed the law might have unintended consequences for victims and impede on voluntary prostitution—but was broadly supported by a long list of prosecutors, law enforcement officers, politicians, and the public as a whole. Prop 35 passed in November 2012 with over 81.3 percent of the more than 10 million votes cast voting in approval, making it the most successful ballot initiative since California began the process in the 1914 election and the first to pass with over 80 percent of the vote.

Today CAS is committed to building on the legacy it helped establish with Prop 35 by encouraging a statewide network of anti–human trafficking organizations and agencies to share resources and expertise and to collaborate in support of common initiatives and legislative action.

Christian Solidarity International

Christian Solidarity International (CSI), originally founded in 1977, is a Christian human rights organization that advocates for and aids victims of religious persecution, enslavement, child abuse, and natural disaster.

CSI played an instrumental role in raising awareness of the thousands of Sudanese who were being captured, brutalized, and forced into slavery by northern Sudanese government-backed militia groups during Sudan's north-south war. Prior to CSI's involvement, Americans and the international community at large knew and cared little about the revival of slavery in Sudan. In the early 1990s, CSI began investigating allegations of human rights violations in the Sudanese civil war and initiated efforts on the ground to liberate Christians and other minorities forced into slavery by the Islamist Khartoum regime. The organization simultaneously urged reporters from around the world to make the dangerous trek to Sudan to document the ongoing slave trade and worked to rouse an Evangelical movement in the United States. This movement eventually inspired the George W. Bush administration to broker a deal to end the 36-year-long Sudanese war.

CSI's slave redemption program, first established in 1995, continues to operate today. CSI representatives first identify and locate individuals held as slaves with the help of Arab retrievers. They then negotiate the liberation of these slaves in exchange for a cattle vaccine (Novidium). Upon their liberation, CSI reunites freed slaves with their families and communities and provides them with medical treatment, food rations, survival and shelter kits, and seed, grain, and hoes for the next harvest. According to CSI's website, more than 100,000 individuals have been liberated through this program. Nevertheless, both the program and CSI's CEO John Eibner have faced criticism for its practice of buying freedom for slaves through goods or money. Some have argued that this practice is counter-productive. James Jacobson of Christian Freedom International, for example, has argued that the financial incentives of slave redemption in a poverty-stricken nation such as Sudan encourage the taking of slaves, that slave redemptions can promote hoaxes, and that the distribution of food and goods creates a magnet for slave raiders.

CNN Freedom Project

In 2011, CNN and CNN International launched the Freedom Project, a humanitarian news media campaign aimed at shining a spotlight on the various forms of modern slavery, giving voice to victims, highlighting success stories, holding businesses and governments accountable, and investigating the criminal enterprises involved in the human trade. The Freedom Project accomplishes this goal by investigating and telling stories of modern slavery through articles, reports, and high-quality documentaries.

In 2012, the Freedom Project released Operation Hope, voted the Best Social Awareness Program at the Asian Television Awards, which tells the story of a seven-year-old Bangladeshi boy who was viciously attacked, castrated, and left for dead by a group of neighborhood men after he refused to be forced into begging. After watching the documentary, U.S. businessman Aram Kovach helped organize and finance the boy's reconstructive surgery at John Hopkins hospital. The documentary drew international attention to the existence and prevalence of mafia-style beggar gangs in South Asia who maim and force children into begging.

Other project documentaries have exposed African slaves in the Sinai desert, sex trafficking rings in Southern California, and child labor and slavery on the cocoa plantations of the Ivory Coast in West Africa. Most recently, in August 2019, the Freedom Project released the documentary Stolen Son: The Child

Traffickers Preying on the Rohingya. The documentary tells the story of a mother's desperate attempt to find her missing 12-year-old son and highlights the problem of the persecuted Rohingya Muslims in Myanmar. The Rohingya are so mistreated in Myanmar that they are often forced to seek refuge in neighboring Bangladesh where they are targeted by human traffickers who lure them away from refugee camps with false promises of employment and better living conditions.

Since its launch, the Freedom Project has generated more than 1,000 investigative stories of modern slavery from across five continents. The project was one of the first to uncover and draw attention to the resurgence of modern-day slave auctions of African migrants in Libya in 2017.

The Freedom Project website provides visitors with educational materials and information on charities and agencies working to eradicate slavery. The site also includes direct links to anonymously report cases of modern slavery and trafficking to the National Trafficking Resource Center and Crime Stoppers, a program that forwards information on unsolved felonies to the appropriate law enforcement agency.

Coalition to Abolish Slavery and Trafficking

The Coalition to Abolish Slavery and Trafficking (CAST) is the United States' largest anti-trafficking partnership between nonprofit service providers, faith-based community groups, healthcare organizations, government agencies and law enforcement dedicated to assisting persons who have been trafficked for the purpose of forced labor and slavery-like practices and working to end such human rights violations.

The CAST was established in 1998 when it opened up the first-ever shelter exclusively for trafficking victims in the wake of the El Monte sweatshop case, in which 72 Thai workers were discovered living in slavery and debt bondage.

Today the CAST directly supports survivors by providing counseling, legal resources, housing, and educational and leadership training and mentorship. The organization also provides specialized training to law enforcement, service providers, government agencies, law firms, corporations, and faith-based groups on how to identify victims of human trafficking as part of its Human Trafficking 101 program.

The CAST offers a pro bono legal program providing survivors with access to critical legal services including immigration advocacy, criminal victim-witness advocacy, and civil litigation, provides comprehensive legal and legal services training, and facilitates the Legal Anti-Trafficking Weekly Working Group. This group provides informal opportunities for attorneys and legal service providers to ask questions and share experiences about handling human trafficking cases. Participants are also able to access updates on anti-trafficking legal and policy issues and to obtain technical assistance from legal professionals across the country. Similarly, CAST's Social Services Monthly Technical Assistance Call enables social service providers and case managers to speak with attorneys to learn about best practices in working with legal service providers such as protecting privilege/confidentiality, accessing public benefits, and potential legal remedies for clients.

In 2014, the CAST was honored by President Obama with the Presidential Award for Extraordinary Efforts to Combat Trafficking in Persons.

DeliverFund

DeliverFund is a nonprofit organization founded and staffed by former elite intelligence operators from the CIA, NSA, FBI, and Navy Seals who use their experience in special operations and counterterrorism to equip, train, and advice law enforcement officers and help them obtain the information they need to dismantle trafficking rings and arrest and prosecute traffickers.

In addition to partnering with police departments to offer elite training to officers, DeliverFund maps out sex trafficking networks with a special technology and disseminates that knowledge to law enforcement agencies. In early 2018, DeliverFund helped take down Backpage.com, the international ad site that notoriously facilitated sex trafficking by hosting ads for trafficked women and coaching traffickers on how to word their ads to avoid drawing the attention of law enforcement. In a twist of fate, DeliverFund consolidated its operations by moving its headquarters to the Dallas office space formerly occupied by Backpage.

DeliverFund currently maintains the International Human Trafficking Analysis Center (iHTAC), which serves as a central knowledge bank for the collection, integration, analysis, and dissemination of intelligence regarding human trafficking activity for use by law enforcement, select nonprofits, and professionals working to end modern slavery. DeliverFund additionally uses private donor money to provide software licenses, hardware, and analytic support directly to law enforcement agencies.

DeliverFund is also one of several nongovernmental organizations that contribute to FBI-spearheaded stings during the Super Bowl. Following the 2019 Super Bowl in Atlanta, Georgia, DeliverFund helped provide the FBI with intelligence that led to the arrest of 26 suspected traffickers and 34 individuals who were allegedly attempting to engage in sex acts with minors.

ECPAT

ECPAT, formerly referred to as End Child Prostitution and Trafficking, was initially established in 1990 as a campaign to end the sexual exploitation of children in Asian tourism. Following a 1996 partnership with UNICEF to organize a global world congress in Stockholm, Sweden, against the sexual exploitation of children, ECPAT transformed from a regional campaign into a global network of over 100 organizations in over 90 countries, with an international secretariat in Bangkok, Thailand.

ECPAT is the only child's rights organization that is solely focused on ending the sexual exploitation of children through trafficking, prostitution, and sextortion, online and in the travel and tourism sector. ECPAT network organizations advocate for stronger legal environments within individual countries and internationally. ECPAT conducts primary research and collects information from various sectors and countries with the goal of providing quality academic resources and data that can be used to guide the decisions of policymakers and governmental and nongovernmental organizations. In 2016, ECPAT initiated the *Global Study on Sexual Exploitation of Children in Travel and Tourism*, which engaged more than 60 nongovernmental and governmental partners in the first comprehensive global study of the topic. ECPAT additionally spearheaded the *Access to Justice and Right to Remedies for Child Victims of Sexual Exploitation Research Project*, a multicountry initiative focusing on child survivors' experiences in accessing judicial remedies and other reparations for sexual exploitation.

In spite of ECPAT's reputation for conducting reliable, cutting-edge research, one of the statistics it helped promulgate has been challenged for accuracy. In 2015, the Washington Post Fact Check drew attention to a widely promulgated statistic found on ECPAT-USA's website that "At least 100,000 children in the U.S. are commercially sexually exploited." The statistic was derived from a 2002 National Incidence Studies of Missing, Abducted, Runaway and Thrownaway Children (NISMART) report that showed that nearly 1.7 million kids in the United States had a runaway episode a year. But according to the same NISMART report, more than 75 percent of these children were away from home less than a week and 99.8 percent of these children were recovered. Furthermore, only 1,700 kids reported having engaged in sexual activity in exchange for money, drugs, food, or shelter during the episode. In response to this revelation, ECPAT-USA removed the faulty data from its website and pledged to no longer promulgate it. A 2016 study, funded by the U.S. Department of Justice, found that the number of juveniles in the sex trade in the United States was about 9,000–10,000. While nowhere near the number cited by ECPAT-USA, the study revealed that child sex trafficking within U.S. borders is still a significant problem.

End It

End It is a campaign designed to draw worldwide attention to the realities of modern-day slavery and to encourage people to raise their voices against it. The End It movement was started by several student leaders in Atlanta, Georgia, in 2013 at the Passion Conference, an annual Christian conference attended by college students from campuses across the nation who are passionate about justice. Since its inception, the End It Movement has grown to a global network of antislavery advocates from all walks of life.

At the beginning of each year, End It, in partnership with other major trafficking organizations, sponsors "Shine a Light on Slavery Day." On this day, individuals are encouraged to write red "X" marks on their hands and to post pictures of the red "X" on social media with the hashtags #enough and #enditmovement. The campaign is widely successful with hundreds of thousands participating, including several celebrities and athletes such as Carrie Underwood, Ashton Kutcher, Peyton Manning, Tony Hawk, and many others.

The End It Movement's social media campaigns have been criticized by some who argue that such campaigns make people feel good about themselves while doing nothing to make a tangible difference. Others, however, have pointed out the value of End It's campaigns arguing, for instance, that the red "X" project results in a drastic rise in donations to anti-trafficking nonprofits. Furthermore, Polaris reported that calls to its anti-trafficking hotline greatly increased in part due to awareness generated by End It.

The Exodus Road

The Exodus Road was founded by a husband and wife team, Matt and Laura Parker. In 2010, the Parkers moved to Thailand to direct a children's home and became aware of the marginalized people groups being targeted by traffickers. For the next two years, the couple began investigating brothels and working to build a relationship with law enforcement and local NGOs. In 2012, they launched The Exodus Road with the goal of rescuing adults and minors from exploitation and slavery in the sex and labor industries.

The Exodus Road primarily focuses on empowering search and rescue teams to work alongside national law enforcement to rescue victims and arrest perpetrators. Search and rescue teams are comprised of highly trained and vetted nationals who utilize cyber forensic technology to gather evidence of human trafficking and facilitate rescue missions and raids with local police. The Exodus Road employs local social workers to advocate for survivors during and following raids and to provide immediate care in their recovery. Today, The Exodus Road, which is headquartered in Colorado Springs, Colorado, supports operatives in India, South East Asia, a confidential country in Latin America, and the United States. The organization has plans to move into Indonesia and Bahrain.

In addition to its search and rescue operations and survivor care programs, The Exodus Road seeks to educate individuals and train national leaders through events and online campaigns, such as Traffickwatch and Online Abolitionists. The Exodus Road additionally strives to highlight the most urgent trafficking issues in the regions in which it operates and to profile cutting-edge research by unassociated individuals working to combat human trafficking. During the summer of 2019, The Exodus Road featured the work of Ian Urbana, an investigative reporter for the *New York Times,* whose project *The Outlaw Ocean* provides an in-depth look at the prevalence of force, fraud, and debt bondage in the lawless environment of international waters.

The Frederick Douglass Family Initiatives

The Frederick Douglass Family Initiatives (FDFI) was cofounded in June 2007 by Robert J. Benz and Nettie Washington Douglass and her son Kenneth B. Morris, direct descendants of Frederick Douglass, a former American slave who became a prominent abolitionist and statesman, and Booker T. Washington, a famous educator and founder of the Tuskegee Institute. The FDFI was formed as an abolitionist organization with the goal of educating the public, especially young people, using the lessons of history to fight against modern forms of slavery.

Under the initiative "One Million Abolitionists," the FDFI aims to give away 1 million copies of "The Narrative of the Life of Frederick Douglass: An American Slave" with the goal of inspiring recipients to create service projects in their communities using Douglass's example of courage. The institute has developed several additional educational initiatives including a coalition project titled PROTECT. This project, based on a partnership with two California nonprofits 3 Stands Global and Love Never Fails, aims to help educators and students identify and prevent instances of human trafficking through a standardized educational curriculum. The group will create grade-level appropriate, state standard compliant materials to allow 5th-, 7th-, 9th-, and 11th-grade teachers to incorporate the topic of human trafficking into their annual educational calendar.

Free the Slaves

Founded in 2000, Free the Slaves (FTS) is a widely regarded leader and pioneer in the modern international abolition movement. Through groundbreaking research, advocacy, and innovative field programs, FTS works to change government policy and business practices and empower local organizations and communities to combat modern slavery in strategically-selected hotspots in India, Nepal, Ghana, Haiti, Senegal, and the Dominican Republic.

In the realm of policy advocacy, FTS works with liberators and frontline workers to gather insight into and evidence of effective interventions and then uses this information to advocate for stronger anti-trafficking laws and increased funding of antislavery programs. FTS's policy agenda focuses on six key goals: increasing corporate transparency and accountability for human rights abuses in the manufacturing and sale of products and providing consumers and investors with the data to make informed choices; reducing the vulnerability of impoverished and marginalized people by strengthening communities through increased investment in economic development, rights awareness, and public services; diminishing the profitability of slavery by promoting awareness of and enforcement of anti-trafficking laws; helping survivors successfully reintegrate into their communities through education, vocational training, access to credit, and a range of additional services; regulating foreign labor recruitment to make it more difficult for traffickers to pose as legitimate labor recruiters; and increasing donor investment in anti-trafficking programs to broaden the scope of antislavery activities worldwide.

In line with its goal of promoting slavery-free and slavery-resistant communities, FTS recently launched the Community Liberation Initiative, which integrates field-tested and rigorously evaluated anti-trafficking strategies into a wide range of international development initiatives in communities where slavery is worst. This initiative has led to remarkable success. The villages of Sakdouri and Kukdaha in India, for example, were once trafficking hotspots with significant percentages of their residents in various forms of slavery. Today, after intervention by FTS and an Indian partner organization, both villages are free. FTS website features this story and other success stories in a series of mini-documentaries on its website.

FTS works in close partnership with a wide range of human rights, corporate accountability, and development organizations and is cochair and secretariat of the Alliance to End Slavery and Trafficking (ATEST), a U.S.-based coalition that advocates for lasting solutions to prevent labor and sex trafficking, hold perpetrators accountable, ensure justice for victims, and provide survivors with the tools they need for recovery.

Recently, FTS programs have been a key part of the anti-trafficking work in both Senegal and Haiti that has contributed to these two countries being removed from the Tier Two Watch List in the U.S. State Department's Trafficking in Persons (TIP) report. In Haiti, FTS joined forces with Beyond Borders, a faith-based nonprofit that works to help people liberate themselves from oppression and isolation, to institute the United to End Child Slavery Program. Together the organizations are working to liberate and protect children exploited as domestic servants.

Freedom United

Freedom United is a digital movement working to unite individuals and organizations throughout the world in the fight against human trafficking and modern slavery. Freedom United provides online resources enabling its global network of more than 70 nonprofit partners and 8 million supporters to learn about modern slavery, to get involved with various anti-trafficking campaigns, and to financially support global efforts to eradicate slavery. Freedom United facilitates an online learning hub called Freedom University where viewers can access interactive lessons, quizzes, videos, presentations, and articles on different topics related to the issue of modern slavery. Among Freedom United's many featured campaigns are efforts to end orphanage trafficking, to stop forced labor of immigrant detainees, to eliminate forced marriage in Niger and Lebanon, to help victims of sex trafficking in the United Kingdom, to suspend loans tainted by Uzbek forced labor, and to help prevent domestic slavery in Delhi.

Girls Not Brides

Girls Not Brides was launched in September 2011 by the Elders, a group of independent leaders, peace activists, and human rights activists founded by Nelson Mandela in 2007. Today, Girls Not Brides is a global partnership of more than 1,300 civil society organizations from more than 100 countries throughout Africa, Asia, the Middle East, Europe, and the Americas working to end child marriage. Members work to bring global awareness to the prevalence of child marriage and to promote laws, policies, and programs to eliminate the exploitive practice that affects millions of children, predominantly girls, every year and to promote a safe, healthier, and more prosperous future for girls around the world.

In line with the UN Convention on the Rights of the Child, Girls Not Brides believes that 18 should be the minimum age for marriage for boys and girls, and in 2015 members lobbied to include ending child marriage in the United Nations Sustainable Development Goals (SDGs) for 2030. In an effort to promote achievement of the SDGs, Girls Not Brides aids governments and local organizations as they develop and implement strategies to reduce child marriage within their borders. Girls Not Brides recently launched the Stop Stealing Her Childhood campaign calling on world leaders to register a UN SDG Accelerator Action plan outlining their specific strategies to address child marriage in their country. As a means of putting international pressure on governments to make such commitments, Girls Not Brides has put together a global petition with a toolkit for citizens to launch their own country-level campaigns calling on their individual governments to reinforce their commitment to end child marriage.

Global Centurion

Global Centurion (GC) is a nonprofit anti-trafficking organization that uniquely seeks to eradicate modern slavery by focusing on reducing the demand from the perpetrators, exploiters, buyers, and end users of human beings who fuel the market for forced labor and commercial sex. GC was founded in 2010 by Laura J. Lederer, JD, who founded the Protection Project at Harvard University's John F. Kennedy School of Government and served as senior adviser on Trafficking in Persons in the U.S. State Department's Office to Combat Trafficking in Persons.

Based on the basic economic principle that supply results from demand and that when demand goes up, supply grows to meet the demand and vice versa, GC has adopted the view that the only effective method for eradicating supply (human trafficking victims) is to target demand (customers, exploiters, and other end users). Consequently, GC has developed a three-pronged approach to combating the demand for sex and labor trafficking. This approach includes developing demand-focused research and programs; providing cutting-edge education, awareness and advocacy training to communities, civic leaders, NGOs, law enforcement, and at-risk populations; and establishing partnerships and collaborative networks to respond to modern slavery.

In the realm of research and development, GC's primary project is the International Case Law Database, a searchable, longitudinal database of all forms of human trafficking including sex trafficking, labor trafficking, forced labor, bonded labor, debt bondage, involuntary domestic servitude, forced child labor, child soldiers, child sex trafficking and tourism, and commercial sexual exploitation of women and children. GC has developed a methodology for identifying, analyzing, and coding data on perpetrators, victims, and the patterns of trafficking crimes within and between countries by extracting relevant data from over 10,000 national and international human trafficking cases. The database includes victim profiles, perpetrator profiles, and crime profiles. GC has also conducted research on over 200 cases in which gang members have been involved in recruiting, transporting, harboring, obtaining, or selling a person for purposes of commercial sexual exploitation or involuntary servitude. GC uses the data collected from these cases to discover patterns, including recruitment methods, methods of coercion and control, and age of victims. This information is used to recommend laws, policies, and actions to government officials, community leaders, and educators.

GC additionally develops maps identifying major hubs of demand for sex and labor trafficking around the world with the goal of helping policymakers, organizations, and individuals understand what drives the human trade. These maps are designed to help viewers better understand and recognize contributing factors of the various types of demand. For instance, national and international sporting events like the Superbowl and World Cup create major demand hubs for sex trafficking as does the presence of military personnel on Rest and Recuperation in economically unstable or war-torn countries. The demand for labor trafficking tends to be high in locations where labor-intensive goods are produced. These include garment factories, agricultural areas, construction sites, and precious gyms, metals, and mineral mines.

Human Trafficking Institute

The Human Trafficking Institute (HTI) was founded in 2017 with the goal of empowering police and prosecutors to stop traffickers by providing experts within criminal justice systems with training, investigative resources, and evidence-based research necessary to free victims.

The HTI's primary strategy is to set up Specialized Human Trafficking Units and fast-track courts and then to equip them to effectively enforce anti-trafficking laws and rescue victims. The institute does this by taking members of the Specialized

Units through the HTI Academy where they learn how to identify cases, use trauma-informed interviewing techniques, and develop successful trial strategies. The HTI then ensures that former FBI agents or prosecutors with experience in human trafficking cases work with the Specialized Units providing staffers with access to their expertise and experience. The HTI helped the Department of Justice's Human Trafficking Prosecution Unit pilot this multipronged strategy through the development of its ACT teams in six federal prosecution districts and saw impressive results. Districts with an ACT team saw an increase in the number of human traffickers charged compared to districts without an ACT team.

The HTI continually works to update its best practices and legal research to provide specialized units and policymakers with evidence to guide practical casework, policymaking, and funding decisions. Each year the institute publishes a Federal Human Trafficking Report with comprehensive data about every criminal and civil human trafficking case handled by federal courts that year.

In memory of Frederick Douglass's commitment to freedom, education, and advocacy and in an effort to develop leaders in the anti-trafficking movement, the HTI sponsors the Douglass Fellowship each year, which provides an opportunity for second- and third-year law students to participate in an eight-month research fellowship. Fellows are paired with a mentor who currently works in the anti-trafficking sector and are given the opportunity to work on a variety of projects including writing amicus briefs to the United State Supreme Court or U.S. Circuit Courts of Appeal, researching current trends in human trafficking law, analyzing successful models of human trafficking enforcement, and more.

In addition to its work in the United States, the HTI runs anti-trafficking collaboration programs in Belize and Uganda. In Belize, the HTI is working to train recruits, to increase the capacity of specialized anti-trafficking police, and to improve trafficking survivors' cooperation with law enforcement.

The HTI recently entered into a formal agreement with the Chief Justice of the Supreme Court of Belize to hire an institute lawyer to help process cases more efficiently. The HTI has also visited Guatemala to explore ways in which Belize and Guatemala might partner in their efforts to combat trafficking. In Uganda, the HTI seeks to equip the government, the newly created Human Trafficking Department, and the Victim Witness Coordination Unit to continue the country's progress in implementing its decade old anti-trafficking law. In March 2018, the HTI had the opportunity to cohost a large-scale training of 140 judges in Kampala to help them understand Uganda's human trafficking law and how to apply it in different scenarios.

In April 2018, the HTI launched TraffickingMatters.com, a first-of-its-kind global resource platform where individual organizations can share trending cases, articles, and resources. Since its launch TraffickingMatters.com has also featured daily news articles available in an email subscription from U.S. and international publications on topics ranging from case updates and arrests to new legislation and advancements in the anti-trafficking field.

Human Trafficking Legal Center

The Human Trafficking Legal Center (HT Legal) is the only U.S. organization systematically working to train attorneys to pursue justice for trafficking survivors in civil courts. Through the generous support of powerful law firms, HT Legal is able to pair survivors with pro bono lawyers and then works to provide technical support and mentorship to survivors and their attorneys through often lengthy court battles. Since 2012, HT Legal has trained more than 3,600 attorneys at leading U.S. law firms and has placed nearly 300 cases for free legal representation. In an effort to further assist those litigating federal human trafficking cases, HT Legal meticulously tracks landmark cases as they develop and collects legal filings from every criminal and civil trafficking case in the United States. This data is compiled in a comprehensive federal case database. Pro bono attorneys can use this resource to research similar cases, draft complaints, and file motions. This resource and the logistical support and training provided by HT Legal has resulted in a 95 percent success rate at securing convictions in civil cases.

International Cocoa Initiative

The International Cocoa Initiative (ICI) is a Swiss-based foundation working in Côte d'Ivoire and Ghana to unite the cocoa and chocolate industry, farming communities, and national governments in an effort to eliminate child labor in cocoa-producing communities and to ensure a better future for children and their families.

The ICI currently works to achieve its mission on several levels. First, at the community level, the ICI carries out awareness-raising activities on child labor and child rights, informing community members on the causes and consequences of child labor, the importance of schooling and vocational training, and the negative effects of child labor on children's health and education. The ICI works at this level to promote education, health, water and sanitation, and rural livelihoods and to help farming communities develop their own Community Action Plans, in which they identify and agree to support a range of activities to protect children.

The second level of the ICI's work is in the cocoa supply chain. The ICI sets up and manages the Child Labor Monitoring and Remediation System (CLMRS). This system works to identify and remediate cases of child labor in the supply chain by sending a community liaison person to visit households and farms within cocoa-growing communities to identify cases of child labor or children engaging in a hazardous activity. The community liaison person enters collected information into a centralized database via a mobile app and requests remediation support. This support is implemented by the ICI working with the chocolate company and cocoa supplier. Children are then monitored to ensure the process is successful. Since it was launched as a pilot program in 2012, the system has been used to identify and assist nearly 25,000 children in child labor.

The next level of the ICI's work is at the national level. At this level, the ICI provides training and technical advice on child labor to the governments of Côte d'Ivoire and Ghana and helps work with government agencies to coordinate the various actors and initiatives aimed at eliminating child labor. The ICI also works at this level to help the private sector change business practices and implement supply chain strategies that minimize the risk of child labor, including setting up their own child labor monitoring and remediation systems.

Finally, the ICI works at the international level to collect and disseminate data, information, and case studies on best practices and strategies in the fight against child labor in the cocoa industry and to help international companies design programs to reduce child labor and integrate responsible supply chain management into their business models.

International Justice Mission

The International Justice Mission (IJM) is the largest antislavery organization in the world. IJM was founded by lawyer Gary Haugen, who is Harvard and University of Chicago educated, in 1997 as an international legal agency with the express purpose of representing and rescuing victims of violence, sexual exploitation, slavery, and oppression. Prior to founding IJM, Haugen spent several years as a trial attorney in the civil rights division of the U.S. Department of Justice (DOJ). During this time, he directed a high-profile war-crimes investigation on behalf of the United Nations. His experience as a human rights investigator stirred in him a passion for working to increase access to effective systems of public justice among the abused poor.

Today, IJM has several hundred full-time staff working from its Washington, DC, headquarters and in field offices throughout Africa, Latin America, and South and South East Asia. While media attention largely focuses on IJM's work rescuing victims of violence, forced labor, and sex trafficking, a large percentage of the organization's efforts are focused on ensuring that local laws against slavery and exploitation are enforced. In particular, IJM employees work with local law enforcement to investigate, arrest, and prosecute slave owners. IJM additionally provides rehabilitation and aftercare programs for victims and sponsors various programs designed to reduce individuals' vulnerability to traffickers, including a successful microenterprise project.

One recent example of IJM's many successes in rescue and rehabilitation involved the freeing of 44 boys, some as young as 10, and 32 men from forced labor in hazardous conditions at several jewelry factories in India in September 2019. The case first arose when a local lawyer passed on an anonymous tip of exploitation to IJM's team in Chennai. IJM then worked with the local government to identify the factory locations and conduct rescue operations at five separate facilities. All the boys and men rescued had been trafficked from West Bengal, a state 1,000 miles away in northern Indian. Thus, following their rescue IJM facilitated their return home and connected them with another local IJM team that will work to assist the men and boys in finding livelihood options so they will be less vulnerable to trafficking in the future.

International Labour Organization

The International Labour Organization (ILO) was founded following World War I as an agency of the League of Nations. Today, the 100-year-old agency is a tripartite body of the United Nations that brings together representatives of governments, employers, and workers from its 187 member states in an effort to set international labor standards, devise policies, and develop programs to protect workers and promote good working conditions. To help ensure that member states are making efforts to comply with the labor standard conventions that they ratify, the ILO operates a supervisory system. Through this system, the ILO regularly examines the application of standards in member states and points out how these efforts might be improved. The ILO works to assist noncompliant states through social dialogue and the provision of technical support.

One of ILO's main priorities is to eliminate forced labor and human trafficking. Pursuant to this goal, the ILO implemented the International Program on the Elimination of Child Labor in 1992 to eliminate the worst forms of child labor, and in 1998 the ILO adopted the Declaration on Fundamental Principles and Rights at Work, which obligates members states to respect and promote: the freedom of association and the right to collective bargaining, the elimination of forced or compulsory labor, the abolition of child labor, and the elimination of discrimination in respect of employment and occupation. Member states who have not yet met this commitment by ratifying a core convention are asked to report on the status of the relevant rights and procedures within their borders, noting impediments to ratification, and areas where assistance may be required. In 2002, the ILO established the Special Action Program to combat Forced Labor (SAP-FL), to aid compliance with various goals of the Declaration on Fundamental Principles and Rights at Work through the provision of training materials, resources, programs, and oversight services.

In 2015, the ILO—in partnership with the International Organization of Employers and the International Trade Union Confederation—launched the "50 for Freedom" campaign to generate public support and encourage countries to ratify its Forced Labor Protocol, which officially went into effect on November 9, 2016. To date, all but nine member states have ratified the protocol that establishes new obligations to prevent forced labor, protect victims, and provide victims with access to remedies. The ILO additionally launched the Fair Recruitment

Initiative in 2014 to address the prevalence of exploitation in labor recruitment practices around the globe.

International Organization for Migration

The International Organization for Migration (IOM) was originally established in 1951 as the Provisional Intergovernmental Committee for the Movement of Migrants from Europe to address the displacement of people in Western Europe following World War II. Today, IOM is an intergovernmental organization that works to promote an orderly and humane management of migration across the globe, by encouraging international cooperation on migration issues, assisting in the search for solution to migration problems, and providing humanitarian assistance to migrants, including refugees and internally displaced peoples. As part of its broader mission, the IOM engages in a variety of counter-trafficking initiatives and has helped provide protection and direct assistance, in the form of shelters medical care, vocational training, and safe repatriation and reintegration, for over 100,000 men, women, and children who were trafficked for sexual and labor exploitation, slavery, and servitude.

In 2017, the IOM launched the Counter Trafficking Data Collaborative (CTDC), the first publicly available global database on human-trafficking victims and the largest collection of case data in the world. The CTDC compiles data from organizations around the world in a central, accessible online platform and now features data available for download and in visual form on over 90,000 cases of identified human trafficking from 172 countries.

KnowTheChain

KnowTheChain is a collaborative partnership between several organizations—the Business & Human Rights Resource Centre, Humanity United, Sustainalytics, and Verité—that each possesses significant expertise in addressing forced labor worldwide. KnowTheChain was established to increase awareness of forced labor risks and to provide resources and tools to assist companies and investors in their efforts to identify and eradicate such risks in their global supply chains.

KnowTheChain additionally operates a benchmarking tool for assessing corporate policies and practices of the largest global companies across three sectors where forced labor is particularly acute: information and communications technology (ICT), food and beverage, and apparel and footwear. Companies in those sectors are sourcing many products and commodities from countries where labor regulation is poor and/or not enforced and where migrant workers who are particularly vulnerable to forced labor and trafficking are common. The benchmarks help identify and share leading practices, reward companies that have taken significant action, and enable and incentivize others to improve their standards and procedures. KnowTheChain published its first set of benchmarks in 2016, and the second set, covering more than 120 companies, in 2018.

Korea Future Initiative

The Korea Future Initiative is a London-based charity that works to combat human rights abuses against North Koreans—with a particular focus on women, children, and minorities—through three steps: rescue, reports, and redress.

The initiative first and foremost raises funds to rescue North Koreans who are at great risk of exploitation and to deliver them to freedom and safety. Such rescue efforts align with the initiative's goal to report on human rights violations in real time and to provide valuable and actionable intelligence for those involved in advocacy, rescue, and welfare work. The core focus of the initiative's reporting is a long-term project to detail patterns of abuses committed against North Korean women and girls in North Korea, China and Southeast Asia, and South Korea. Recently, the initiative published a report presented to the British House of Commons documenting how thousands of North Korean women and girls as young as 12 are being tricked into escaping North Korea only to be subjected to forced marriage, prostitution, and cybersex slavery by trafficking gangs running a multi-million-dollar illicit sex industry in China.

Finally, the Korea Future Initiative strives to provide redress to victims by supporting programs that offer transitional and conventional justice to survivors, memorial projects that seek to honor victims by telling their individual and collective stories in online memorials, global exhibitions, and commemorative activities, and outreach efforts to exiled North Korean communities in Europe and South Korea.

La Strada International

La Strada International (LSI) is a network of eight independent member organizations that work at the grassroots level to address human trafficking. For nine years after its inception in 1995, the organization functioned as a joint program and network coordinated by the former Dutch Foundation against Trafficking of Women. In 2004, it was officially established as an independent international association with a general secretariat based in Amsterdam.

The organization, which takes its name from a Federico Fellini film *La Strada* about a young girl who is sold to work in a circus, was launched as a result of a trilateral anti-trafficking project between the Czech Republic, the Netherlands, and Poland. This project involved a joint training seminar between the three countries to exchange information, knowledge, and experience and to develop prevention and support services for women who had been trafficked and returned home, either by choice or because they had been deported from Western Europe. The seminar eventually led to the first LSI project, "Prevention of the Trafficking of Women in Central and Eastern Europe." By 2001, Ukraine, Bulgaria, Belarus, Bosnia and Herzegovina, Moldova, and Macedonia, had joined the program, but the General Assembly revoked Bosnia and Herzegovina's membership in 2012 after it determined that the country's La Strada organization had made no improvements in its anti-trafficking work.

LSI's activities primarily emphasize the protection of the human rights of trafficking victims in three main areas: information and lobbying, prevention and education, and social and legal services to victims and at-risk groups.

LSI closely monitors trends and developments related to human trafficking in Europe and regularly publishes statements and opinion pieces on proposed and adopted policies on human trafficking, migration, and sex work. For example, in the past, LSI has been highly critical of laws that equate sex work in general with human trafficking or that call for the criminalization of clients of sex workers, arguing that such laws lower the chance of identifying individuals who have been trafficked and do not prevent or stop human trafficking.

LSI engages in a variety of independent and joint campaigns and projects. One of the primary focus areas is ensuring that victims receive compensation. While most European countries have legal provisions for victims of crime to claim compensation or otherwise to be compensated for material and nonmaterial damages, evidence shows that very few trafficked persons have the information and means to seek compensation, and even fewer actually receive a compensation payment. Thus, in an effort to increase access to compensation for trafficked and exploited persons, LSI recently carried out the "Know Your Rights: Claim Compensation" campaign. Similarly, LSI's "Justice at Last" project aims to identify and analyze remaining barriers for compensation claims, as well as best practices in overcoming such barriers. This project additionally strives to raise awareness among policymakers, service providers, and victims about the most effective mechanisms for obtaining access to compensation.

LSI is involved in several projects carried out in conjunction with nonaffiliated partners. One such project, "DemandAT," is implemented by an international consortium coordinated by International Centre for Migration Policy Development. This project investigates different approaches to addressing and reducing demand through anti-trafficking efforts and policies. Among many other joint projects, LSI works in conjunction with NGOs in the 27 European Union countries on "The European NGOs Observatory on Trafficking, Exploitation, and Slavery (E-Notes)" project. This project was set to establish a Europe-wide permanent monitoring and reporting observatory on measures against trafficking, exploitation, and slavery in Europe in order to enhance and support public institutions' policy in the field of protection and assistance of trafficked persons. The report, including the tool used for monitoring, can be downloaded online.

Liberty Shared

Liberty Shared, also referred to as Liberty Asia, was established in Hong Kong in 2012 by British business lawyer and documentary filmmaker Duncan Jepson to improve technological interventions and facilitate better communication and strategic collaboration between NGOs, corporations, and financial institutions seeking to fight human trafficking across Asia. Liberty Shared compiles intelligence on slavery in particular regions and shares that information with the private and public sector.

In 2016, Liberty Shared launched the Freedom Collaborative, a password-protected, interactive online networking platform for the counter-trafficking community, which provides users with a space to read and share relevant news, updates, and best practices; to connect with new partners and service providers; to obtain legal support; and to access a considerable catalogue of resources and open research tools. Liberty Shared, in conjunction with Salesforce Asia, also administers the Victim Case Management System (VCMS), a multifunctional, cloud-based shared platform for survivor case management and data that addresses challenges in data collection, record keeping, standardization, aggregation, dissemination, and protection. More than 50 NGOs currently share data on VCMS, and the platform has been used to contribute more than 25,000 cases of trafficking to the International Organization for Migrations Counter Trafficking Data Collaborative. The analytics provided by the VCMS also enable NGOs to better track patterns of human trafficking and identify high-risk territories

In addition to facilitating shared data and collaboration in the anti-trafficking community, Liberty Shared runs a Legal Resource Center that compiles briefings on local cases involving sexual exploitation, debt bondage, forced labor, forced marriage, and domestic servitude and on the implications of the United Kingdom's Modern Slavery Act for Asia. The center also provides information on best practices and analyzes how future cases might be more successfully prosecuted. Recently, the center launched Project Safe, a program that focuses on the identification and safe repatriation of children trafficked from Laos, Cambodia, and Myanmar to Thailand, while providing legal solutions to diminish these children's exposure to abuse.

Made in a Free World

Made in a Free World (MIAFW) is a nonprofit established by Justin Dillon, a musician turned activist, with the goal of using the free market to free slaves by encouraging collaboration between consumers and the companies that manufacture the goods they purchase and use in their daily lives. In 2008, Dillon directed the human trafficking documentary "Call + Response." After viewing the film, representatives of the U.S. State Department commissioned Dillon to develop a model similar to carbon footprinting that would educate consumers on their connection to human trafficking and modern slavery and encourage them to take action. On September 22, 2011, MIAFW launched the website SlaveryFootprint.org that asks visitors the question "How many slaves work for you?" The site provides an online lifestyle survey in which consumers can enter in details about the food they eat, the products they use, and the hobbies they engage in to find out approximately how many forced laborers are involved in their everyday lives. The goal is to enlighten consumers so that they can pressure the companies and brands they love to eradicate slave practices in their supply chains. Once they are enlightened to their personal connection to modern-day slavery, consumers are encouraged to act through an Online Action Center or the "Free World" Mobile App that enables users to send an open letter to their personal Facebook and Twitter networks and to company executives asking them to provide products made without slave labor.

Today, MIAFW focuses on developing and implementing high-impact solutions to human trafficking and strives to provide businesses with the tools and support they need to meet the growing consumer demand for products created without forced labor. Recently, MIAFW partnered with Harvard-educated mathematician Mira Bernstein to launch FRDM, a software platform that allows businesses to upload data on all the items they buy and the location of their suppliers. FRDM then generates a dashboard identifying the riskiest suppliers in those areas, enabling businesses to reassess their suppliers.

Not for Sale Campaign

In 2000, after learning of a human-trafficking ring at a San Francisco Bay Area restaurant he frequented, professor and business entrepreneur David Batstone set out on a quest to investigate and raise awareness of the millions of human beings held in modern bondage. During this time, Batstone met a woman named Kru Nam, who was actively rescuing children from forced labor and sex trafficking and caring for them in an empty field in northern Thailand. Batstone and cofounder Max Wexler initially founded the Not for Sale Campaign to raise funds to shelter Kru Nam's rescued children in Thailand. Eventually, Not for Sale expanded into other countries, including Peru and Romania, using funds raised through anti-trafficking awareness campaigns to provide direct services for local victims.

Several years after its founding, Not for Sale changed its model from a traditional charity funded by individual donations to one that develops income producing enterprises that create economic opportunities in vulnerable communities while simultaneously working to raise awareness and prevent exploitation. Each company that Not for Sale runs or partners with commits a portion of its revenue to understanding and combating the root causes of slavery in a region and to providing shelter, education, healthcare, legal services, and job training for victims of exploitation. Partner companies and ventures include: Square Organics, a producer of organic protein bars made with nutrient dense ingredients; Spence Diamonds, a manufacturer of artisan-created diamonds that have the exact physical, chemical, and optical properties as natural diamonds, but are created in a plasma chamber rather than mined from the earth; Rebbl, a marketer of drinks made with super herbs; Dignita, a naturally recognized culinary program and restaurant that serves as a training center for individuals who have come from exploitive situations; St. Clare, a San Francisco–based café and coffee company that works to develop and source coffees from the Akha tribes in Northern Thailand, whose people live without citizenship to any nation and are particularly vulnerable to traffickers; Not For Sale Ale, a craft beer produced by Monks Brewery in Sweden; Zshoes, a producer of high-quality shoes made of rubber and cotton from the Peruvian Amazon; and AllSaints a British fashion retailer.

Today, Not for Sale operates in the United States, Thailand, the Netherlands, Vietnam, Romania, Peru, Uganda, and the

Democratic Republic of the Congo. Recent projects have been established in Rwanda, Mozambique, and Bulgaria.

Operation Underground Railroad

Operation Underground Railroad (O.U.R.), named after the network of secret routes and safe houses in the United States used by African American slaves to escape to freedom during the early to mid-nineteenth century, is a nonprofit founded in December 2013 by former U.S. Department of Homeland Security special agent Tim Ballard. Ballard, who served on DHS's Internet Crimes against Children Task Force and the U.S. Child Sex Tourism Jump Team, sought to develop an organization that would bring together experts in extraction operations and anti–child trafficking efforts, both in the United States and around the world, to rescue children and prosecute those who violate them.

O.U.R. primarily focuses on enhancing existing law enforcement efforts by providing resources and child exploitive investigation training to departments whose budgets don't allow for a child pornography, child exploitation, or human trafficking operation. O.U.R. additionally runs an ops team consisting of former CIA, past and current law enforcement, and U.S. Special Operations Forces members and other highly skilled operatives that lead coordinated identification and extraction efforts in collaboration with local law enforcement agencies.

O.U.R. operatives follow a five-step process in their rescue efforts. First, they access the feasibility of the rescue. This includes the willingness of local authorities to work with O.U.R. and arrest the perpetrators. Second, operatives research the location, the children, and the background of those running trafficking rings. Operatives also identify vetted care facilities where rescued children can be placed for food, shelter, and rehabilitation and then work to build partnerships with these aftercare centers. Third, operatives develop a logistical strategy for a safe, efficient, and legal rescue and provide training for local law enforcement to sustain and support rescue operations. The fourth stage involves the actual rescue. In some instances, operatives will go undercover and arrange to "buy" a child as if they are customers and will move in with police to arrest perpetrators after the purchase. In other cases, operatives may pose as "clients." Following arrests, operatives ensure that recovered children are moved to pre-screened facilities for aftercare. Finally, operatives will work with local law enforcement to arrest, try, and convict the perpetrators.

O.U.R.'s website includes stories from many successful rescue operations. One story highlights the plight of young sisters Lucy and Ella (names changed) who were rescued in the Dominican Republic in 2017 after being exploited by their mother, who would livestream their sexual abuse to paying Westerners. This rescue operation resulted in the mother's arrest and Lucy and Ella's safe placement in an O.U.R. aftercare home partner. Today, the girls are thriving in the home where they are cared for and are being taught important vocational skills.

Polaris Project

The Polaris Project was founded in 2002 by Brown University students Katherine Chon and Derek Ellerman who were inspired to start a nonprofit after studying a criminal forced labor case occurring in Providence, Rhode Island. Named after the North Star that guided slaves using the Underground Railroad as they navigated their way to freedom, the Polaris Project was one of the first NGOs in the United States to focus on both labor and sex trafficking of men, women, and children. It has since grown into one of the largest antislavery organizations in the United States.

Polaris operates on a four-part model of serving victims and survivors by connecting them with referral partners nationwide, by collecting data that can be used to better understand how the business of human trafficking really works, by using this knowledge to design strategies for preventing and responding to different types of human trafficking in specific industries, and by enlisting law enforcement and other public- and private-sector partners to apply these strategies in their efforts to disrupt human trafficking and support survivors.

In 2007, Polaris set up the National Human Trafficking Resource Center Hotline. This hotline is manned 24 hours a day, 365 days a year by anti-trafficking advocates who are able to connect callers to services and organizations in their geographical area, provide actionable tips, and refer cases to relevant law enforcement agencies. In 2013, Polaris expanded its hotline service to include BeFree, a texting shortcode that victims and concerned citizens can use to send text messages for help. Through the hotline and textline, Polaris has learned of and responded to more than 31,000 instances of human trafficking across the United States and has reported more than 6,500 cases to local law enforcement entities after individuals have requested law enforcement support. Many of these referrals have resulted in the successful arrest and prosecution of traffickers.

Polaris maintains the Global Modern Slavery Directory, an online, publicly accessible database of organizations from around the world that work on the issue of human trafficking, exploitation, and forced labor. The directory now includes nearly 3,000 advocacy organizations and direct service providers that address all types of human trafficking and slavery in 199 countries. Advocates at the National Human Trafficking Resource Center Hotline are able to use the directory to connect potential victims to anti-trafficking organizations in their home country that are more likely to understand the local context and be able to connect victims to direct service providers.

In addition to its hotline and data dissemination activities, Polaris is heavily involved in legal advocacy and has played a pivotal role in the drafting, introduction, and support of more than 127 anti-trafficking bills at the state and federal level.

In recent years, Polaris has established collaborative partnerships with governments, law enforcement, service providers, and businesses worldwide. Because hotels are a common venue for sex and labor trafficking, Polaris has partnered with Wyndham Hotel Group, the world's largest hotel company with over 7,500 hotels in an effort to prevent human trafficking within its business. As part of this joint effort, Wyndham and Polaris are developing comprehensive training and educational tools for hotel owners and franchises, property-level staff and employees at its corporate offices, and call centers. Among its many other projects, Polaris has also begun working with governments and organizations across the world to set up and conduct hotlines training. In 2013, Polaris was awarded Google's $3 million Global Impact Award, which it used to support the launch of the Global Human Trafficking Hotline Network.

Remember Nhu

Remember Nhu, a nonprofit committed to ending child sex slavery by preventing children from entering the sex trade, was conceived in 2003–2004 by business owner Carl Ralston after he attended a Christian and Missionary Alliance Conference in Cambodia. At this conference, Ralston learned more about the horrific problem of sex trafficking and heard a local missionary tell the story of Nhu. Nhu was a 12-year-old girl who had committed her life to Jesus Christ, was baptized, and had publicly began to share her faith when her Buddhist grandmother sold her virginity. At the time, the missionary speaker did not know what had become of Nhu. After hearing this story, Ralston determined that he would do everything in his power to "Remember Nhu" and to fight against the use of children in the sex trade.

In 2004, as his final project for a master's degree in religion, Ralston launched Remember Nhu. In the meantime, Ralston took six trips to Cambodia to look for Nhu and finally found her in 2006 when she was 17. Ralston and his wife Laurie welcomed Nhu into their family, and she became Remember Nhu's first official employee. In January 2007, she helped open Remember Nhu's first Prevention Home for Children. A year later, she opened the organization's first business, the Agape Beauty Salon in Phnom Penh, Cambodia, and in 2014, she helped open and became manager at the first Remember Nhu Vocational Training Center. In May of 2016, Ralston experienced one of the greatest joys of his life as he walked Nhu down the aisle at her wedding, where she entered into marriage as free woman, by her own choice.

Today, Remember Nhu continues to identify children who are at risk of behind sold and provides them with a home staffed by house parents, interns, and instructors in which their physical, educational, emotional, and spiritual needs are met. After graduating from school, children living in these homes continue to be supported as they enter college or one of Remember Nhu's Vocational Training Centers. Remember Nhu operates over 100 homes in 16 countries, where over 1,650 children are currently protected from being sold. These homes are financed primarily by sponsors who commit to supporting a particular child, whom they may correspond with and encourage through letters, gifts, and even visits. To date, Remember Nhu has prevented more than 2,000 children from entering the sex trade.

Shared Hope International

Shared Hope International (SHI) is a Christian nonprofit working to prevent the conditions that foster sex trafficking, to restore victims of sex slavery, and to bring justice to vulnerable women and children. SHI was founded in 1998 by U.S. representative Linda Smith after she traveled to Mumbai, India, and visited one of the worst brothel districts in the world. The slavery and exploitation Smith witnessed inspired her to establish SHI and to fight trafficking outside of Congress.

Initially, SHI used grants from the U.S. State Department to research international sex trafficking and to facilitate mutual efforts by governments, law enforcement, and the private sector in several countries to protect victims, prosecute perpetrators, and prevent further trafficking. Today, SHI focuses on combating trafficking in the United States and abroad through a three-pronged approach of prevention, restoration, and bringing justice.

In the realm of prevention, SHI aims to train first responders and community members to identify warning signs of trafficking and to employ intervention techniques to rescue child victims. Every year, SHI hosts the Juvenile Sex Trafficking Conference, a several-day event that highlights the most pressing issues in the anti-trafficking field and features presentations and workshops by experts and professionals from across the United States on skill building, survivor experiences, cross-discipline collaboration, task force development, case studies, and lessons learned. SHI additionally operates CHARLI, an interactive online platform for professionals, advocates, and the general public that features webinars and self-paced training, delivering collaboration, advocacy, resources, and learning on juvenile sex trafficking.

SHI sponsors several ongoing campaigns to equip and empower the public to identify trafficking and take preventative action. One such campaign, Ambassadors of Hope, works to train volunteers to prevent trafficking through various awareness raising efforts such as hosting a table at a local event, speaking to students and advocating online for state legislation. In an effort to empower people of faith and faith communities to fight trafficking, SHI put together a Faith-in-Action Toolkit to equip church leaders to raise awareness in their community. The tools provided in the kit can be used in sermons or Sunday School, on retreats, or at youth camps.

In 2006, SHI launched one of its most well-known preventative campaigns The Defenders, a coalition of men committed to doing everything in their power to ending commercial sexual exploitation and to bringing dignity, honor, and respect to women and children. Members of this coalition first take a pledge not to purchase or participate in pornography, prostitution, or any form of commercial sex. They also pledge to take a public stand against exploitation and to hold their friends and family members accountable for their actions toward women and children.

In the realm of restoration, SHI provides business mentorship, financial support, and technical assistance to local organizations around the world to facilitate the development of programs and facilities that offer holistic, long-term care to vulnerable and exploited women and children. SHI has built and continues to support Villages or Homes of Hope in Nepal, India, and Jamaica that offer safe communities of refuge and restoration to rescued victims of sexual slavery and their children. In other locations, including South Africa and Japan, SHI has funded the establishment of self-sustaining restoration facilities. In Nepal, India, Japan, and the United States, SHI operates the Women's Investment Network (WIN), a nine-month training program that provides survivors of exploitation with the opportunity to learn job skills so they can enter or reenter the workforce and support themselves and their families. Recently, SHI launched the National Restoration Initiative to develop shelters and services for trafficked youth in the United States.

Finally, SHI works to bring justice to victims of trafficking by lobbying for the passage of laws that protect survivors and increase offender accountability. SHI's The Protected Innocence Challenge grades each state on the strength of its laws addressing child sex trafficking and produces legal analysis for stakeholders. In 2013, SHI launched the Demanding Justice Project to study the outcomes of federal and state arrests, charges, and prosecutions of buyers of sex acts with children. The purpose of the research, which is published in a report on a corresponding website, is to inform advocacy efforts and to strengthen anti-demand legislation and enforcement.

Thomas Reuters Foundation

The Thomas Reuters Foundation is the London-based philan-thropic arm of Thomas Reuters, the world's largest news and information provider. The foundation was created in 1983 to advance quality journalism worldwide through media train-ing and humanitarian reporting. In 1997, in the aftermath of the Rwandan genocide, the foundation launched AlertNet, a humanitarian news service. The scope of AlertNet's coverage was expanded over the years to eventually include a focus on human trafficking in 2013.

Today, the foundation plays a thought leadership role in the fight against slavery and trafficking by raising awareness of the crime through authoritative reporting, by providing world-class training, mentoring, and fellowships to journalists in an effort to empower them to produce a wider range of accurate, quality coverage, and by providing free legal assistance and research to antislavery organizations. The foundation additionally hosts an annual flagship event, The Trust Conference, a human rights forum that brings together more than 600 key players in the global fight against modern-day slavery from diverse sectors representing more than 60 countries.

In 2015, the foundation began granting the Stop Slavery Award to recognize companies considered "best in class" for the policies and processes they have implemented to limit the risk of slavery in their supply chains and operations and to high-light the key roles such companies are playing in the global fight against slavery. In 2020, the award was expanded to recog-nize the contributions of small to mid-size enterprises, NGOs, grassroots organizations, the public sector, and journalists.

Transparentem

Transparentem is a nonprofit global investigation team based in Brooklyn, New York, and Washington, DC, that was estab-lished to encourage transparency and ethical behavior in important global industries. Transparentem works to achieve this goal by identifying and investigating endemic human and environmental abuses in manufacturing supply chains through frontline reporting and other forensic methods. Once investigators and analysts gather sufficient evidence of abuse, they put together a Primary Intelligence Note (PIN) documenting their findings, which they initially present to brands, retailers, and importers in hopes that they will make significant voluntary efforts to eliminate abuses in their supply chains. Transparentem representatives provide PIN recipients a time-bound grace period, during which they agree to temporarily delay further release of the contents of the PINs and the identities of the companies named in them so recipients have the opportunity to develop and implement an initial remedial action plan. If recipients make no effort to correct abuses, Transparentem releases evidence contained in the PINs along with any additional findings to investors, regulators, and journalists.

Once information is disclosed, Transparentem provides a brief summary of their work on their website. One published project involved an 18-month investigation into Malaysia's garment industry. During this investigation, Transparentem discovered significant indicators of forced labor. Migrant workers from poor countries such as Bangladesh, Nepal, and Indonesia told members of the team that they had gone deep into debt to pay fees to recruitment agents for jobs in Malaysia, in hopes of securing a better live for themselves and their families. Upon arrival, however, many workers discovered that they had been deceived by recruitment agents who confiscated their passports and forced them to live in squalid conditions and to work in abusive conditions at garment factories. Beginning in the spring of 2018, Transparentem investigators contacted 23 major apparel brands that they had identified as likely having an ongoing buying relationship with the investigated factories. Of the 23 companies Transparentem approached, most initiated remediation efforts. To date, these efforts have resulted in initiation of the return of workers' recruitment fees and travel documents as well as the implementation of policies requiring that workers are informed of the terms of their employment in writing before leaving home.

U.S. State Department, Office to Monitor and Combat Trafficking in Persons

The Office to Monitor and Combat Trafficking in Persons (TIP Office) was created as an agency within the U.S. State Department in 2001 under mandate by the passage of the Trafficking Victims Protection Act of 2000. The primary mission of the TIP Office—which is led by the U.S. Ambassador-at-Large to Monitor and Combat Trafficking in Persons—is to enforce all laws applying the 13th Amendment of the Constitution, outlawing slavery in the United States, and to motivate and support governments to address their own participation in the global slave trade. The TIP office works with international organizations, foreign governments, and the private sector to raise awareness of human trafficking and to promote the implementation of policies and practices that strengthen efforts to prevent modern slavery and human trafficking, protect victims, and prosecute offenders. The TIP Office additionally manages a foreign assistance program that has provided millions of dollars in assistance to hundreds of anti-trafficking programs around the world.

Every year, the TIP Office publishes the Trafficking in Persons (TIP) Report, which provides the latest information on the status of human trafficking around the world and a comprehensive assessment of what governments are doing to combat it. When the TIP Report was first issued in 2001, it ranked 82 nations according to their efforts to fight human trafficking within their borders and provide an overview of human trafficking in each country and the factors affecting vulnerability to trafficking of the country's nationals abroad. In 2019, the TIP Report provided a narrative for and ranked 187 nations.

As mandated by the TVPA, the TIP Office places each country in the Report onto one of four tiers based on the extent of the governments' efforts to meet the TVPA's minimum standards for the elimination of human trafficking. A Tier 1 ranking indicates that a country's government fully meets the TVPA's standards for elimination of trafficking. To maintain a Tier 1 ranking governments must demonstrate each year that they are not only maintaining but also increasing their efforts to combat trafficking. A Tier 2 ranking indicates that a country is making significant efforts to bring itself into compliance with TVPA standards. Tier 3 rankings are assigned to countries that are not making significant efforts to comply with the TVPA's minimum standards. Pursuant to the TVPA, the U.S. president may deny loans or financial assistance to Tier 3 ranked countries.

Walk Free Foundation

The Walk Free Foundation, which was launched in May 2012, is an initiative of the Minderoo Foundation, an Australian philanthropic organization founded by Andrew Forrest and his wife Nicola that strives to solve major global challenges. The Walk Free Foundation aims to eradicate modern slavery in all its forms through research, education, and global advocacy. The foundation's projects include: The Bali Process Government and Business Forum, which connects business and government leaders to advocate for the eradication of slavery in the Asia Pacific; the Global Freedom Network, which empowers faith leaders to educate and advocate for the abolition of modern slavery; the Freedom Fund, which partners with investors, governments, antislavery organizations, and those at risk of exploitation to identify and invest in the most effective frontline efforts to eradicate modern slavery in the countries and sectors where it is most prevalent; and Promising Practices, a comprehensive global database of antislavery practices designed to establish the most effective efforts and initiatives in the fight against modern slavery.

The foundation is best known for its publication of the Global Slavery Index, the world's leading research tool measuring the size and scale of modern slavery. Approaching its fifth edition, the index provides a country-by-country analysis of the number of individuals enslaved, vulnerability factors, and governmental action. In 2017, the foundation additionally partnered with the International Labour Organization and the International Organization for Migration to publish the inaugural Global Estimates of Modern Slavery report, which combines data on modern slavery from the United Nations, the Gallup World Poll, and the Global Slavery Index.

Introduction

This chapter contains figures and primary resources for further research on the topic of modern slavery. The first section presents global data on modern slavery focusing on region, type, migration, and sex distribution. The second section provides excerpts from international and U.S. law, speeches, testimony, and other government documents pertaining to modern slavery organized in chronological order.

The handmade woolen carpet industry is fast growing in many parts of the developing world and is particularly rife with child labor. Children like this young girl are prized in the carpet industry for their small, fast fingers. Defenseless, they do what they're told, toiling in cramped, dark, airless village huts from sunrise until well into the night. (Kay Chernush for the U.S. State Department)

Data

This figure shows the prevalence of modern slavery (per 1,000 population) by region and category.

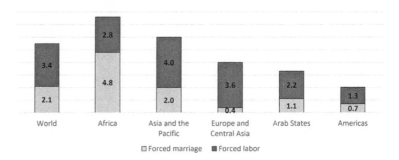

Figure 5.1 Regional Prevalence of Modern Slavery
Source: International Labour Organization and Walk Free Foundation. "Global Estimates of Modern Slavery: Forced Labour and Forced Marriage." Geneva: International Labour Office, 2017. Available online at https://www.ilo.org/global /publications/books/WCMS_575479/lang--en/index.htm

This pie chart shows the number and percentage distribution of victims of forced labor, by subcategory.

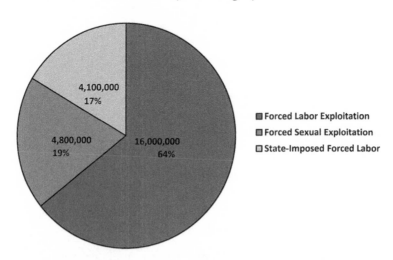

Figure 5.2 Forced Labor
Source: International Labour Organization and Walk Free Foundation. "Global Estimates of Modern Slavery: Forced Labour and Forced Marriage." Geneva: International Labour Office, 2017. Available online at https://www.ilo.org/global /publications/books/WCMS_575479/lang--en/index.htm

This figure shows the percentage of victims of forced labor living outside their country of residence, by form of forced labor.

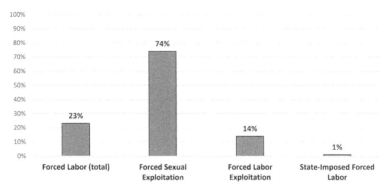

Figure 5.3 Forced Labor and Migration

Source: International Labour Organization and Walk Free Foundation. "Global Estimates of Modern Slavery: Forced Labour and Forced Marriage." Geneva: International Labour Office, 2017. Available online at https://www.ilo.org/global /publications/books/WCMS_575479/lang--en/index.htm

This figure shows the differences by sex in the typology of forced labor exploitation.

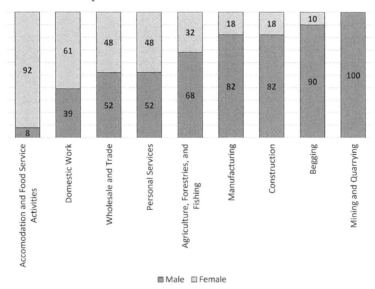

Figure 5.4 Sex Distribution of Victims of Forced Labor Exploitation, by Sector of Economic Activity

Source: International Labour Organization and Walk Free Foundation. "Global Estimates of Modern Slavery: Forced Labour and Forced Marriage." Geneva: International Labour Office, 2017. Available online at https://www.ilo.org/global /publications/books/WCMS_575479/lang--en/index.htm

This figure shows the differences by sex in the typology of means of coercion at both the recruitment and employment stages.

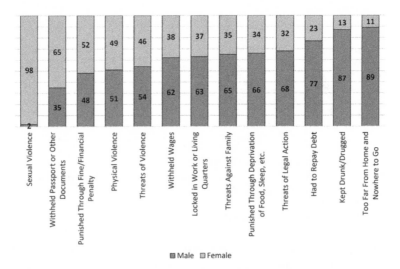

Figure 5.5   Percentage Distribution of Means of Coercion, by Sex
Source: International Labour Organization and Walk Free Foundation. "Global Estimates of Modern Slavery: Forced Labour and Forced Marriage." Geneva: International Labour Office, 2017. Available online at https://www.ilo.org/global /publications/books/WCMS_575479/lang--en/index.htm

Documents
The International Slavery Convention (1926) (Excerpts)

The International Slavery Convention was an agreement under the authority of the League of Nations that required all signatory states to enact and enforce laws against slavery, forced labor, and the slave trade in their territories, to intercept slave traffic in their territorial waters and on ships flying their flag, and to assist other states in anti-slavery efforts. The Convention was signed at Geneva on September 25, 1926, and entered into force a year later.

. . . Whereas the signatories of the General Act of the Brussels Conference of 1889-90 declared that they were equally animated by the firm intention of putting an end to the traffic in African slaves,

Whereas the signatories of the Convention of Saint-Germain-en-Laye of 1919, to revise the General Act of Berlin of 1885 and the General Act and Declaration of Brussels of 1890, affirmed their intention of securing the complete suppression of slavery in all its forms and of the slave trade by land and sea,

Taking into consideration the report of the Temporary Slavery Commission appointed by the Council of the League of Nations on June 12th, 1924,

Desiring to complete and extend the work accomplished under the Brussels Act and to find a means of giving practical effect throughout the world to such intentions as were expressed in regard to slave trade and slavery by the signatories of the Convention of Saint-Germain-en-Laye, and recognising that it is necessary to conclude to that end more detailed arrangements than are contained in that Convention,

Considering, moreover, that it is necessary to prevent forced labour from developing into conditions analogous to slavery,

Have decided to conclude a Convention and have accordingly appointed as their Plenipotentiaries [names omitted] ... have agreed as follows:

Article 1

For the purpose of the present Convention, the following definitions are agreed upon:

1. Slavery is the status or condition of a person over whom any or all of the powers attaching to the right of ownership are exercised.

2. The slave trade includes all acts involved in the capture, acquisition, or disposal of a person with intent to reduce him to slavery; all acts involved in the acquisition of a slave with a view to selling or exchanging him; all acts of disposal

by sale or exchange of a slave acquired with a view to being sold or exchanged, and, in general, every act of trade or transport in slaves.

Article 2

The High Contracting Parties undertake, each in respect of the territories placed under its sovereignty, jurisdiction, protection, suzerainty or tutelage, so far as they have not already taken the necessary steps:

(a) To prevent and suppress the slave trade;

(b) To bring about, progressively and as soon as possible, the complete abolition of slavery in all its forms.

Article 3

The High Contracting Parties undertake to adopt all appropriate measures with a view to preventing and suppressing the embarkation, disembarkation and transport of slaves in their territorial waters and upon all vessels flying their respective flags . . .

Article 4

The High Contracting Parties shall give to one another every assistance with the object of securing the abolition of slavery and the slave trade.

Article 5

The High Contracting Parties recognise that recourse to compulsory or forced labour may have grave consequences and undertake, each in respect of the territories placed under its sovereignty, jurisdiction, protection, suzerainty or tutelage, to take all necessary measures to prevent compulsory or forced labour from developing into conditions analogous to slavery . . .

Source: United Nations, Office of the High Commissioner, Human Rights. https://www.ohchr.org/Documents/Profession alInterest/slavery.pdf

The Universal Declaration of Human Rights (1948) (Excerpts)

The United Nations adopted the Universal Declaration of Human Rights (UDHR) in the wake of the wartime atrocities against slave workers that had been carried out during World War II. The Declaration identified fundamental rights that ought to be universally protected, including the right to life and liberty. Article 4 of the Declaration specially declares that slavery ought to be abolished in all of its forms. Abolitionists have successfully used Article 4 of the UDHR to put legal pressure on governments to act against slavery within their borders. Nevertheless, the Human Rights Council— the United Nations' body responsible for promoting and protecting human rights around the globe—has been heavily criticized for its inclusion of notorious human rights abusers and authoritarian regimes. In 2019, the UN General Assembly elected Mauritania to the Human Rights Council, a country that has blatantly imprisoned abolitionists and where up to 20 percent of the population remains enslaved.

Preamble
Whereas recognition of the inherent dignity and of the equal and inalienable rights of all members of the human family is the foundation of freedom, justice and peace in the world,

Whereas disregard and contempt for human rights have resulted in barbarous acts which have outraged the conscience of mankind, and the advent of a world in which human beings shall enjoy freedom of speech and belief and freedom from fear and want has been proclaimed as the highest aspiration of the common people,

Whereas it is essential, if man is not to be compelled to have recourse, as a last resort, to rebellion against tyranny and oppression, that human rights should be protected by the rule of law,

Whereas it is essential to promote the development of friendly relations between nations,

Whereas the peoples of the United Nations have in the Charter reaffirmed their faith in fundamental human rights, in the dignity and worth of the human person and in the equal rights of men and women and have determined to promote social progress and better standards of life in larger freedom,

Whereas Member States have pledged themselves to achieve, in co-operation with the United Nations, the promotion of universal respect for and observance of human rights and fundamental freedoms,

Whereas a common understanding of these rights and freedoms is of the greatest importance for the full realization of this pledge,

Now, therefore, The General Assembly, Proclaims this Universal Declaration of Human Rights as a common standard of achievement for all peoples and all nations, to the end that every individual and every organ of society, keeping this Declaration constantly in mind, shall strive by teaching and education to promote respect for these rights and freedoms and by progressive measures, national and international, to secure their universal and effective recognition and observance, both among the peoples of Member States themselves and among the peoples of territories under their jurisdiction.

Article 1

All human beings are born free and equal in dignity and rights. They are endowed with reason and conscience and should act towards one another in a spirit of brotherhood.

Article 2

Everyone is entitled to all the rights and freedoms set forth in this Declaration, without distinction of any kind, such as race, colour, sex, language, religion, political or other opinion, national or social origin, property, birth or other status . . .

Article 3

Everyone has the right to life, liberty and security of person.

Article 4

No one shall be held in slavery or servitude; slavery and the slave trade shall be prohibited in all their forms . . .

Source: United Nations, Office of the High Commissioner, Human Rights. https://www.ohchr.org/EN/UDHR/Docume nts/UDHR_Translations/eng.pdf

United Nations Supplementary Convention on the Abolition of Slavery, the Slave Trade, and Institutions and Practices Similar to Slavery (1956)

The Supplementary Convention on the Abolition of Slavery was adopted in Geneva to expand the definition of contemporary slavery to include debt bondage, serfdom, forced or servile marriage, and the buying and selling of children for labor or prostitution. The Convention additionally imposed more extensive prohibitions against practices contributing to slave trafficking and the slave trade and encouraged collaboration between state parties in efforts to end such practices. The Economic and Social Council within the United Nations was tasked with exploring ways in which the Convention might be effectively carried out and with creating proposals for addressing issues.

Preamble

The States Parties to the present Convention,

Considering that freedom is the birthright of every human being,

Mindful that the peoples of the United Nations reaffirmed in the Charter their faith in the dignity and worth of the human person,

Considering that the Universal Declaration of Human Rights, proclaimed by the General Assembly of the United Nations as a common standard of achievement for all peoples and all nations, states that no one shall be held in slavery or servitude and that slavery and the slave trade shall be prohibited in all their forms,

Recognizing that, since the conclusion of the Slavery Convention signed at Geneva on 25 September 1926, which was designed to secure the abolition of slavery and of the slave trade, further progress has been made towards this end,

Having regard to the Forced Labour Convention of 1930 and to subsequent action by the International Labour Organisation in regard to forced or compulsory labour,

Being aware, however, that slavery, the slave trade and institutions and practices similar to slavery have not yet been eliminated in all parts of the world,

Having decided, therefore, that the Convention of 1926, which remains operative, should now be augmented by the conclusion of a supplementary convention designed to intensify national as well as international efforts towards the abolition of slavery, the slave trade and institutions and practices similar to slavery,

Have agreed as follows:

Section I. - Institutions and practices similar to slavery

Article 1

Each of the States Parties to this Convention shall take all practicable and necessary legislative and other measures to bring about progressively and as soon as possible the complete abolition or abandonment of the following institutions and practices, where they still exist and whether or not they are covered by the definition of slavery contained in article 1 of the Slavery Convention signed at Geneva on 25 September 1926:

(a) Debt bondage, that is to say, the status or condition arising from a pledge by a debtor of his personal services or of those of a person under his control as security for a debt, if the value of those services as reasonably assessed is not applied towards the liquidation of the debt or the length and nature of those services are not respectively limited and defined;

(b) Serfdom, that is to say, the condition or status of a tenant who is by law, custom or agreement bound to live and labor on land belonging to another person and to render some determinate service to such other person, whether for reward or not, and is not free to change his status;

(c) Any institution or practice whereby:

    (i) A woman, without the right to refuse, is promised or given in marriage on payment of a consideration in money or in kind to her parents, guardian, family or any other person or group; or

    (ii) The husband of a woman, his family, or his clan, has the right to transfer her to another person for value received or otherwise; or

    (iii) A woman on the death of her husband is liable to be inherited by another person;

(d) Any institution or practice whereby a child or young person under the age of 18 years, is delivered by either or both of his natural parents or by his guardian to another person, whether for reward or not, with a view to the exploitation of the child or young person or of his labour.

Article 2

With a view to bringing to an end the institutions and practices mentioned in article 1 (c) of this Convention, the States Parties undertake to prescribe, where appropriate, suitable minimum ages of marriage, to encourage the use of facilities whereby the consent of both parties to a marriage may be freely expressed in the presence of a competent civil or religious authority, and to encourage the registration of marriages.

Section II. - The slave trade

Article 3

1. The act of conveying or attempting to convey slaves from one country to another by whatever means of transport, or of being accessory thereto, shall be a criminal offence under the laws of the States Parties to this Convention and persons convicted thereof shall be liable to very severe penalties.

2. (a) The States Parties shall take all effective measures to prevent ships and aircraft authorized to fly their flags from conveying slaves and to punish persons guilty of such acts or of using national flags for that purpose. (b) The States Parties shall take all effective measures to ensure that their ports, airfields and coasts are not used for the conveyance of slaves.

3. The States Parties to this Convention shall exchange information in order to ensure the practical co-ordination of the measures taken by them in combating the slave trade and shall inform each other of every case of the slave trade, and of every attempt to commit this criminal offence, which comes to their notice.

Article 4

Any slave who takes refuge on board any vessel of a State Party to this Convention shall ipso facto be free.

Section III. - Slavery and institutions and practices similar to slavery

Article 5

In a country where the abolition or abandonment of slavery, or of the institutions or practices mentioned in article 1 of this Convention, is not yet complete, the act of mutilating, branding or otherwise marking a slave or a person of servile status in order to indicate his status, or as a punishment, or for any other reason, or of being accessory thereto, shall be a criminal offence under the laws of the States Parties to this Convention and persons convicted thereof shall be liable to punishment.

Article 6

1. The act of enslaving another person or of inducing another person to give himself or a person dependent upon him into slavery, or of attempting these acts, or being accessory thereto, or being a party to a conspiracy to accomplish any such acts, shall be a criminal offence under the laws of the States Parties to this Convention and persons convicted thereof shall be liable to punishment.

2. Subject to the provisions of the introductory paragraph of article 1 of this Convention, the provisions of paragraph 1 of the present article shall also apply to the act of inducing another person to place himself or a person dependent upon him into the servile status resulting from any of the institutions or practices mentioned in article 1, to any attempt to perform such acts, to being accessory thereto, and to being a party to a conspiracy to accomplish any such acts.

Section IV. - Definitions

Article 7

For the purposes of the present Convention:

(a) "Slavery" means, as defined in the Slavery Convention of 1926, the status or condition of a person over whom any or all of the powers attaching to the right of ownership are exercised, and "slave" means a person in such condition or status;

(b) "A person of servile status" means a person in the condition or status resulting from any of the institutions or practices mentioned in article 1 of this Convention;

(c) "Slave trade" means and includes all acts involved in the capture, acquisition or disposal of a person with intent to reduce him to slavery; all acts involved in the acquisition of a slave with a view to selling or exchanging him; all acts of disposal by sale or exchange of a person acquired with a view to being sold or exchanged; and, in general, every act of trade or transport in slaves by whatever means of conveyance.

Section V. - Cooperation between States Parties and communication of information

Article 8

1. The States Parties to this Convention undertake to co-operate with each other and with the United Nations to give effect to the foregoing provisions.

2. The Parties undertake to communicate to the Secretary-General of the United Nations copies of any laws, regulations and administrative measures enacted or put into effect to implement the provisions of this Convention.

3. The Secretary-General shall communicate the information received under paragraph 2 of this article to the other Parties and to the Economic and Social Council as part of the

documentation for any discussion which the Council might undertake with a view to making further recommendations for the abolition of slavery, the slave trade or the institutions and practices which are the subject of this Convention . . .

Source: United Nations, Office of the High Commissioner, Human Rights. https://www.ohchr.org/EN/ProfessionalInter est/Pages/SupplementaryConventionAbolitionOfSlavery.aspx

ILO Convention Concerning the Prohibition and Immediate Action for Elimination of the Worst Forms of Child Labor (1999) (Excerpts)

The International Labour Organization (ILO) was first established in 1919 with the aim of bringing dignity to all workers and promoting safe working conditions, reasonable hours, adequate wages, no child labor, and social security in old age. In 1946, the ILO became a specialized agency of the United Nations, and, in the early 1990s, it began to devote particular attention to the problem of child labor and modern slavery. In 1999, the ILO adopted the Convention Concerning the Prohibition and Immediate Action for the Elimination of the Worst Forms of Child Labour, known in short form as the Worst Forms of Child Labour Convention. Countries ratifying the convention pledge to take immediate action to prohibit and eliminate the worst forms of child labor. With financial help from the United States, the ILO established the International Program on the Elimination of Child Labour (IPEC) to assist countries in meeting their goals and to monitor compliance.

Preamble
The General Conference of the International Labour Organization,

Having been convened at Geneva by the Governing Body of the International Labour Office, and having met in its 87th Session on 1 June 1999, and

Considering the need to adopt new instruments for the prohibition and elimination of the worst forms of child labor, as the main priority for national and international action, including international cooperation and assistance, to complement the Convention and the Recommendation concerning Minimum Age for Admission to Employment, 1973, which remain fundamental instruments on child labor . . .

adopts this seventeenth day of June of the year one thousand nine hundred and ninety-nine the following Convention, which may be cited as the Worst Forms of Child Labor Convention, 1999.

Article 1

Each Member which ratifies this Convention shall take immediate and effective measures to secure the prohibition and elimination of the worst forms of child labor as a matter of urgency.

Article 2

For the purposes of this Convention, the term **child** shall apply to all persons under the age of 18.

Article 3

For the purposes of this Convention, the term **the worst forms of child labor** comprises:

(a) all forms of slavery or practices similar to slavery, such as the sale and trafficking of children, debt bondage and serfdom and forced or compulsory labor, including forced or compulsory recruitment of children for use in armed conflict;

(b) the use, procuring or offering of a child for prostitution, for the production of pornography or for pornographic performances;

(c) the use, procuring or offering of a child for illicit activities, in particular for the production and trafficking of drugs as defined in the relevant international treaties;

(d) work which, by its nature or the circumstances in which it is carried out, is likely to harm the health, safety or morals of children . . .

Article 6

1. Each Member shall design and implement programmes of action to eliminate as a priority the worst forms of child labor.

2. Such programs of action shall be designed and implemented in consultation with relevant government institutions and employers' and workers' organizations, taking into consideration the views of other concerned groups as appropriate.

Article 7

1. Each Member shall take all necessary measures to ensure the effective implementation and enforcement of the provisions giving effect to this Convention including the provision and application of penal sanctions or, as appropriate, other sanctions.

2. Each Member shall, taking into account the importance of education in eliminating child labor, take effective and time-bound measures to:

   (a) prevent the engagement of children in the worst forms of child labor;

   (b) provide the necessary and appropriate direct assistance for the removal of children from the worst forms of child labor and for their rehabilitation and social integration;

(c) ensure access to free basic education, and, wherever possible and appropriate, vocational training, for all children removed from the worst forms of child labor;

(d) identify and reach out to children at special risk; and

(e) take account of the special situation of girls.

3. Each Member shall designate the competent authority responsible for the implementation of the provisions giving effect to this Convention.

Article 8

Members shall take appropriate steps to assist one another in giving effect to the provisions of this Convention through enhanced international cooperation and/or assistance including support for social and economic development, poverty eradication programs and universal education . . ..

Source: International Labour Organization. https://www.ilo .org/dyn/normlex/en/f?p=NORMLEXPUB:12100:0::NO::P1 2100_ILO_CODE:C182. Used by permission of the International Labour Organization.

Trafficking Victims Protection Act (2000) (Selections)

The Trafficking Victims Protection Act (TVPA) is the cornerstone of federal anti-trafficking legislation in the United States. Signed into law by President Clinton in the final days before the 2000 election, the TVPA represented the first time that an American president had committed the nation to fighting global trafficking in all its forms. The TVPA established human trafficking and related offenses as federal crimes with severe penalties and implemented several programs aimed at eradicating slavery and restoring victims. The act additionally called for the establishment of an Office to Monitor and Combat Trafficking in Persons within the State Department tasked with annually ranking countries based on their efforts to eradicate slavery. Reauthorizations and expansions of the law have since been signed by presidents Bush, Obama, and Trump.

PUBLIC LAW 106-386—OCT. 28, 2000

DIVISION A—TRAFFICKING VICTIMS PROTECTION ACT OF 2000

SEC. 102. PURPOSES AND FINDINGS.

(a) PURPOSES.—The purposes of this division are to combat trafficking in persons, a contemporary manifestation of slavery whose victims are predominantly women and children, to ensure just and effective punishment of traffickers, and to protect their victims.

(b) FINDINGS.—Congress finds that:

(1) As the 21st century begins, the degrading institution of slavery continues throughout the world. Trafficking in persons is a modern form of slavery, and it is the largest manifestation of slavery today. At least 700,000 persons annually, primarily women and children, are trafficked within or across international borders. Approximately 50,000 women and children are trafficked into the United States each year.

(2) Many of these persons are trafficked into the international sex trade, often by force, fraud, or coercion. The sex industry has rapidly expanded over the past several decades. It involves sexual exploitation of persons, predominantly women and girls, involving activities related to prostitution, pornography, sex tourism, and other commercial sexual services. The low status of women in many parts of the world has contributed to a burgeoning of the trafficking industry.

(3) Trafficking in persons is not limited to the sex industry. This growing transnational crime also includes forced labor and involves significant violations of labor, public health, and human rights standards worldwide. . . .

(12) Trafficking in persons substantially affects interstate and foreign commerce. Trafficking for such purposes as involuntary servitude, peonage, and other forms of forced labor has an impact on the nationwide employment network and labor market. Within the context of slavery, servitude, and labor or services which are obtained or maintained through coercive conduct that amounts to a condition of servitude, victims are subjected to a range of violations.

(13) Involuntary servitude statutes are intended to reach cases in which persons are held in a condition of servitude through nonviolent coercion. In United States v. Kozminski, 487 U.S. 931 (1988), the Supreme Court found that section 1584 of title 18, United States Code, should be narrowly interpreted, absent a definition of involuntary servitude by Congress. As a result, that section was interpreted to criminalize only servitude that is brought about through use or threatened use of physical or legal coercion, and to exclude other conduct that can have the same purpose and effect.

(14) Existing legislation and law enforcement in the United States and other countries are inadequate to deter trafficking and bring traffickers to justice, failing to reflect the gravity of the offenses involved. No comprehensive law exists in the United States that penalizes the range of offenses involved in the trafficking scheme. Instead, even the most brutal instances of trafficking in the sex industry are often punished under laws that also apply to lesser offenses, so that traffickers typically escape deserved punishment.

(15) In the United States, the seriousness of this crime and its components is not reflected in current sentencing guidelines, resulting in weak penalties for convicted traffickers.

(16) In some countries, enforcement against traffickers is also hindered by official indifference, by corruption, and sometimes even by official participation in trafficking.

(17) Existing laws often fail to protect victims of trafficking, and because victims are often illegal immigrants in the destination country, they are repeatedly punished more harshly than the traffickers themselves.

(18) Additionally, adequate services and facilities do not exist to meet victims' needs regarding health care, housing, education, and legal assistance, which safely reintegrate trafficking victims into their home countries.

(19) Victims of severe forms of trafficking should not be inappropriately incarcerated, fined, or otherwise penalized solely for unlawful acts committed as a direct result of being trafficked, such as using false documents, entering the country without documentation, or working without documentation.

(20) Because victims of trafficking are frequently unfamiliar with the laws, cultures, and languages of the countries into which they have been trafficked, because they are often subjected to coercion and intimidation including physical detention and debt bondage, and because they often fear retribution and forcible removal to countries in which they will face retribution or other hardship, these victims often find it difficult or impossible to report the crimes committed against them or to assist in the investigation and prosecution of such crimes.

(21) Trafficking of persons is an evil requiring concerted and vigorous action by countries of origin, transit or destination, and by international organizations.

(22) One of the founding documents of the United States, the Declaration of Independence, recognizes the inherent dignity and worth of all people. It states that all men are created equal and that they are endowed by their Creator with certain unalienable rights. The right to be free from slavery and involuntary servitude is among those unalienable rights. Acknowledging this fact, the United States outlawed slavery and involuntary servitude in 1865, recognizing them as evil institutions that must be abolished. Current practices of sexual slavery and trafficking of women and children are similarly abhorrent to the principles upon which the United States was founded.

(23) The United States and the international community agree that trafficking in persons involves grave violations of human rights and is a matter of pressing international concern. The international community has repeatedly condemned slavery and involuntary servitude, violence against women, and other elements of trafficking, through declarations, treaties, and United Nations resolutions and reports . . .

(24) Trafficking in persons is a transnational crime with national implications. To deter international trafficking and bring its perpetrators to justice, nations including the United States must recognize that trafficking is a serious offense. This is done by prescribing appropriate punishment, giving priority to the prosecution of trafficking offenses, and protecting rather than punishing the victims of such offenses. The United States must work bilaterally and multilaterally to abolish the trafficking industry by taking steps to promote cooperation among countries linked together by international trafficking routes. The United States must also urge the international community to take strong action in multilateral fora to engage recalcitrant countries in serious

and sustained efforts to eliminate trafficking and protect trafficking victims . . .

Source: United States Government Printing Office. https://www.govinfo.gov/content/pkg/PLAW-106publ386/pdf/PLAW-106publ386.pdf

Protocol to Prevent, Suppress and Punish Trafficking in Persons, Especially Women and Children, Supplementing the United Nations Convention against Transnational Organized Crime (November 2000)

The Protocol to Prevent, Suppress, and Punish Trafficking in Persons Especially Women and Children (The Trafficking Protocol) is one of the three Palermo Protocols that were adopted by the United Nations General Assembly to supplement the 2000 Convention against Transnational Organized Crime (The Palermo Convention). The Trafficking Protocol introduced the "3P" paradigm of prevention, victim protection, and prosecution efforts to fight modern slavery. The Protocol—which has been ratified by 175 state parties since it entered into force on December 25, 2003—was the first legally binding global agreement with an internationally agreed-upon definition of trafficking in persons that established international guidelines for investigating and prosecuting traffickers and protecting and aiding victims.

Preamble
The States Parties to this Protocol,

Declaring that effective action to prevent and combat trafficking in persons, especially women and children, requires a comprehensive international approach in the countries of origin, transit and destination that includes measures to prevent such trafficking, to punish the traffickers and to protect the victims of such trafficking, including by protecting their internationally recognized human rights . . .

Convinced that supplementing the United Nations Convention against Transnational Organized Crime with an international instrument for the prevention, suppression and punishment of trafficking in persons . . .

Have agreed as follows:

I. General provisions
Article 1
Relation with the United Nations Convention against Transnational Organized Crime

1. This Protocol supplements the United Nations Convention against Transnational Organized Crime. It shall be interpreted together with the Convention.

2. The provisions of the Convention shall apply, mutatis mutandis, to this Protocol unless otherwise provided herein.

3. The offences established in accordance with article 5 of this Protocol shall be regarded as offences established in accordance with the Convention.

Article 2
Statement of purpose
The purposes of this Protocol are:

(a) To prevent and combat trafficking in persons, paying particular attention to women and children;

(b) To protect and assist the victims of such trafficking, with full respect for their human rights; and

4. (c) To promote cooperation among States Parties in order to meet those objectives.

Article 3
Use of terms
For the purposes of this Protocol:

(a) "Trafficking in persons" shall mean the recruitment, transportation, transfer, harbouring or receipt of persons, by means of the threat or use of force or other forms of coercion, of abduction, of fraud, of deception, of the abuse of power or of a position of vulnerability or of the giving or receiving of payments or benefits to achieve the consent of a person having control over another person, for the purpose of exploitation. Exploitation shall include, at a minimum, the exploitation of the prostitution of others or other forms of sexual exploitation, forced labour or services, slavery or practices similar to slavery, servitude or the removal of organs;

(b) The consent of a victim of trafficking in persons to the intended exploitation set forth in subparagraph (a) of this article shall be irrelevant where any of the means set forth in subparagraph (a) have been used;

(c) The recruitment, transportation, transfer, harbouring or receipt of a child for the purpose of exploitation shall be considered "trafficking in persons" even if this does not involve any of the means set forth in subparagraph (a) of this article;

(d) "Child" shall mean any person under eighteen years of age.

Article 4
Scope of application
This Protocol shall apply, except as otherwise stated herein, to the prevention, investigation and prosecution of the offences established in accordance with article 5 of this Protocol, where those offences are transnational in nature and involve an organized criminal group, as well as to the protection of victims of such offences.

Article 5
Criminalization

1. Each State Party shall adopt such legislative and other measures as may be necessary to establish as criminal offences

the conduct set forth in article 3 of this Protocol, when committed intentionally.

2. Each State Party shall also adopt such legislative and other measures as may be necessary to establish as criminal offences:

   (a) Subject to the basic concepts of its legal system, attempting to commit an offence established in accordance with paragraph 1 of this article;

   (b) Participating as an accomplice in an offence established in accordance with paragraph 1 of this article; and

   (c) Organizing or directing other persons to commit an offence established in accordance with paragraph 1 of this article.

II. Protection of victims of trafficking in persons
Article 6
Assistance to and protection of victims of trafficking in persons

1. In appropriate cases and to the extent possible under its domestic law, each State Party shall protect the privacy and identity of victims of trafficking in persons, including, inter alia, by making legal proceedings relating to such trafficking confidential.

2. Each State Party shall ensure that its domestic legal or administrative system contains measures that provide to victims of trafficking in persons, in appropriate cases:

   (a) Information on relevant court and administrative proceedings;

   (b) Assistance to enable their views and concerns to be presented and considered at appropriate stages of criminal proceedings against offenders, in a manner not prejudicial to the rights of the defence.

3. Each State Party shall consider implementing measures to provide for the physical, psychological and social recovery of victims of trafficking in persons, including, in appropriate cases, in cooperation with non-governmental organizations, other relevant organizations and other elements of civil society, and, in particular, the provision of:

(a) Appropriate housing;

(b) Counselling and information, in particular as regards their legal rights, in a language that the victims of trafficking in persons can understand;

(c) Medical, psychological and material assistance; and

(d) Employment, educational and training opportunities.

4. Each State Party shall take into account, in applying the provisions of this article, the age, gender and special needs of victims of trafficking in persons, in particular the special needs of children, including appropriate housing, education and care.

5. Each State Party shall endeavour to provide for the physical safety of victims of trafficking in persons while they are within its territory.

6. Each State Party shall ensure that its domestic legal system contains measures that offer victims of trafficking in persons the possibility of obtaining compensation for damage suffered.

Article 7
Status of victims of trafficking in persons in receiving States

1. In addition to taking measures pursuant to article 6 of this Protocol, each State Party shall consider adopting legislative or other appropriate measures that permit victims of trafficking in persons to remain in its territory, temporarily or permanently, in appropriate cases.

2. In implementing the provision contained in paragraph 1 of this article, each State Party shall give appropriate consideration to humanitarian and compassionate factors.

Article 8
Repatriation of victims of trafficking in persons

1. The State Party of which a victim of trafficking in persons is a national or in which the person had the right of permanent residence at the time of entry into the territory of the receiving State Party shall facilitate and accept, with due regard for the safety of that person, the return of that person without undue or unreasonable delay.

2. When a State Party returns a victim of trafficking in persons to a State Party of which that person is a national or in which he or she had, at the time of entry into the territory of the receiving State Party, the right of permanent residence, such return shall be with due regard for the safety of that person and for the status of any legal proceedings related to the fact that the person is a victim of trafficking and shall preferably be voluntary.

3. At the request of a receiving State Party, a requested State Party shall, without undue or unreasonable delay, verify whether a person who is a victim of trafficking in persons is its national or had the right of permanent residence in its territory at the time of entry into the territory of the receiving State Party.

4. In order to facilitate the return of a victim of trafficking in persons who is without proper documentation, the State Party of which that person is a national or in which he or she had the right of permanent residence at the time of entry into the territory of the receiving State Party shall agree to issue, at the request of the receiving State Party, such travel documents or other authorization as may be necessary to enable the person to travel to and re-enter its territory.

5. This article shall be without prejudice to any right afforded to victims of trafficking in persons by any domestic law of the receiving State Party.

6. This article shall be without prejudice to any applicable bilateral or multilateral agreement or arrangement that governs, in whole or in part, the return of victims of trafficking in persons.

III. Prevention, cooperation and other measures
Article 9
Prevention of trafficking in persons

1. States Parties shall establish comprehensive policies, programs and other measures:

    (a) To prevent and combat trafficking in persons; and

    (b) To protect victims of trafficking in persons, especially women and children, from revictimization.

2. States Parties shall endeavor to undertake measures such as research, information and mass media campaigns and social and economic initiatives to prevent and combat trafficking in persons.

3. Policies, programs and other measures established in accordance with this article shall, as appropriate, include cooperation with non-governmental organizations, other relevant organizations and other elements of civil society.

4. States Parties shall take or strengthen measures, including through bilateral or multilateral cooperation, to alleviate the factors that make persons, especially women and children, vulnerable to trafficking, such as poverty, underdevelopment and lack of equal opportunity.

5. States Parties shall adopt or strengthen legislative or other measures, such as educational, social or cultural measures,

including through bilateral and multilateral cooperation, to discourage the demand that fosters all forms of exploitation of persons, especially women and children, that leads to trafficking.

Article 10
Information exchange and training

1. Law enforcement, immigration or other relevant authorities of States Parties shall, as appropriate, cooperate with one another by exchanging information, in accordance with their domestic law, to enable them to determine:

    (a) Whether individuals crossing or attempting to cross an international border with travel documents belonging to other persons or without travel documents are perpetrators or victims of trafficking in persons;

    (b) The types of travel document that individuals have used or attempted to use to cross an international border for the purpose of trafficking in persons; and

    (c) The means and methods used by organized criminal groups for the purpose of trafficking in persons, including the recruitment and transportation of victims, routes and links between and among individuals and groups engaged in such trafficking, and possible measures for detecting them.

2. States Parties shall provide or strengthen training for law enforcement, immigration and other relevant officials in the prevention of trafficking in persons. The training should focus on methods used in preventing such trafficking, prosecuting the traffickers and protecting the rights of the victims, including protecting the victims from the traffickers. The training should also take into account the need to consider human rights and child- and gender-sensitive issues and it should encourage cooperation with

non-governmental organizations, other relevant organizations and other elements of civil society.

3. A State Party that receives information shall comply with any request by the State Party that transmitted the information that places restrictions on its use.

Article 11
Border measures

1. Without prejudice to international commitments in relation to the free movement of people, States Parties shall strengthen, to the extent possible, such border controls as may be necessary to prevent and detect trafficking in persons.

2. Each State Party shall adopt legislative or other appropriate measures to prevent, to the extent possible, means of transport operated by commercial carriers from being used in the commission of offences established in accordance with article 5 of this Protocol.

3. Where appropriate, and without prejudice to applicable international conventions, such measures shall include establishing the obligation of commercial carriers, including any transportation company or the owner or operator of any means of transport, to ascertain that all passengers are in possession of the travel documents required for entry into the receiving State.

4. Each State Party shall take the necessary measures, in accordance with its domestic law, to provide for sanctions in cases of violation of the obligation set forth in paragraph 3 of this article.

5. Each State Party shall consider taking measures that permit, in accordance with its domestic law, the denial of entry or revocation of visas of persons implicated in the commission of offences established in accordance with this Protocol.

6. Without prejudice to article 27 of the Convention, States Parties shall consider strengthening cooperation among border control agencies by, inter alia, establishing and maintaining direct channels of communication . . .

Source: United Nations, Office of the High Commissioner, Human Rights. https://www.ohchr.org/en/professionalinterest/pages/protocoltraffickinginpersons.aspx

George W. Bush's Speech to the UN General Assembly (2003) (Selection)

On September 23, 2003, President George W. Bush delivered a speech before the United Nations, in which he identified three challenges requiring "urgent attention" and "moral clarity" among the international community: fighting the war against terror, ending the proliferation of weapons of mass destruction and instituting democracy in Iraq, and fighting trafficking of victims for sex slavery. He also pledged an extra $50 million in U.S. funds to help combat sex trafficking. With this speech, Bush became the first world leader to call on the General Assembly to fight modern slavery. The speech, however, focused worldwide attention almost exclusively on sex trafficking as opposed to other more prevalent forms of modern slavery.

THE PRESIDENT: Mr. Secretary General; Mr. President; distinguished delegates; ladies and gentlemen: Twenty-four months ago—and yesterday in the memory of America—the center of New York City became a battlefield, and a graveyard, and the symbol of an unfinished war. Since that day, terrorists have struck in Bali, Mombassa, in Casablanca, in Riyadh, in Jakarta, in Jerusalem—measuring the advance of their cause in the chaos and innocent suffering they leave behind . . .

There's another humanitarian crisis spreading, yet hidden from view. Each year, an estimated 800,000 to 900,000 human beings are bought, sold or forced across the world's borders.

Among them are hundreds of thousands of teenage girls, and others as young as five, who fall victim to the sex trade. This commerce in human life generates billions of dollars each year—much of which is used to finance organized crime.

There's a special evil in the abuse and exploitation of the most innocent and vulnerable. The victims of sex trade see little of life before they see the very worst of life—an underground of brutality and lonely fear. Those who create these victims and profit from their suffering must be severely punished. Those who patronize this industry debase themselves and deepen the misery of others. And governments that tolerate this trade are tolerating a form of slavery.

This problem has appeared in my own country, and we are working to stop it. The PROTECT Act, which I signed into law this year, makes it a crime for any person to enter the United States, or for any citizen to travel abroad, for the purpose of sex tourism involving children. The Department of Justice is actively investigating sex tour operators and patrons, who can face up to 30 years in prison. Under the Trafficking Victims Protection Act, the United States is using sanctions against governments to discourage human trafficking.

The victims of this industry also need help from members of the United Nations. And this begins with clear standards and the certainty of punishment under laws of every country. Today, some nations make it a crime to sexually abuse children abroad. Such conduct should be a crime in all nations. Governments should inform travelers of the harm this industry does, and the severe punishments that will fall on its patrons. The American government is committing $50 million to support the good work of organizations that are rescuing women and children from exploitation, and giving them shelter and medical treatment and the hope of a new life. I urge other governments to do their part.

We must show new energy in fighting back an old evil. Nearly two centuries after the abolition of the Transatlantic Slave Trade, and more than a century after slavery was officially ended in its last strongholds, the trade in human beings for any purpose must not be allowed to thrive in our time.

All the challenges I have spoken of this morning require urgent attention and moral clarity. Helping Afghanistan and Iraq to succeed as free nations in a transformed region, cutting off the avenues of proliferation, abolishing modern forms of slavery—these are the kinds of great tasks for which the United Nations was founded. In each case, careful discussion is needed, and also decisive action. Our good intentions will be credited only if we achieve good outcomes.

As an original signer of the U.N. Charter, the United States of America is committed to the United Nations. And we show that commitment by working to fulfill the U.N.'s stated purposes, and give meaning to its ideals. The founding documents of the United Nations and the founding documents of America stand in the same tradition. Both assert that human beings should never be reduced to objects of power or commerce, because their dignity is inherent. Both require—both recognize a moral law that stands above men and nations, which must be defended and enforced by men and nations. And both point the way to peace, the peace that comes when all are free. We secure that peace with our courage, and we must show that courage together.

May God bless you all. (Applause.)

Source: The White House Archives. https://georgewbush-white house.archives.gov/news/releases/2003/09/20030923-4.html

Testimony of Gary Haugen to the United States Senate Committee on Foreign Relations (2015)

On February 15, 2015, International Justice Mission President and CEO Gary Haugen testified before the Senate Foreign Relations Committee at a hearing entitled "Ending Modern Slavery: What Is the Best Way Forward?" Haugen's testimony highlighted how violence is at the core of modern slavery and emphasized the importance of building the political will to end impunity for perpetrators of modern slavery.

Thank you for this opportunity to testify, Chairman Corker. My name is Gary Haugen, and I am the President of International Justice Mission (IJM). We are grateful that you have chosen to make the issue of global slavery one of your top priorities.

As you know, slavery is a crime that inflicts great suffering on tens of millions of victims every year. It takes many forms, including forced sexual exploitation, exploitative labor, domestic servitude, and debt bondage. But all forms of slavery, past and present, share certain characteristics.

First, slavery is unspeakably violent. Over the past fifteen years, International Justice Mission has investigated thousands of cases of slavery and worked with local authorities to rescue tens of thousands of children, men and women. In virtually every case, perpetrators use violence and the threat of violence to terrorize victims into submission and servitude. IJM's clients have experienced kidnapping, brutal beatings, sexual assault and gang rape, mutilation, humiliation, and starvation. Many of our clients report that slave owners and managers will go to great lengths to track down escaped slaves and bring them back to the facility to be beaten or whipped in front of the other slaves to sow terror and docility.

Second, slavery is an economically-motivated crime. This orgy of violence and abuse that factory managers, labor recruiters, brothel owners, and crew bosses inflict on the vulnerable is for a very specific purpose. It is for the purpose of generating profits for the abusers. The simple economic model of reducing labor costs to virtually nothing by coercing labor generates upwards of $150 billion in profits.

A conversation between my staff and a Ghanaian slave owner illustrates this simple calculation. IJM's team was conducting a prevalence study of child labor slavery on Lake

Volta in Ghana recently. The team asked a fisherman who had several young child slaves on his boat why he didn't use older children for the dangerous and back-breaking work. He answered without hesitation: "Older kids eat too much. And they start to have their own ideas. The young kids are much easier to control."

A third common characteristic of present day and historic slavery is that in all cases there is a perpetrator. Human beings do not naturally or willingly offer up their bodies and their labor for the abusive enrichment of another. In all cases, slavery occurs when vulnerable people are preyed upon by others possessing slightly more power than they do. Vulnerability alone does not enslave; it requires an enslaver.

One characteristic that modern day slavery does *not* share with historic slavery is its legal status. During the 400 years of the trans-Atlantic slave trade, slavery was legal. It was legal in the U.S. from earliest Colonial days to its legal abolition in 1865. Today, in contrast, slavery is legal virtually nowhere in the world. Yet there are more human beings in slavery today than at any previous time in history.

The first half of the abolition agenda—outlawing the crime of slavery has been accomplished. The second half of the abolition agenda—making these laws meaningful to slavery's victims—has barely been attempted.

According to the latest State Department Trafficking in Persons Report, the governments of the 3 countries reported to have the most number of slaves (totaling over 19.5 million, or over half the world's slaves) reported zero convictions in anti-trafficking cases in 2013. Zero.

The obvious question for the Committee is this: Why are laws against slavery so seldom enforced?

In our work, IJM has found that anti-slavery or anti-trafficking laws are not enforced because the victims are poor and powerless and have little access to judicial institutions. Perpetrators, in contrast, frequently have ties to local authorities.

In some cases, local police are paid by local traffickers to look the other way or are actively complicit in the crime. The overwhelming failure of effective law enforcement against trafficking and slavery has persuaded many policy makers that it is simply impossible for police to change. They have simply given up on the dream of making the protection of law real for poor people. Thus, the bulk of U.S. anti-trafficking assistance is for programs to prevent the crime by making the victim less vulnerable. Tens of millions of dollars have been spent in public education programs to teach poor communities about the risks of trafficking and slavery. Hundreds of millions of dollars are spent on education, health and job creation in hopes of insulating potential victims from exploitation and abuse.

Education, health and income generation programs are valuable in their own right. But these funds have not had a measurable impact on slavery. Why? Because they do not affect the behavior of the central player in every situation of enslavement and exploitation: the perpetrator. Perpetrators of trafficking, slavery, and debt bondage, whether they are unscrupulous labor recruiters in Qatar, brothel owners in Southeast Asia, or pimps in the U.S. have one thing in common. They are making money from the subjugation of others. If they are not at risk for going to jail for their crime, they will go to whatever village, slum, city or state in the world to find the poor and the vulnerable. But they will stop even trying to enslave the poor if they are afraid of going to jail.

Consider Ghana, a lower-middle income, democratic nation that has had robust economic growth for the past five years. Ghana is a favored partner of the World Bank, whose current grants, loans, and credits total $3.49 billion. The U.S. Government is a generous donor, as well, providing $154 million for health and development last year.

But a third of Ghana's children work, and neither economic growth nor foreign assistance protects thousands of them from actual enslavement in fishing, domestic servitude, artisanal gold mining, begging, and prostitution. Prevalence studies conducted by International Justice Mission (IJM) on Lake Volta over the past 18 months revealed that 60 percent of the children fishing on the lake were clearly slaves, bearing tell-tale signs of violence, depredation, and terror.

Ghanaian law prohibits slavery, but slave owners and traffickers told IJM undercover investigators that they had no fear whatsoever of Ghana's anti-trafficking police, a force of 150 officers. They have little reason to: the unit does not own a boat and does not patrol Lake Volta. Fortunately, the Government of Ghana is committed to ending this scourge. With training and assistance, the anti-trafficking police unit is an excellent candidate for funding and technical assistance from the U.S. and other donors. Once it begins to rescue kids and apprehend perpetrators, child slavery prevalence will go down—not because Ghana is less economically disadvantaged but because traffickers will respond to increasing prospects of apprehension, conviction and stiff jail terms. Fishing and other enterprises will have to hire—and pay—adult workers.

We've seen and measured the impact of professional law enforcement on the crime of child trafficking elsewhere. In 2007, IJM received a grant from the Bill and Melinda Gates Foundation to begin operations to reduce child sex trafficking in the Philippines second largest city of Cebu. With that support, IJM initiated collaboration with the Philippines National Police in the country's second largest city, Cebu, to rescue minor girls from sexual exploitation and apprehend perpetrators. IJM contracted with an independent criminal data collection firm to execute a baseline prevalence of commercial exploitation of minors in Cebu's substantial sex industry. Over the next three years, IJM and its PNP partners investigated hundreds of establishments, rescued over 225 victims of trafficking, and apprehended 77 suspected perpetrators. Because trafficking is a non-bail offense under Philippines law, those suspects remained in jail, many of their businesses shuttered. The independent investigators conducted a mid-term study and a final study at the end of the 4-year period. They found that the availability of minor girls had plummeted by 79 percent in Cebu.

International Justice Mission has also seen dramatic reduction in the prevalence of child prostitution elsewhere in Southeast Asia as a consequence of professional policing. In Cambodia, very young, prepubescent children were commonly available for sexual exploitation in the early 2000's. A Cambodian government study at the time estimated that 30 percent of those in prostitution were minor children. A decade later, professional policing by a well-trained and well-led anti-trafficking unit had transformed the sex industry in Cambodia. A prevalence study by IJM in late 2012 revealed no children under fifteen being sold for sex and very few minors age 15-17 in commercial sex venues.

Cambodia's transformation with regard to commercial sexual exploitation of children is noteworthy because broader human rights standards did not improve. Cambodia's government was not comprehensively transformed, and it is still a poor country. Change occurred because the government made a conscious political decision to enforce its own laws against child prostitution and proceeded to equip and empower the police anti-trafficking unit to do its job. Over 100 perpetrators of child trafficking were convicted and jailed. And Cambodia's criminal class responded with alacrity: they got out of the business of selling children.

IJM's experience working with local law enforcement has shown us that police *can* improve quite dramatically and are equal to the task of changing the calculations of those profiting from the sale of others. As we've seen in Southeast Asia, it is not necessary for police to apprehend every brothel owner, madam, pimp, or trafficker. A relatively small number of arrests, prosecutions, and convictions have a disproportionate impact on criminals who buy, sell, and exploit children.

The United States has led in the worldwide fight against slavery, and is fortunate to have some excellent tools with which to do it. The Trafficking Victims Protection Act of 2000 and the establishment of the State Department Office to Monitor and Combat Trafficking in Persons have helped make the issue of slavery a top U.S. foreign policy concern. The annual Trafficking in Persons Report has been the catalyst for positive changes by governments on every continent, as has the leadership of many very fine American diplomats around the world.

We are grateful for Congress authorizing and funding an anti-trafficking innovation: Child Protection Compacts. We have seen what is possible in our own work when we partnered with local law enforcement in a collaborative casework model, and stayed in the fight with them. The Child Protection Compacts reflects this approach, and offers an opportunity to see real change in the prevalence of child trafficking in selected focus countries.

But even with the substantial diplomatic and financial resources the United States has offered over the past fifteen years, the global scourge of slavery requires a global response. IJM is very encouraged by discussions between the Senate, the executive branch, and representatives of the private sector about the creation of a new funding mechanism that would bring new resources to the fight. We look forward to working with you on this historic initiative.

Source: United States Senate. Committee on Foreign Relations. "Prepared Testimony of Gary Haugen, International Justice Mission," *Ending Modern Slavery: What Is the Best Way Forward.* 114th Cong., 1st Sess. February 4, 2015. https://www .foreign.senate.gov/download/haugen-testimony-02-04-15

"The National Nature of Human Trafficking: Strengthening Government Responses and Dispelling Misperceptions," U.S. State Department *Trafficking in Persons Report* (June 2019)

In compliance with the Trafficking Victims Protection Act (TVPA), the U.S. State Department publishes an annual Trafficking in

Persons Report *(TIP Report), which provides the latest informa-tion on the status of human trafficking around the world and a comprehensive assessment of what governments are doing to combat it. Despite major progress, many countries adopt inadequate inter-vention strategies and have gaps in their legal response to modern slavery. One such gap occurs because governments commonly focus on transnational human trafficking cases at the expense of cases occurring within their own boarders. Thus, the 2019 TIP Report specifically highlights human trafficking that takes place exclusively within the borders of a country, absent any transnational elements, to emphasize the need for governments to implement laws that address all forms of trafficking whether they involve movement across borders or not.*

Each instance of human trafficking takes a common toll; each crime is an affront to the basic ideals of human dignity, inflict-ing grievous harm on individuals, as well as on their families and communities. Yet, if it were possible to hold human traf-ficking up to a light like a prism, each facet would reflect a different version of the crime, distinct in context but the same in essence. Together they would show the vast and varied array of methods traffickers use to compel adults and children of all genders, education levels, nationalities, and immigration statuses into service in both licit and illicit sectors. Traffick-ers may be family members, recruiters, employers, or strangers who exploit vulnerability and circumstance to coerce victims to engage in commercial sex or deceive them into forced labor. They commit these crimes through schemes that take victims hundreds of miles away from their homes or in the same neigh-borhoods where they were born.

This multifaceted crime can challenge policy makers. The foundational elements of human trafficking are difficult to grasp and the real world instances of this exploitation are even harder to identify. Importantly, how governments address human trafficking depends heavily on the way authorities perceive the crime. When officials view trafficking as a crime and have a precise understanding of its core elements, they are better equipped to identify and combat it, regardless of the particular scheme the trafficker uses.

Over the last two decades, the international community has benefited from an improved understanding of and response to human trafficking. Working together, governments, NGOs, international organizations, academics, communities, and survivors of human trafficking have built a more complete picture of human trafficking—a picture that rejects a narrow understanding of traffickers and victims, in favor of one that encompasses the full range of ways traffickers exploit their victims.

Despite major progress, a number of countries still struggle with gaps in their domestic legal responses, often because they do not recognize and address human trafficking using the wider view described above. In practice, this may mean that governments overlook certain forms of human trafficking when the conditions do not meet their narrower presumptions. For example, authorities may not consider men and boys as victims of sex trafficking due to a common misperception that sex traffickers only exploit women and girls. This may also result in governments arresting and prosecuting trafficking victims for the unlawful acts their traffickers compelled them to engage in, instead of offering them the support of protective services. Where this happens, anti-trafficking interventions are inadequate and the potential for productive criminal justice, protection, and prevention efforts is threatened.

This year the TIP Report introduction takes a deeper dive into one such gap, common in many countries around the world, whereby governments concentrate on transnational human trafficking cases at the expense of cases taking place within their borders. This spotlight is not intended to suggest that transnational human trafficking is not also important, or that the many other forms of trafficking that may go unaddressed due to similar oversight are of lesser consequence, but rather to call on governments to ensure they are addressing all forms of human trafficking and finding a balanced approach. In that vein and in the interest of de-emphasizing movement, this year's report no longer refers to countries by the nomenclature "source, transit, and destination country."

THE NATIONAL NATURE OF HUMAN TRAFFICKING

Prevalence of human trafficking is difficult to measure; however, a number of international organizations have estimated that traffickers exploit a majority of human trafficking victims without moving them from one country to another. For example, the ILO estimated that traffickers exploit 77 percent of all victims in the victims' countries of residence. Likewise, UNODC reported in 2018 that, for the first time ever, a majority of victims had been identified in their countries of citizenship, stating: "While transnational trafficking networks are still prevalent and must be responded to through international cooperation, national justice measures, strategies and priorities should acknowledge the increasingly national nature of the trafficking problem." The same UNODC report also found that the clear majority of traffickers were citizens of the countries where they were convicted.

It should be noted that these numbers are not uniform across regions or even types of human trafficking. For example, UNODC found that the number of victims identified domestically was high compared to foreign victims in most areas of the world, except for Western and Central Europe, the Middle East, and some countries in East Asia. In addition, the ILO found that victims of sex trafficking more likely faced transnational human trafficking while victims of forced labor typically experienced exploitation in their country of residence.

Frequently, human trafficking within a country is found in sectors that are common nearly everywhere, such as the commercial sex industry and others like farming, construction, manufacturing, and mining. The latter are also often referred to as "dirty, dangerous, and difficult" and rely on low-skilled and vulnerable local labor forces. At the same time, instances of human trafficking within a country may be more characteristic of that specific country or region, such as child domestic work or exploitative sham marriages. Indeed, examples vary greatly:

- Traffickers in Brazil, under the guise of religious mandates, exploit Brazilian victims in forced labor, including on farms and in factories and restaurants, after the victims join certain churches or religious cults.

- In Cambodia, a lack of jobs leads some women and girls to leave their homes in rural areas to try to find work in tourist destination cities. In many cases, traffickers exploit them in sex trafficking, including in massage parlors, karaoke bars, and beer gardens.

- In Ethiopia, traffickers often deceive parents of children living in rural areas into sending their children to major cities to work as domestic workers. The traffickers promise families that the children will go to school and receive wages for their work, thereby enabling them to send money home.

- In India, the government officially abolished bonded labor in 1976, but the system of forced labor still exists. For example, under one scheme prevalent in granite quarries in India, quarry owners offer wage advances or loans with exorbitant interest rates, trapping workers in debt bondage—in some cases for their entire lives.

- In the United Kingdom (UK), gangs force British children to carry drugs. According to the UK National Crime Agency data in 2017, the largest group of potential victims referred to the National Referral Mechanism was UK nationals.

- In the United States, traffickers prey upon children in the foster care system. Recent reports have consistently indicated that a large number of victims of child sex trafficking were at one time in the foster care system.

- In Yemen, the ongoing conflict has led to many human rights violations, with many parties using child soldiers. According to a UN report, there have been 842 verified cases of the recruitment and use of boys as young as 11 years old.

Given the recent global estimates related to the national nature of human trafficking and the various forms it can take, all governments must acknowledge and take targeted steps to address human trafficking that takes place within one country without any movement across an international border.

There may be complicated reasons why a government would fail to address this form of human trafficking. It is easier to look outward and call on other governments to act; it takes much more resolution and political will for governments to look inward and stop traffickers, including their own citizens, from exploiting victims who have not crossed an international border. Governments should also examine the varying political and economic systems that make it easier for traffickers to commit the crime. What is clear is that governments have an obligation to address all forms of human trafficking, those both with and without a transnational element. When governments overlook this reality and ignore human trafficking at home, they risk being blinded to—and neglecting—an often significant crime within their own borders.

THE PALERMO PROTOCOL AND TRANSNATIONALITY

In 2000, the Protocol to Prevent, Suppress and Punish Trafficking in Persons, Especially Women and Children (the Palermo Protocol), supplementing the UN Convention against Transnational Organized Crime (UNTOC), marked an important transition into the modern movement against human trafficking. Over the years, the Palermo Protocol has been the source of much clarification—but also some confusion—about human trafficking, particularly regarding the issue of transnationality.

It was the first international instrument to define "trafficking in persons" and provide insight into the many different ways traffickers commit this crime. The Palermo Protocol uses "trafficking in persons" as an umbrella term that covers a wide variety of offenses, such as maintaining someone in forced labor or recruiting someone for compelled commercial sexual exploitation. It also provided a much-needed foundation on which governments could build policies that criminalize human trafficking and stop traffickers, protect victims and prevent victimization, and promote cooperation among countries.

Thus, three elements are needed to establish the crime of human trafficking under Palermo—the trafficker's action, the means of force, fraud or coercion, and the purpose of exploitation. As of March 31, 2019, 173 parties ratified the Palermo Protocol and 168 countries have passed domestic legislation criminalizing human trafficking according to this framework. In addition, a number of best practices in protection for victims have emerged including the importance of a victim-centered and trauma-informed approach in both law enforcement and service provision.

According to the UNODC's 2018 Global Report on Trafficking in Persons, there has been an upward trend in the last decade in the number of victims identified and traffickers convicted globally. These data are not uniform across regions and types of human trafficking, yet the report suggests an overall positive correlation between the implementation of anti-trafficking strategies and increased identification of victims and conviction of traffickers. Similarly, the TIP Report's data on prosecutions, convictions, and victim identification are significantly higher now than they were ten years ago, when the TIP Report first began to note an upward global trend. It is clear that government efforts stemming from the adoption of the Palermo Protocol are working.

Many governments deserve credit for their serious efforts to address modern slavery. Yet, much work remains. Persistent gaps in governments' understanding of the issue continue to impede global progress, as do stubborn misperceptions about human trafficking and inconsistencies in the implementation of domestic legislation.

One common misperception generates ongoing confusion—that human trafficking requires movement across borders and cannot occur solely within a country's borders. A possible explanation for this confusion may stem from the use of the word "trafficking" in the term "trafficking in persons," which connotes movement, and the fact that the Palermo Protocol and its parent convention the UNTOC are intended to foster international cooperation in combating organized crime networks, which typically operate transnationally. The Palermo Protocol also calls on parties to meet its objectives through interstate cooperation. This context could imply that human trafficking is exclusively transnational, requires movement, and necessarily is tied to organized crime. Yet the UNTOC itself and a number of UNODC publications interpreting the Palermo Protocol make it clear that, when drafting domestic legislation, governments should consider human trafficking independently of both transnationality and the involvement of an organized criminal group. Each state party must establish in its domestic law the crime of human trafficking both within and between countries.

> *It is important for drafters of legislation to note that the provisions relating to the involvement of transnationality and organized crime do not always apply. . . . The Trafficking in Persons Protocol also applies to protection of victims regardless of transnationality or involvement of an organized group.*
> —The Legislative Guide for Implementation of the Palermo Protocol

Another related misunderstanding about human trafficking is that a trafficker must move or transport a victim. Even though the term "trafficking in persons" connotes movement, no language in the definition requires movement to constitute a trafficking crime. Indeed, the Palermo Protocol's definition specifically refers to actions by traffickers that do not entail or require any movement, such as recruitment, which quite often takes place locally. Harboring, in particular, has been frequently interpreted to mean the maintenance of an individual in compelled service, including by a United Nations and Council of Europe publication that defined harboring as "accommodating or housing persons," including at their place of exploitation. In such cases, the three elements clearly are met—by the actions of housing or keeping an individual by coercive means for the purpose of exploitation—without the trafficker ever moving the person.

As reflected in their laws, most governments recognize this view of human trafficking. This is a major success that, in just two decades, 168 governments have implemented domestic legislation criminalizing all forms of human trafficking whether the crime happens transnationally or nationally. That said, even upon the adoption of the Protocol, supporters emphasized that the true challenge would lie in the implementation of the laws in each country.

FUNDAMENTALS OF IMPLEMENTING THE PALERMO PROTOCOL

In creating and implementing legislation, governments have the power to shape reality. Legislation that protects all victims and criminalizes all forms of human trafficking, including those that take place exclusively within a country's borders, gives governments the platform and opportunity to embrace fully their responsibilities under the Palermo Protocol.

As noted above, the majority of governments around the world already have in place comprehensive laws to address trafficking in persons. Yet, law alone can do little to end human trafficking. Translating legislation into meaningful action demands dedication, focus, and resources and requires that those implementing it truly understand both the underlying letter and the spirit of the law.

Governments can and should adopt and implement the promising practices below. Their value lies in their power not only to help governments better address human trafficking within their borders, but also to help combat all manner of misconceptions, biases, and misunderstandings about what constitutes human trafficking.

Institutionalizing a clear understanding of human trafficking

A clear understanding of the underlying exploitative nature of human trafficking and the unique ways it affects a country is a critical foundation on which governments can build a truly comprehensive strategy.

As noted above, the Palermo Protocol defines human trafficking by its three elements—a trafficker's action taken through the means of force, fraud, or coercion for the purpose of exploitation. Understanding it as such leaves little room for interpretation based on the incidental attributes of the victim or the trafficker, such as gender, age, nationality, legal status, or occupation, or on other circumstances surrounding the crime, such as movement or connection to organized crime.

Messaging from the highest levels of government should be clear and consistent and preclude overly restrictive interpretations of human trafficking or perceptions of its victims. Governments should make every effort to ensure that those addressing human trafficking, both in policy and practice, frame the issue correctly to avoid limiting the applicability of anti-trafficking laws and protection efforts.

For example, governments should prosecute human trafficking crimes as such and not under other criminal provisions—or, worse, civil laws—that may come with weaker or no criminal penalties. Characterizing an offense as less severe, such as penalizing human traffickers for labor violations under employment law instead of charging them for labor trafficking, may mean that traffickers are given penalties substantially lower than those prescribed under anti-trafficking law, limiting their potential deterrent effects.

In addition, governments should encourage or mandate comprehensive training for victim identification, especially for those most likely to come into contact with trafficking victims. This includes law enforcement officers, prosecutors, and judicial officials, healthcare providers, educators, child welfare officials, labor inspectorates, and many others. Training should be designed to help such stakeholders identify all forms of human trafficking. Without such an education, those best positioned to spot the signs of human trafficking may not be able to identify victims when they encounter them or know the appropriate way to respond.

Institutionalizing a clear understanding of human trafficking may also require governments to invest in research and data collection. Over the years, data collection by national governments has improved substantially, but gaps still exist and evidence suggests that anti-trafficking efforts lag where less is known about trafficking. An evidence-driven and unbiased understanding of human trafficking in a country is imperative to the creation of a well-balanced and tailored anti-trafficking response.

For example, in the Netherlands in 2017, the Dutch National Rapporteur on Trafficking in Human Beings worked with UNODC to develop the "first reliable estimate of actual number of victims in the Netherlands." Using multiple systems estimation, a methodology that helped to find hidden populations of trafficking victims, the Netherlands found the estimated number of trafficking victims is four to five times higher than the average number of those identified. It also found that the most common form of human trafficking in the Netherlands (46%) is sex trafficking of Dutch nationals in the Netherlands, while the least visible victims in the Netherlands are Dutch girls. The National Rapporteur further acknowledged the findings exposed "gaps and blind spots" in the Dutch approach to combating human trafficking and the need to pursue evidence-driven policies.

Developing a robust anti-trafficking coordination process
Due to its complexity, combating human trafficking requires
a multidisciplinary effort. For governments this means incorpo-
rating the expertise of stakeholders from a range of agencies or
ministries that may have a nexus to human trafficking. To facilitate an approach that addresses human trafficking regardless of
where or how it takes place, government scan take steps to ensure
that all appropriate authorities understand human trafficking,
the various ways they may come into contact with victims or
perpetrators, and the appropriate response when they do.

Cambodia funds an interagency committee, the National
Committee for Counter Trafficking, to coordinate anti-
trafficking activities and implement its national action plan.
Subsidiary provincial anti-trafficking committees coordinate
efforts at the local level to mirror the activities of the national
action plan with modest central government funds and assistance from NGOs. With the help of international donors, six
out of nine of these committees created their own provincial-level
action plans. A working group monitors the efforts of both the
interagency committee and its provincial subsidiary committees.

Establishing ongoing coordination can also help to ensure
that the appropriate agencies or ministries have the authority
to investigate cases of human trafficking.

For example, **Serbia** is consolidating jurisdiction to investigate human trafficking under the Criminal Police Directorate—
Serbia's domestic law enforcement agency. Previously, the
Border Police and Foreigners Office Police split this responsibility, which complicated investigations and implied that a
human trafficking crime needed a transnational element.

In addition, intra-governmental partnerships can be incred-
ibly effective for information-sharing and helping governments
to expand the number and types of trafficking schemes found
in their country. For example, when considering trafficking
crimes in-country, labor ministries must collaborate and learn
from law enforcement to be fully engaged in inspecting local

economies and knowing how to alert the appropriate authorities when they identify instances of human trafficking.

In an effort to combat the commercial sexual exploitation of children in **Japan**, the Tokyo Metropolitan Assembly passed an ordinance in July 2017 prohibiting girls younger than 18 from working in compensated dating—or "JK"—services and requiring such businesses to register their employee rosters with the city. Authorities identified 114 of these operations nationwide in2017, and closed 14 for violating the terms of the ordinance. Courts then initiated prosecution under the Labor Standards Act against the owner of one such establishment for child sex trafficking.

In **Greece**, the Anti-Trafficking Unit of the Hellenic Police Unit maintains several teams of officers across Greece that investigate human trafficking and other crimes and also conduct joint inspections with labor inspectors and social workers.

Confronting harmful cultural norms and local practices

Cultural norms and practices play an important role in defining a country or society, but human traffickers have also used them to support, hide, or attempt to justify human trafficking. The Palermo Protocol specifically notes that exceptions cannot be made to the criminalization requirement based on cultural variations. It is important that governments examine how traffickers may exploit cultural practices to conduct criminal activity. In some cases, traffickers may take advantage of religious beliefs to coerce victims into servitude and it is important that governments seek help from and offer support to cultural and religious leaders taking strides to protect their communities from human traffickers.

For example, in **Nigeria**, traffickers use fraud to recruit women and girls for jobs in Europe and force them into commercial sex when they get there. Many traffickers force victims to take a *juju* oath to ensure compliance and threaten death resulting from the *juju* curse if they break their oath, disobey their traffickers, and try to leave their exploitative situations. In early 2018, the National Agency for the Prohibition of

Trafficking in Persons and the governor of Edo State partnered with the Oba of Benin, the traditional religious leader of the Benin kingdom in Nigeria, to publicize a ceremony where the Oba performed a ritual dissolving all previous *juju* curses performed by traffickers.

In other cases, deeply ingrained practices may make it difficult for governments to see and address human trafficking in their own backyards. For example, many countries in South Asia face the practice of debt bondage, a form of human trafficking in which traffickers use debt to force an individual into forced labor.

Pakistan's largest human trafficking problem is bonded labor—in which employers use an initial debt to force people to work and trap them and often their family members, sometimes for generations. Although Pakistani laws criminalize this form of forced labor, enforcement of these laws remains inadequate and many landowners continue to exploit bonded laborers with impunity.

In addition, officials across government should work to challenge stereotypes of a typical victim of human trafficking. For example, in many cases, traffickers force their victims to commit crimes. Forced criminality takes the form of begging, prostitution, cannabis cultivation, and theft, among others. An untrained law enforcement officer or benefits adjudicator may not realize an individual is a victim of human trafficking before making an arrest or a decision on available benefits. These assumptions can also make victims more reluctant to seek help. Proactive efforts to recognize and mitigate these assumptions are therefore critical.

For example, in **Finland** the non-discrimination ombudsman is the national rapporteur on human trafficking. She began a new research project assessing trafficking cases in Finland to evaluate how victims access the assistance system. The findings of this type of study could serve as an important barometer for how national assumptions and blind spots among law enforcement, service providers, and society shape a country's response to human trafficking.

Empowering communities to recognize and address human trafficking

When the public views trafficking crimes as common local or cultural practices that do not warrant criminal investigation or prosecution, it is critically important for governments to raise awareness and foster initiatives for communities to help address it.

The 2018 TIP Report covered the issue of supporting community efforts to find local solutions. It is worth noting again the value in reinforcing and empowering communities as full partners in the fight against human trafficking. Public perceptions about human trafficking have a major impact on the way governments address it. If well informed about the various forms of human trafficking, the public can be the eyes and ears of their communities and can put pressure on law enforcement to make it a priority.

For example, in **Ghana**, where forced child labor is prevalent in the fishing industry on Lake Volta, NGOs have worked to change community perceptions so that many now view the use of children in fishing as an illegal activity. Many communities have formed local watchdog groups that know how to identify human trafficking, go door-to-door raising awareness about its harmful effects, and report cases to authorities. Community members are also essential in providing follow-on support and reintegration services.

In addition, governments can design public awareness campaigns to target a particular issue and motivate communities to get involved. In design, these types of campaigns should have clear objectives that promote sound anti-trafficking policies.

For example, in **Benin**, some traffickers subject children to forced labor in street and market vending. Recently, the Beninese government led a public awareness campaign focused on potential exploitation in Benin's large open-air markers in Cotonou, Porto-Novo, and Parakou. This community-oriented campaign also incorporated an inspection program conducted at the markets and along roads connecting major cities, which resulted in the identification of more than 800 potential child trafficking victims.

In addition, governments can design community-based approaches to enhance their law enforcement efforts. For example, across **Moldova**, teams of local officials and NGOs coordinate victim identification and assistance efforts resulting in an increased number of shelter referrals.

Conclusion

Since the adoption of the Palermo Protocol, a growing number of stakeholders, including a majority of the world's governments, have enacted comprehensive laws to hold human traffickers criminally accountable and provide care to survivors. Over time, it has become clear that stopping traffickers and ensuring protections for all victims, including victims of internal trafficking in persons, requires governments to truly comprehend what constitutes human trafficking and to proactively use those laws.

At times, governments may need to go even further. In particular, addressing human trafficking at home also takes political courage—in inspecting local sectors and industries, investigating official power structures that may condone or facilitate such activities, and ending impunity for crimes that have long been seen as accepted local and cultural practices. Governments may find it easier to blame sex trafficking on those who come to their countries to engage in foreign sex tourism than to address local demand; or to blame foreign government and power structures for failing to protect their nationals working abroad from labor trafficking, than to address the exploitative activities of labor recruiters in their jurisdiction.

Acknowledging human trafficking within the borders of a country is not easy. Governments should be willing to admit its existence and rise to their responsibility to address it. In doing so, governments not only protect those within their borders but also contribute to the greater global fight against human trafficking.

Source: U.S. State Department 2019 Trafficking in Persons Report. https://www.state.gov/wp-content/uploads/2019/06/2019-Trafficking-in-Persons-Report.pdf

6 Resources

This chapter provides an annotated list of selected books, articles, and reports on a variety of topics related to modern slavery, which offers readers a starting point for further research. Several nonprint sources are listed and annotated as well.

Books

Bales, Kevin. 2005. *Understanding Global Slavery: A Reader.* Berkeley, CA: University of California Press.

Although slavery is illegal throughout the world, millions still live in bondage. In this exposé, renowned scholar Kevin Bales seeks to understand the various manifestations of slavery that persist in the twenty-first century and the most effective efforts at eradication. Bales astutely demonstrates that for many slaves, the first step out of bondage is to open individuals' eyes to the reality of their bondage and the possibility of freedom. He additionally argues, however, that, in an era where the problem is not necessarily indifference or apathy, but ignorance, rethinking slavery must also occur within entire populations. In each chapter, Bales explores a different facet of global slavery with the goal of promoting a more comprehensive awareness and understanding of this largely hidden crime.

The Donaldina Cameron House was established in 1874 as a Presbyterian Mission Home in San Francisco`s Chinatown to help girls and women escape indentured servitude and prostitution. When Donaldina herself finally took over, she worked tirelessly, often risking her own life to help these same girls and women. (David Edelman/Dreamstime.com)

Bales, Kevin. 2007. *Ending Slavery: How We Free Today's Slaves.* Berkeley, CA: University of California Press.

After years of traveling the world, researching the scope and nature of contemporary slavery, and publishing his findings, renowned scholar Kevin Bales authored this book outlining a concrete plan for freeing millions of slaves and ultimately eradicating global slavery. Bales argues that, like many other crimes, slavery takes on the culture of its surroundings and is entangled with both local and global economies. Ending slavery will thus require attacking its all levels and will ultimately depend on the collaboration between local police, governments, the United Nations, businesses, and churches.

Bales, Kevin. 2012. *Disposable People: New Slavery in the Global Economy.* 3rd edition. Berkeley, CA: University of California Press.

Now, in its third edition, the inaugural edition of this book published in 1999 provided the first global analysis of modern slavery and its role in the global economy. It consequently established researcher Kevin Bales as one of the leading authorities on modern slavery and drew international attention to the importance of studying and responding to the global scourge. In this exposé, Bales contends that although slavery is illegal throughout the world, 27 million slaves—whom he defines as human beings forced to work, under threat of violence, for no pay—are still held in captivity worldwide. Through an investigation of conditions in Mauritania, Brazil, Thailand, Pakistan, and India, and the use of vivid case studies, Bale demonstrates how—in contrast with slaves of the past who were often viewed as long-term investments—today's slaves are cheap, require little care, and are disposable. Bale maintains that three interrelated factors have contributed to the growth of new slavery: an enormous population explosion that has flooded the world's labor markets with millions of impoverished, desperate people; economic globalization and modernized agriculture that have displaced farmers, making them and their families vulnerable to slavery; and rapid economic change in developing countries, which has contributed to corruption, violence, and a lack of legal protection for the vulnerable. Bales additionally offers suggestions for combatting contemporary slavery and highlights the successful efforts of organizations, such as Anti-Slavery International, the Pastoral Land Commission in Brazil, and the Human Rights Commission in Pakistan.

Bales, Kevin, and Ron Soodalter. 2009. *The Slave Next Door: Human Trafficking and Slavery in America Today.* 2nd edition. Berkeley, CA: University of California Press.

Coauthored by prominent antislavery scholar Kevin Bales and historian Ron Soodalter, this book exposes the multiple forms of contemporary slavery that are thriving in the United States. Through individual stories and profiles, Bales and Soodalter reveal how slaves are often "hidden in plain sight" in homes, farms, businesses, and on the street. The book concludes with an assessment of various eradication efforts. In this second edition, Bales and Soodalter include a new preface that examines positive improvements and significant developments in the fight against human trafficking in the United States, as well as areas that still need improvement.

Batstone, David. 2010. *Not for Sale: The Return of the Global Slave Trade—and How We Can Fight It.* Revised and Updated Edition. New York: HarperCollins.

In this revised and updated edition of his groundbreaking study originally published in 2007, David Batstone—business professor and cofounder and president of the Not for Sale Campaign—highlights the courageous efforts of modern-day abolitionists to end the scourge of modern slavery.

The book chronicles several manifestations of modern slavery, including rural and urban trafficking in Burma and Thailand, bonded labor in India, forced conscription of child soldiers in Uganda, sex trafficking in Europe, exploitation of children in Peru, and forced labor in various economic sectors of the United States. Interwoven with personal accounts, the book additionally provides insight into contributing factors of modern slavery and specific strategies abolitionists adopt to promote emancipation in particular settings. The book concludes with an overview of the Not for Sale Campaign and a prescription for how readers can join the fight for abolition.

Bok, Francis. 2003. *Escape from Slavery: The True Story of My Ten Years in Captivity and My Journey to Freedom in America.* New York: St. Martin's Press.

In this autobiography, antislavery activist Francis Bok recounts the remarkable story of his captivity and his eventual escape to freedom. Bok was captured at the age of 7 years by Arab militiamen during a slave raid at a local marketplace in Southern Sudan. Bok spent 10 years in brutal bondage in northern Sudan before he finally succeeded in escaping to Cairo using a black-market passport. After several years living in refugee camps, Bok was able to secure passage to America where he joined the antislavery movement, while working to earn a high school diploma. Bok has testified before Congress about the horrors of contemporary slavery in Sudan and has shared his story with audiences around the country.

Cadet, Jean-Robert. 1998. *Restavec: From Haitian Slave Child to Middle-Class American.* Austin, TX: University of Texas Press.

Following independence from the French rule in 1804, former African slaves in Haiti created the first independent black republic in the Western Hemisphere. Nevertheless, slavery remains widespread in Haiti today. According to the 2018 Global Slavery Index, Haiti has the highest vulnerability to slavery in the America and is second only to Venezuela in overall prevalence of slavery. One of the most prominent manifestations of modern slavery in Haiti is the *restavec* system, which uses children of the poor as the unpaid servants of the well-off. In this memoir, Jean-Robert Cadet recounts the oppression and abuse he endured as a youth in the Haitian *restavec* system and tells the inspiring story of his subsequent life in the United States, where he became free, put himself through college, and eventually founded the Jean R. Cadet Organization to provide relief to children trapped as *restavecs* and to bring an end to child slavery in Haiti through increased global awareness.

Cox, Caroline, and John Marks. 2006. *This Immoral Trade: Slavery in the 21st Century.* Grand Rapids, MI: Monarch Books.

In commemoration of the bicentenary celebration of the International Slavery Convention, which banned slavery worldwide, Caroline Cox and John Marks document the continuation of the barbaric practice in the modern world and call on readers to imitate the efforts of one of history's most valiant antislavery crusaders, William Wilberforce.

This book paints a general picture of the various forms and contexts of modern slavery by focusing on three detailed case studies of Sudan, Uganda, and Burma. It additionally highlights the real-life experiences of slaves and slavery's life-long effects by providing first-hand testimony from more than one hundred former slaves. The book concludes with an overview of the history of slavery and the main types and causes of slavery in the modern world.

Haugen, Gary A., and Victor Boutros. 2014. *The Locust Effect: Why the End of Poverty Requires the End of Violence.* New York: Oxford University Press.

Written by founder and CEO of the International Justice Mission Gary Haugen and federal prosecutor Victor Boutros, this book is a searing exposé of how order and civilization are non-existent for most of the world's poor because they live in a state of de facto lawlessness. As a result, they are plagued by the daily reality of predatory violence, including rape, forced labor, illegal detention, land theft, police abuse, and other brutality.

Haugen and Boutros refer to the pestilence of violence and the destructive impact it has on efforts to lift the global poor out of poverty as *the locust effect.* Like a horde of locusts, unchecked violence devours everything in its path—it ruins lives, blocks the road out of poverty, and undercuts development. Haugen and Boutros point out that while the world is aware that poor people suffer from hunger, disease, homelessness, illiteracy, dirty water, and so forth, and the well-intended are busy trying to meet those needs, few are paying attention to the chronic vulnerability to violence that lies hidden underneath the more visible deprivations of the poor. This is particularly tragic, they argue, because data demonstrates that everyday violence significantly undermines economic development and reduces the effectiveness of poverty alleviation efforts. Goods and services to the poor are nearly useless so long as they continue to be plagued by brutalization and theft. Thus, Haugen and Boutros contend that for the global poor in this century, there is no higher-priority need than the provision of basic justice systems. Unless, the poor are protected from the devastation of daily violence, none of the other efforts that people of goodwill seek to do, such as providing food, healthcare, education, and micro-loans, will ultimately matter.

Although criminal justice systems in many places have been designed to protect the well connected and powerful, but not the common people, Haugen and Boutros offer hope for change by drawing attention to examples in which cities plagued by even the worse police corruption and violence have managed to reform and change.

Kara, Siddharth. 2017. *Modern Slavery: A Global Perspective.* New York: Columbia University Press.

This volume is the culmination of author and activist Siddharth Kara's 16 years of research into modern slavery—during this time, he investigated slavery in 51 countries and documented 5,439 individual cases of slavery. Based on this extensive research, Kara provides an overview of the most pervasive and salient manifestations of contemporary slavery around the globe. He focuses in particular on a handful of case studies that manifest many of the most important realities of slavery as they exist in the world today—from sex trafficking in Nigeria, to labor trafficking in California agriculture, to organ trafficking in South Asia and across the U.S.-Mexico border, to the use of technology in the sexual trafficking of young girls in Europe, to debt bondage in the construction sectors of Malaysia and Singapore, and finally to slavery in the Thai seafood industry. While Kara continues to rely in some degree on the data-driven approach that informed his earlier works, his main aim in this book is to convey the clearest possible picture of slavery in all its depravity, greed, and disdain. Thus, much of the work focuses on transmitting the torment of slaves, the forces that perpetuate their servitude, and the difficulty of accurately documenting their suffering.

Kelley, Judith G. 2017. *Scorecard Diplomacy: Grading States to Influence Their Reputation and Behavior.* Cambridge, United Kingdom: Cambridge University Press.

Judith G. Kelley, the dean of Duke University's Sanford School of Public Policy, analyzes the growing phenomenon of using rankings as a foreign policy tool for influencing countries' behavior. Kelley demonstrates that in the absence of traditional force, public grades and rankings are a powerful means of encouraging countries motivated by a concern for their own reputation to address a public problem. In particular, she analyzes the United States' foreign policy on human trafficking using a global survey of NGOs, case studies, thousands of diplomatic cables, media stories, worldwide interviews, and other documents. Kelley quantitatively documents how the tier rankings issued through the U.S. State Department's Trafficking in Persons (TIP) Report have contributed to the improvement of various laws and governmental conduct.

Lederer, Laura J. 2018. *Modern Slavery: A Documentary and Reference Guide*. Santa Barbara, CA: Greenwood Press.

In this comprehensive reference book, Laura J. Lederer—president of Global Centurion, former Senior Advisor on Trafficking in Persons in the U.S. State Department's Office to Combat Trafficking in Persons, and founder of the Protection Project at Harvard University's John F. Kennedy School of Government—presents a sobering account of the scope and various manifestations of modern slavery and documents the development of the modern-day antislavery movement, from early survivor voices and grassroots activism to the passage of national and international antislavery laws. Lederer combines her own analysis with primary source material—including survivor stories, witness testimony, case law, speeches, and other writings—to provide an overview of the historical antecedents to the modern antislavery movement, the various and sometimes opposing schools of thought about how to combat modern slavery, and the legislative processes that have led to groundbreaking antislavery laws. The book specifically focuses on how the foundation for today's antislavery laws was laid in the early efforts of four separate traditions: *religious, abolitionist, feminist, and human rights.*

Miers, Suzanne. 2003. *Slavery in the Twentieth Century: The Evolution of a Global Problem.* Lanham, MD: AltaMira Press.

In a unique contribution to the scholarly literature, Professor Emerita Suzanne Miers, a leading authority on the slave trade in Africa, breaks with the bulk of previous historical scholarship that focuses almost exclusively on slavery in the eighteenth and nineteenth centuries in the New World. Miers instead draws attention to modern slavery in its historical context. Linking the extensive scholarship of historical slavery with the growing literature on contemporary slavery, Miers traces the development of the international antislavery movement during the last century, focusing specifically on Great Britain's efforts to suppress the slave trade since the late eighteenth century. She demonstrates how the problems of eradication seem greater and more intractable today than ever, showing how slavery has expanded to include newer forms—some even crueler in nature than historic chattel slavery.

Skinner, E. Benjamin. 2008. *A Crime So Monstrous: Face-to-Face with Modern-Day Slavery.* New York: Free Press.

In this account of contemporary slavery, journalist Benjamin Skinner recounts his more than four years traveling the globe reporting from places where slavery flourishes—including Haiti, Sudan, India, Eastern Europe, the Netherlands, and suburban America. Based on his direct encounters infiltrating trafficking networks, Skinner tells the personal stories of individuals who are held in slavery as well as those involved in trafficking and holding slaves. He additionally highlights the narratives of individuals who, after escaping years of previous bondage, struggle to regain their humanity and live a fulfilling life.

Weaved throughout his first-hand accounts of modern slavery in action, Skinner assesses various contexts, contributing factors, and solutions, as well as the mixed political motives of those involved in abolition efforts.

Tiano, Susan, Moira Murphy-Aguilar, and Brianne Bigej, eds. 2012. *Borderline Slavery: Mexico, United States, and the Human Trade.* Burlington, VT: Ashgate Publishing.

This book is a compilation of 15 articles exploring the ongoing issue of human trafficking between the United States and the Mexican border written by various experts with the goal of exposing the realities of the human trade both regionally and globally. The book is divided into four sections. *Part I: The Global Context: Setting the Stage for Sex and Labor Trafficking* explores the historical and theoretical context of the modern slave trade and presents arguments that modernization, globalization, and misguided policies have contributed to the booming illicit trade of human beings. *Part II: Human Trafficking in Mexico* examines violence, inequality, and extreme poverty as causes of trafficking and the extent to which Mexico is a source, a destination, and a layover route for victims. *Part III: Human Trafficking along the U.S.-Mexico Border* focuses on the regional problem of trafficking at the border and argues that law enforcement and border control officers are more focused on drugs, undocumented migrants, and smuggling than they are on trafficking. *Part IV: Combatting Human Trafficking: Coordinated Responses across Communities and Borders* draws attention to various political and legal obstacles to ending trafficking and protecting victims and puts forth several recommendations for policymakers.

Articles and Reports

Aitken, Jonathan. 2007. "The Broken and Crushed." *American Spectator* 40, no. 5: 56–57.

In this brief article, columnist and biographer Jonathan Aitken contends that while no one denies that thousands are trapped in exploitive and slave-like conditions across the globe, individual situations of human bondage differ in nature from the systematic African slavery of the eighteenth century, which was characterized by the horrors of the middle passage and the degradation of the slave auctions. Aitken thus questions whether there are any cases of modern slavery that a latter-day William Wilberforce might be able to abolish through the process of parliamentary campaigning and the pressure of public opinion on an accountable democracy? He determines that the Dalits in India provide such a case. Aitken highlights how a respected modern democracy turns a blind eye to systemic exploitation and slavery of a sizeable percentage of its population.

Frank, Michael J., and G. Zachary Terwilliger. 2015. "Gang-Controlled Sex Trafficking." *Virginia Journal of Criminal Law* 3: 342–352.

In this law review article, Michael J. Frank and G. Zachary Terwilliger, Assistant United States Attorneys in the Eastern District of Virginia, draw attention to the growing involvement of street gangs in sex trafficking. The authors point out that sex trafficking has become an appealing source of revenue for street gangs because it is highly profitable, it entails relatively minimal risk of detection by the police, and gangs already possess many of the tools and connections necessary to operate a sex trafficking venture. The article provides an overview of the means by which gangs recruit and maintain victims, the tools they use to market victims to customers, and the methods they employ to prevent victims from escaping. The authors additionally explain how gangs' structure, discipline, and reputation for violence make them formidable sex traffickers and contend that, absent aggressive intervention, gangs are likely to expand their domain in the world of sex trafficking.

Haarr, Robin. 2017. "Evaluation of the Program to Combat Sex Trafficking of Children in the Philippines: 2003-2015." *International Justice Mission.* August. Accessed March 23, 2020. https://www.ijm.org/documents/studies/philippines-csec -program-evaluation.pdf

This report aims to assess the relevance, effectiveness, and impact of International Justice Mission's (IJM's) Program to Combat Sex Trafficking of Children in the Philippines during the period of 2003 to June 2016 and to assess the potential for sustainability of results achieved. The program was designed to support and build the capacity of public justice system actors to enforce antihuman trafficking laws and to provide quality aftercare to child sex trafficking victims through the government and other relevant stakeholders. The program focused specifically on three desired outcomes: increasing the capacity, will, and mandate of regional and national Philippine law enforcement to investigate and intervene in suspected sex trafficking cases; increasing the quantity and quality of child sex trafficking prosecutions in the Philippines, resulting in an increase in the number of convictions; and increasing the capacity of the Philippine government and private social service providers to process sex trafficking survivors immediately post-rescue, to provide trauma-informed care, and to reintegrate sex trafficking survivors into local communities. Based on a variety of evaluation methods and processes, the report found that IJM's program was successful in achieving all three desired outcomes and that the program contributed to a substantial reduction in the availability of sexually trafficked and commercially exploited minors. The report concluded, however, that more time is necessary to assess the long-term impact and sustainability of the program.

Harroff-Tavel, Hélène, and Alix Nasri. 2013. "Tricked and Trapped: Human Trafficking in the Middle East." *The*

International Labour Organization and Heartland Alliance International. Accessed March 23, 2020. https://www.ilo.org/wcmsp5/groups/public/---arabstates/---ro-beirut/documents/publication/wcms_211214.pdf

The International Labour Organization (ILO) calculated that in 2012, there were some 600,000 forced labor victims in the Middle East and that 3.4 in every 1,000 of the region's inhabitants were compelled to work against their will. Nevertheless, the region has seen an increase in recent years in the numbers of governments and civil society actors engaged in attempts to combat the problem. In an effort to fill the gaps in understanding human trafficking in the Middle East, the ILO embarked on a qualitative research project from June 2011 to December 2012 to map the processes of human trafficking for labor and sexual exploitation and to document national efforts to combat it. The study found that the reliance on the *kafala* (sponsorship) system in the region is inherently problematic. The *kafala* system, a legal employment system used in the Middle Eastern Gulf States and in Lebanon and Jordon, requires that migrant workers are sponsored by a national entity to reside in the country. The sponsors, either individuals or companies, control the mobility of migrant workers through their ability to prevent them from changing jobs or exiting the country. This system facilitates forced labor by establishing an unequal power dynamic that is rife for abuse. Employers under this system are able to threaten employees with deportation, withhold wages and personal documents, and prevent their employees from leaving by requiring them to pay high fees for their release. Oftentimes, fraudulent *kafeels* (sponsors) will recruit foreign workers for non-existent jobs and will then auction off the visas of these workers to the highest bidder. Thus, combatting trafficking and forced labor in the Middle East will require a shift in legal and social protections for migrant workers, in particular.

International Justice Mission. 2016. "Labor Trafficking in Cambodia: A Review of the Public Justice System's Response." November. Accessed March 23, 2020. https://www.ijm.org/documents/studies/labor_trafficking_in_cambodia_-_a_review_of_the_pjss_response_ijm_2016.pdf

Cambodia is a source, transit, and destination country for men, women, and children subjected to labor trafficking. Until recently, the bulk of effort and international, NGO, and government attention has been directed at the commercial sexual exploitation of children. While this focused attention has yielded a significant reduction in commercial sexual exploitation and trafficking over the past decade, there have been fewer initiatives focused on the criminal justice response to labor trafficking. Since a vast majority (over 75 percent) of Cambodians living in modern slavery are victims of labor trafficking, specific attention is needed to ensure that improvements in the public justice system's (PJS's) ability to address sex trafficking are expanded to combat labor trafficking as well.

This report reviews the performance of Cambodia's PJS in cases of labor trafficking, identifying strengths and recent improvements, gaps in response that could be further improved upon, and areas where more data or research is needed in order to inform future initiatives for the PJS and its partners. The report calls for enhanced, expanded and institutionalized training, specific guidelines to be issued where laws or best practices are unclear, the implementation of international instruments and innovations for cross-border collaboration, and continuing to improve collaboration between government and nongovernment agencies within Cambodia.

International Labour Organization and Walk Free Foundation. 2017. "Global Estimates of Modern Slavery: Forced Labour and Forced Marriage." Geneva. Accessed March 23, 2020.

https://www.ilo.org/global/publications/books/WCMS
_575479/lang--en/index.htm
A report published by the International Labour Organization and the Walk Free Foundation, in partnership with
the International Organization for Migration, providing
comprehensive global estimates on the numbers of individuals trapped in forced labor and forced marriage, the
main forms of forced labor and forced marriage, their
extent and characteristics, the means by which persons are
trapped in them, and the duration of abuse. The second
part of the report discusses key policy priorities emerging
from the Global Estimates in the drive to rid the world of
modern slavery.

The report is part of a broader multi-partner effort to
measure and monitor progress towards Target 8.7 of the
United Nation's 2030 Sustainable Development Goals
(SDGs), which calls for effective measures to end forced
labor, modern slavery, and human trafficking, as well as
child labor in all its forms.

KnowTheChain. 2019. "Three Sectors, Three Years Later:
Progress and Gaps in the Fight against Forced Labor."
April. Accessed March 23, 2020. https://knowthechain.org
/wp-content/uploads/KTC_Cross_sector_2019.pdf
KnowTheChain (KTC) is a collaborative partnership
established to increase awareness of forced labor risks and
to provide resources and tools to assist companies and
investors in their efforts to identify and eradicate such
risks in their global supply chains. In 2016, KTC evaluated efforts to address forced labor in their supply chains
of 60 companies in three high-risk sectors—information
and communications technology (ITC), food and beverage, and apparel and footwear. In 2018, this endeavor was
repeated and expanded to 119 companies. This report
aims to provide both an evidence-based barometer for
assessing corporate practices and a resource to companies

and investors for improved policy and action to address forced labor risks. The report presents findings from the KTC's benchmarks on the progress in corporate efforts to address forced labor in high-risk sectors and the most severe gaps in action that persist even among companies with more advanced supply chain labor practices. Finally, the report offers recommendations for companies in any sector and at any stage of developing their policies and processes for addressing forced labor.

Lederer, Laura J. 2011. "Addressing Demand: Why and How Policy Makers Should Utilize Law and Law Enforcement to Target Customers of Commercial Sexual Exploitation." *Regent University Law Review* 23: 297–310.

In this law review article, Laura J. Lederer—president of Global Centurion, former Senior Advisor on Trafficking in Persons in the U.S. State Department's Office to Combat Trafficking in Persons, and founder of the Protection Project at Harvard University's John F. Kennedy School of Government—points out that in human trafficking, as in drug trafficking, there is a triangle of activity consisting of *supply, demand,* and *distribution.* This triangle for purposes of commercial sexual exploitation includes the women, men, and children trafficked into or trapped in commercial sexual exploitation (supply side); the traffickers, pimps, and brothel owners or operators (distribution side); and the customers/consumers and legitimate businesses who facilitate trafficking such as the tourism industry, hotels, and electronic media outlets (demand side). Since the passage of the Trafficking Victims Protection Act in 2000, governmental and NGO activities have largely focused on the supply and distribution sides— that is, providing comprehensive services, including food, clothing shelter, medical attention, and legal aid to those rescued and investigating, arresting, prosecuting, and convicting traffickers. Very little attention and few programs are designed to combat the demand side of the triangle. Lederer, thus, addresses some strategies for demand reduction and suggests a four-point program that jurisdictions can apply in different ways. The four points include: (1) drafting laws that penalize, patronize, and target customers and consumers of commercial sex; (2) creating first-offender programs, colloquially known as "John Schools" to educate first offenders about the deleterious effects of commercial sexual exploitation; (3) creating sting and reverse-sting operations to assist law enforcement in identifying, arresting, and prosecuting buyers; and (4) developing social marketing campaigns that not only target exploiters but also impress upon the general public the message of "no tolerance" for their actions.

Rousseau, David. 2019. "Review of Models of Care for Trafficking Survivors in Thailand." *USAID and Winrock International.* Accessed March 23, 2020. https://www.traffickingmatters.com/wp-content/uploads/2019/11/20191023-Thailand-CTIP-Shelter-Report.pdf

Thailand is a country of origin, destination, and transit for forced labor and human trafficking. Although the Royal Thai Government (RTG) has made progress in the fight against trafficking over the last few years, which has resulted in an improved Trafficking in Persons (TIP) Report ranking, its current model for sheltercare provision does not always fully consider survivors' individual needs and may discourage victims from identifying themselves and participating in prosecutions. This report summarizes the findings of a Review of Models of Care for Trafficking Survivors conducted by the international nonprofit Winrock International under the USAID's Thailand Counter Trafficking-in-Persons Project. The research contained in the report compares models of care available to trafficked persons in Thailand and assesses their relative effectiveness in victim recovery. The report additionally provides recommendations for improvement and explores how models that have been successfully implemented elsewhere could be applied by the RTG to the Thailand context.

Skinner, E. Benjamin. 2009. "The Fight to End Global Slavery." *World Policy Journal* (Summer 2009). Accessed March 23, 2020. https://www.brandeis.edu/investigate /selectedwork/docs/skinner/skinner-final-wpj.pdf
Investigative journalist and fellow at the Carr Center for Human Rights Policy at Harvard's Kennedy School, E. Benjamin Skinner highlights some of what he has learned about the nature of modern slavery since he first began investigating the issue in 2001. Skinner particularly emphasizes the tendency of international law and global abolitionists to focus narrowly on cross-border trafficking and commercial sexual exploitation at the exclusion of more prevalent forms of forced labor. Skinner concludes that the ending global slavery will require both the adoption of a clear definition of what constitutes slavery and the implementation of comprehensive development programs that focus on liberating slaves, prosecuting traffickers, and providing survivors and vulnerable populations with access to basic health services, education, and formal microcredit structures to combat their future susceptibility to slavery.

UK Home Office. 2019. "UK Annual Report on Modern Slavery." *Modern Slavery Unit.* Accessed March 23, 2020. https: //assets.publishing.service.gov.uk/government/uploads/system /uploads/attachment_data/file/840059/Modern_Slavery _Report_2019.pdf
This is a report produced by the United Kingdom (UK) Home Office, providing an overview of modern slavery in the UK, an assessment of the steps taken by the UK government, the Scottish government, and the Northern

Ireland Executive to combat modern slavery and human trafficking in 2018, and an overview of planned future response efforts. Although modern slavery is a complex and largely hidden crime, the Home Office estimates that, in 2013, there were between 10,000 and 13,000 victims of modern slavery in the UK. According to the report, the UK government adopted a Modern Slavery Strategy in 2014 structured around the four Ps' framework: pursue—prosecuting and disrupting individuals and groups responsible for modern slavery; prevent—preventing people from engaging in modern slavery, either as victims or offenders; protect—strengthening safeguards against modern slavery by protecting vulnerable people from exploitation and increasing awareness of and resilience against this crime; and prepare—reducing the harm caused by modern slavery through improved victim identification and enhanced support. The strategy also commits the UK government to step up its international response to modern slavery. The report highlights various concrete actions and successes in each of these areas.

In an effort to better implement the Modern Slavery Act of 2015, going forward the UK government identifies its commitment to strengthen transparency requirements in supply chain laws, to appoint an International Modern Slavery and Migration Envoy, and to continue to roll out Independent Child Trafficking Guardians.

U.S. Department of State. 2019. "Trafficking in Persons Report." June. Accessed March 23, 2020. https://www.state.gov /wp-content/uploads/2019/06/2019-Trafficking-in-Persons -Report.pdf

In compliance with the Trafficking Victims Protection Act (TVPA), the U.S. State Department publishes an annual Trafficking in Persons Report (TIP Report), which provides the latest information on the status of human trafficking around the world and a comprehensive assessment of what governments are doing to combat it. It is a valuable resource for policymakers at home and abroad.

Despite major progress, many countries adopt inadequate intervention strategies and have gaps in their legal response to modern slavery. One such gap occurs because governments commonly focus on transnational human trafficking cases at the expense of cases occurring within their own borders. Thus, the 2019 TIP Report specifically highlights human trafficking that takes place exclusively within the borders of a country, absent any transnational elements, to emphasize the need for governments to implement laws that address all forms of trafficking whether they involve movement across borders or not. The report specifically calls on governments to implement several promising practices including: adopting a clear understanding of human trafficking to aid in prosecution and victim identification, developing a robust anti-trafficking coordination process, confronting harmful cultural norms and local practices, and empowering communities to recognize and address human trafficking. The report concludes with 187 country narratives that provide an overview of human trafficking in each country and the factors affecting vulnerability to trafficking of the country's nationals abroad. The narratives additionally summarize the extent to which each country's respective government has exerted effort to meet the TVPA's minimum standards for the elimination of human trafficking and highlight prioritized recommendations for how each government can better meet TVPA standards.

Walk Free Foundation. 2018. "Global Slavery Index." Accessed March 23, 2020. https://www.globalslaveryindex.org/resources /downloads/

The Global Slavery Index, published by the Walk Free Foundation, is the world's leading research tool measuring the size and scale of modern slavery. The index provides a country-by-country analysis of the number of individuals enslaved, vulnerability factors, and governmental action. The 2018 Index for the first time additionally draws high-GDP countries into focus by providing a picture of the factors that contribute to modern slavery—migration, conflict, repressive regimes, unethical business, environmental destruction, and discrimination. While the responsibility for most of these factors belongs to the countries where modern slavery is occurring, some of these factors are directly linked to the policy decisions of high-GDP countries, where the products of the crime are sold and consumed. The 2018 Index finds that although citizens of most G20 countries enjoy relatively low levels of vulnerability to the crime of modern slavery within their borders, and many aspects of their governments' responses to it are strong, businesses and governments in G20 countries are importing products that are at risk of modern slavery on a significant scale. The analysis found that G20 countries are collectively importing $354 billion USD worth of the products most at risk of modern slavery, which includes common items such as laptops, computers and mobile phones, apparel and accessories, fish, cocoa, and timber. Thus, the 2018 Index calls on businesses and governments in high-GDP countries to increase their efforts to address the risk of modern slavery in supply chains and to provide transparency to investors and consumers.

Walk Free Foundation. 2019. "Measurement, Action, Freedom: An Independent Assessment of Government Progress Towards Achieving UN Sustainable Development Goal 8.7." Accessed March 23, 2020. https://cdn.globalslaveryindex.org /2019-content/uploads/2019/07/17123602/walk.free _.MAF_190717_FNL_DIGITAL-P.pdf

On September 25, 2015, the United Nations General Assembly officially adopted 17 Sustainable Development Goals (SDGs) intended to be achieved by 2030 to guide their global development efforts and policies. Target 8.7 of the SDGs called on all governments to "take immediate and effective measures to eradicate forced labor, end modern slavery and human trafficking, and secure the prohibition and elimination of the worst forms of child labor, including recruitment and use of child soldiers, and by 2025 to end child labor in all its forms." The *Measurement Action Freedom* report published by the Walk Free Foundation provides an independent assessment of whether meaningful action has been taken to achieve Target 8.7 and outlines a roadmap for progress. The report identifies encouraging examples of governments taking actions that have led to increased prosecutions and victim support services, but overall the report finds that global progress in tackling modern slavery has been hugely disappointing. According to the report: 47 countries globally still do not recognize human trafficking as a crime in line with international standards; nearly 100 countries fail to criminalize forced labor or, if they do, the penalty for exploitation amounts to nothing more than a fine; and less than one-third of countries protect women and girls from the exploitation inherent in forced marriage. The report concludes that if progress is to be made in eradicating modern slavery, governments will need to redouble efforts to identify victims, arrest perpetrators, and address the driving factors.

Nonprint Sources

The Abolitionists. 2016. Directed by Darrin Fletcher and Chet Thomas. Ojai, CA: FletChet Entertainment. DVD.
A documentary film that recounts the story of Special Agent Tim Ballard, who—after a decade of rescuing children domestically and overseas working with the Department of Homeland Security—decides to turn in his badge and orchestrate sting missions from outside the

government. Ballard assembles a jump team of highly specialized individuals to infiltrate trafficking organizations and rescue victims. The film chronicles the team's exploits as they rescue 57 children from slavery and contribute to the arrest of seven traffickers.

Britain's Modern Slave Trade. 2016. Directed by Jason Gwynne. Al Jazeera. Accessed March 23, 2020. https://interactive.aljazeera .com/aje/2016/uk-slavery-sex-slave-smuggling-investigation /index.html

An undercover investigation by Al Jazeera that shines the light on the underground system of human rights abuses that continue to thrive while hidden in plain sight. *Britain's Modern Slave Trade* offers raw interviews with victims of the slave trade working in high-profile industries in the UK and provides insight into how criminal enterprises engaging in slave-like practices continue to flourish in spite of the passage of Britain's Modern Slavery Act in 2015.

The Chocolate Case (Tony). 2016. Directed by Benthe Forrer. The Netherlands: Benthe Forrer Studios. Accessed March 23, 2020. https://www.amstelfilm.nl/tony

Like previous documentaries such as *The Dark Side of Chocolate* (2010) and *Cocoa-nomics* (2014), *The Chocolate Case* exposes forced child labor occurring within the chocolate industry. Written and directed by filmmaker and actress Benthe Forrer, the documentary follows a group of three cheeky journalists who uncover child labor in the cocoa production chain and work to create a "chocolate case," a legal precedent to help abolish child slavery in the chocolate plantations of the Ivory Coast. After facing scorn and rejection from the industry, the trio decides to develop the first "slave-free" chocolate bar named "Tony's Chocolonely," which is now one of The Netherlands' leading chocolate brands.

CNN Freedom Project. Accessed March 23, 2020. https://www
.cnn.com/interactive/2018/specials/freedom-project/
    The Freedom Project, a humanitarian news media cam-
    paign launched by CNN and CNN International in
    2011, has produced a large number of documentaries
    highlighting various manifestations of contemporary slav-
    ery around the globe.

The Deep Place. 2017. Directed by Lindsay Branham and
Andrew Michael Ellis. Telluride, CO: Mountainfilm.
Accessed March 23, 2020. https://www.mountainfilm.org
/media/the-deep-place
    A short film recounting the true story of a young boy
    who was abducted by his uncle and trafficked into slavery
    on Ghana's Lake Volta, where thousands of children are
    forced to labor on fishing boats. After two years, the boy
    was rescued by International Justice Mission.
    The film first launched on Facebook in time for the 2017
    holiday season. In just under two months, it helped raise
    more than a million dollars to fund nearly 200 Interna-
    tional Justice Mission rescue operations.

The Hidden. 2018. Directed by Lindsay Branham. Washington,
DC: International Justice Mission and Novo. Accessed March 23,
2020. http://www.novofilm.co/portfolio/the-hidden/
    A virtual reality investigative film about an International
    Justice Mission (IJM) rescue operation in southern India.
    In an effort to highlight the plight of individuals whose
    brutalization often goes unseen, *The Hidden* takes viewers
    on the real-life journey of a family that was forced into
    bonded labor over a paltry debt of $70 USD and bru-
    tally enslaved in a rock quarry for 10 years. The film also
    follows government representatives, supported by IJM, as
    they stage a daring raid to free the family. The film pre-
    miered at the Tribeca Film Festival in 2018 and has been
    touring the festival circuit ever since.

India's Untouchables. 2013. Directed by Michael Lawson. Worcester, PN: Vision Video. DVD.

India's Untouchables is a set of three documentary films—*India's Hidden Slavery, India's Forgotten Women,* and *India's New Beginnings*—that expose the systematic oppression of the Dalit people while offering practical solutions for healing and change. Initially produced in 2008, the first documentary, *India's Hidden Slavery,* is an award-winning film shot in villages and cities across India that exposes how the Dalits, the lowest layer of India's hierarchal caste system, are routinely oppressed and abused as modern-day slaves: in bonded labor, the sex industry, temple prostitution, manual labor, and other brutal forms of exploitation. The film further exposes how contemporary slavery among the Dalits is made possible by a social structure that reinforces segregation, poverty, and injustice.

Journey to Freedom. 2012. Directed by Justin Dillon. Cincinnati, OH: National Underground Freedom Center. Accessed March 23, 2020. https://freedomcenter.org/enabling-freedom /journey-to-freedom
> A documentary that brings to life the striking similarities between historic and contemporary slavery by chronicling the true stories of two men who were sold into slavery more than 150 years apart—twenty-first Century Cambodian Vannak Prum and nineteenth Century American Solomon Northup. The film also highlights the common characteristics shared by abolitionists of the past and their networks and today's freedom fighters.

The Madonna Case. 2014. Directed by Nadia Dyberg. Sweden: Kibera Production. Accessed March 23, 2020. https:// kiberaproduction.exposure.co/the-madonna-case
> A documentary film shot in Thailand, Sweden, and Romania in which journalist Nadia Dyberg follows the thrilling inside story of a police investigation of the largest

ever trafficking network operating in Sweden. Dyber joins up with two police detectives as they work to uncover and bust the brutal network and free victims.

Slavery: A Global Investigation. 2000. Directed by Kate Blewett and Brian Woods. United Kingdom: True Vision. DVD

A documentary film, inspired by Free the Slaves President Kevin Bale's award-winning book *Disposable People*, that aims to expose the continued existence of slave markets around the world. Focusing particularly on three separate industries where slaves are still to be found—the cocoa industry in the Ivory Coast, domestic slavery in the United States and Great Britain, and the carpet industry in northern India—filmmakers Kate Blewett and Brian Woods weave together small, personal stories of slavery to tell the larger story of slavery in the global economy. They also examine effective ways of fighting slavery at home and abroad. The film received a Peabody Award and two Emmy Awards.

Slavery: A 21st Century Evil. 2011. Directed by Rageh Omaar. Al Jazeera. Accessed March 23, 2020. https://www.aljazeera .com/programmes/slaverya21stcenturyevil/2011/10/201110101 2574599955.html

It is an eight-part documentary series in which Rageh Ommar uncovers the truth about the flourishing modern slave trade. Weaving the testimony of current and former slaves with investigations into some of the biggest global slave masters, Omaar explores why this evil continues to flourish. Each episode focuses on a different topic: episode one covers food chain slaves; episode two covers sex slaves; episode three covers bonded slaves; episode four covers child slaves; episode five covers charcoal slaves; episode six covers bridal slaves; episode seven covers prison slaves; and episode eight covers a panel of experts debating different aspects of the trade.

The Storm Makers. 2014. Directed by Guillaume Suon. France: Tipasa Production. DVD.
This is a documentary film about human trafficking in Cambodia. Titled the "Storm Makers" in reference to traffickers and the damage they inflict on Cambodian villages and families, the film follows the lives of women who have returned home after being enslaved overseas and those preparing to make the journey home, as well as a trafficker who claims he has sold more than 500 Cambodian girls, some as young as 14. The film premiered at the 2015 Busan International Film Festival and won the Mecenat Award for Best Asian Documentary.

Why Slavery? 2018. Denmark: The Why Foundation. Accessed March 23, 2020. https://www.thewhy.dk/about
This is a series of six documentaries uncovering the stories of men, women, and children trapped in slavery in the modern age. The documentaries cover a variety of manifestations of modern slavery including the Kafala system in the Middle East, where migrant women have their passports confiscated and are forced to work as maids, the trafficking of Yazidi women by the Islamic State, and the selling of thousands of children for forced labor in India. The series has been aired by major broadcasters around the globe.

7 Chronology

Below is a chronological list of some of the major events impacting slavery in the twentieth and twenty-first centuries and the enactment of key conventions, treaties, and governmental policies and actions intended to help alleviate the global epidemic of modern slavery.

1910 The International Convention for the Suppression of the White Slave Traffic is signed in Paris on May 4 and ratified by 41 states. The convention, which was one of the first multilateral treaties to address the issue of modern slavery and human trafficking, obligates state parties to work to protect women from being deceived or forced into prostitution.

1919 The League of Nations is created. It becomes the first international organization to assemble major conventions regulating modern slavery.

The International Labour Organization (ILO) is founded to establish international labor standards and to bring together governments and employers to address labor exploitation, including forced labor, human trafficking, and other forms of

---

Two hands in handcuffs, representing the concept of slave labor. Combating the various manifestations of modern slavery will require a multifaceted approach based on strong partnerships between international organizations, sovereign governments and law enforcement personnel, public service providers, businesses, and private philanthropic and faith-based organizations. (Piyamas Dulmunsumphun/Dreamstime.com)

slavery. The ILO later becomes a part of the United Nations in 1946.

1923   The British colonial government in Hong Kong passes a law banning the widespread practice of keeping young girls as household slaves.

1924   The League of Nations establishes the Temporary Slave Commission. The commission determines that slavery is widespread and calls on member states to consider the "abolition of the legal status of slavery."

1926   The League of Nations sponsors the International Slavery Convention that requires all signatory states to enact and enforce laws against slavery, forced labor, and the slave trade in their territories, to intercept slave traffic in their territorial waters and on ships flying their flag, and to assist other states in antislavery efforts. The convention is signed at Geneva on September 25 and entered into force a year later.

Burma (later known as Myanmar) abolishes legal slavery.

1927   The League of Nations officially changes the term "white slavery" to "trafficking in women" in recognition of the fact that trafficking affects women of all races.

1928   The British colonial government officially abolishes slavery in Sierra Leone.

1930   The International Labour Organization adopts the Convention Concerning Forced or Compulsory Labour in Geneva on June 28 requiring signatories to take effective measures to prevent and eliminate the use of forced labor. The convention defines forced labor as "all work or service which is exacted from any person under the menace of penalty and for which the said person has not offered himself voluntarily."

1945   The United Nations is established as the successor of the League of Nations.

1948   The United Nations adopts the Universal Declaration of Human Rights identifying fundamental rights that ought to be universally protected. Article 4 of the Declaration states that

"No one shall be held in slavery or servitude; slavery and the slave trade shall be prohibited in all their forms."

1949 The Convention for the Suppression of the Traffic in Persons and of the Exploitation of the Prostitution of Others is adopted. The convention, which prohibits any person from procuring, enticing, or leading away another person for the purposes of prostitution, even with the other person's consent, is the first legally binding instrument establishing procedures for combating international trafficking and prostitution. The convention goes into effect in 1951.

1956 The Supplementary Convention on the Abolition of Slavery, Slave Trade and Institutions and Practices Similar to Slavery updates the 1926 Slavery Convention to criminalize practices involving debt bondage, the sale of wives, serfdom, and child servitude.

1962 Slavery is legally abolished in Saudi Arabia and Yemen.

1964 The Sixth World Muslim Congress pledges global support for all antislavery movements.

1974 The UN Working Group on Contemporary Forms of Slavery is formed to collect information and make recommendations on slavery and slavery-like practices around the world.

1976 India passes legislation banning bonded labor.

1981 Mauritania abolishes slavery by presidential decree; however, no criminal laws are passed to enforce the ban until 2007.

1990 Antislavery advocates from across Asia gather in Chiang Mai, Thailand, with the objective of ending child sex tourism. This meeting leads to the establishment of ECPAT (End Child Prostitution in Asian Tourism).

1996 The Stockholm Declaration is adopted at the First World Congress against Commercial Sexual Exploitation of Children held in Stockholm, Sweden.

1997 The UN establishes a Commission of Inquiry to investigate reports of widespread enslavement of people by the

Myanmar government. Myanmar refuses to allow the Commission of Inquiry to enter its borders. Despite being barred from entry, the commission collects significant evidence of government-sponsored slavery. Two years later, in 1999, the commission releases an official report stating that the Myanmar government "treats the civilian population as an unlimited pool of unpaid forced laborers and servants at their disposal as part of a political system built on the use of force and intimidation to deny the people of Myanmar democracy and the rule of law."

Gary Haugen founds the International Justice Mission (IJM) as an international legal agency with the express purpose of representing and rescuing victims of violence, sexual exploitation, slavery, and oppression. Today, IJM is the largest antislavery organization in the world with several hundred full-time staff working from its Washington D.C. headquarters and in field offices throughout Africa, Latin America, and Southeast Asia.

1999   The ILO passes the Convention on the Worst Forms of Child Labour, which establishes widely recognized international standards protecting children against forced or indentured labor, child prostitution, and pornography, their use in drug trafficking and other harmful work.

2000   The United Nations approves "The Protocol to Prevent, Suppress and Punish Trafficking in Persons, Especially Women and Children" (The Palermo Protocol) as part of the Convention against Transnational Organized Crime in November. Signed by 117 countries, the Protocol is the first legally binding global agreement with an internationally agreed-upon definition of trafficking in persons that establishes international guidelines for investigating and prosecuting traffickers and protecting and aiding victims.

Congress passes and President Clinton signs into law the Trafficking Victims Protection Act. The law mandates the creation of an Interagency Task Force to Combat Trafficking and an Office to Monitor and Combat Trafficking. The law is reauthorized and expanded in 2003, 2005, 2008, 2013, and 2019.

The Netherlands appoints Anna Korvinus as the first independent National Rapporteur on Trafficking in Human Beings to report on the nature and extent of human trafficking and to evaluate the progress and effectiveness of Dutch eradication policies.

Free the Slaves, widely regarded as a leader and pioneer in the modern international abolition movement, is established as an offshoot of the United Kingdom's AntiSlavery International. It eventually becomes an independent organization.

The government of Nepal bans all forms of debt bondage after a concerted campaign carried out by former slaves and human rights organizations.

2001 The Office to Monitor and Combat Trafficking in Persons is established within the U.S. State Department in October as mandated by the Trafficking Victims Protection Act of 2000. The office is charged with investigating and creating programs to combat human trafficking domestically and internationally. The office publishes its inaugural global Trafficking in Persons (TIP) Report, which has since been published annually.

The countries of the Economic Community of Western African States agree on a plan to combat slavery and human trafficking in the region.

2002 The International Cocoa Initiative is established through a collaborative agreement between antislavery NGOs and major chocolate companies to work towards the elimination of slavery and child labor in the cocoa supply chain. The initiative marks the first time that members of an entire industry join forces to address slavery in supply chains.

Brown University students Katherine Chon and Derek Ellerman found the Polaris Project. Named after the North Star that guided slaves using the Underground Railroad as they navigated their way to freedom, the Polaris Project is one of the first NGOs in the United States to focus on both labor and sex trafficking of men, women, and children. It has since grown into one of the largest antislavery organizations in the United States, and it maintains the National Human Trafficking Resource Center Hotline.

2003 The U.S. Congress creates a high-level position at the State Department to head the Office to Monitor and Combat Trafficking and Persons and to work specifically to combat the slave industry in the United States and around the world. President Bush appoints former congressman John Miller to the post in March and elevates the position to that of an U.S. Ambassador.

The U.S. government imposes its first economic sanctions under the Trafficking Victims Protection Act against Myanmar for their widespread use of forced labor.

The Organization for Security and Cooperation in Europe establishes the Office of the Special Representative and Coordinator for Combating Trafficking in Human beings to assist participating States in the development and implementation of effective eradication policies.

2004 Brazil launches the National Pact for the Eradication of Slave Labor to bring together civil organizations, businesses, and governments to pressure companies to commit to the prevention and eradication of forced labor in their supply chains. The pact includes a provision to create a "dirty list" of companies found to be selling products produced by slaves.

The United Nations appoints a Special Rapporteur on Human Trafficking.

The Organization of American States (OAS) appoints an Anti-Tip Coordinator to foster national action and advance best practices among governments and to implement new projects and training programs.

The Association of SouthEast Asia Nations (ASEAN) pledges to combat human trafficking and adopts the Declaration against Trafficking in Persons Particularly Women and Children.

2005   The International Labour Organization publishes its first Global Report on Forced Labour estimating that 12.3 million individuals are held in forced labor. A 2012 update to the report increased that number to 21 million.

2007   Mauritania passes a law criminalizing slavery. Slavery, nevertheless, remains a widely sanctioned practice. Antislavery activists are more likely to be jailed than slaveholders and 10–20 percent of the country's population remains enslaved.

2008   The Council of Europe Convention on Action against Trafficking in Human Beings goes into effect. The convention is the first international law to define trafficking as a violation of human rights and guarantee minimum standards of protection to victims.

Former slave Hadijatou Mani becomes the first to pursue legal action against her government for failing to protect her from slavery. Mani brought her case to the Economic Community of Western African States (ECOWAS), which required the government of Niger to provide Mani with $19,000 USD in compensatory damages.

Congress passes and President George W. Bush signs into law The Child Soldiers Prevention Act (CSPA). The CSPA requires publication in the annual Trafficking in Persons Report of a list of foreign governments identified during the previous year as having governmental armed forces or government-supported armed groups that recruit and use child soldiers, as defined in the act.

2010   The United Nations General Assembly adopts the Global Plan of Action to Combat Trafficking in Persons. The plan calls for the establishment of a trust fund for the victims of trafficking and aims at integrating efforts to eradicate trafficking into broader development goals.

President Barack Obama issues a Presidential Proclamation designating January as National Slavery and Human

Trafficking Prevention Month to be recognized beginning in January, 2011.

2011   California enacts the California Transparency in Supply Chains Act, requiring major manufacturing and retail firms to disclose the efforts they are taking to eliminate forced labor from their supply chains. The law goes into effect on January 1, 2012.

CNN launches the Freedom Project, a humanitarian news media campaign designed to investigate and raise awareness of modern slavery around the globe.

2012   Australian philanthropist Andrew Forrest and his wife Nicola launch the Walk Free Foundation to produce research and encourage collaboration between activists and businesses in the fight to end modern slavery. The foundation is best known for its publication of the Global Slavery Index, the world's leading research tool measuring the size and scale of modern slavery. Approaching its fifth edition, the index provides a country-by-country analysis of the number of individuals enslaved, vulnerability factors, and governmental action.

2013   The Walk Free Foundation releases the first Global Slavery Index estimating that there are 29.8 million slaves globally. Estimates from the most recent index put that number at 40.3 million.

2014   The International Labour Conference adopts The Protocol of 2014 to the Forced Labour Convention, which obligates state parties to provide protection and remedies to victims of forced labor, to prosecute the perpetrators, and to develop "a national policy and plan of action for the effective and sustained suppression of forced or compulsory labor."

2015   The United Kingdom enacts the Modern Slavery Act. The act requires businesses to report what actions they have taken to ensure that their supplies chains are free of slave labor; it increases the maximum jail sentence for traffickers from 14 years to life; it allows authorities to force traffickers to pay compensation to their victims; and it adopts measures to protect those at risk of being enslaved.

The UK Home Office appoints the first ever independent AntiSlavery Commissioner to help oversee enforcement of the Modern Slavery Act.

The UN adopts 17 Sustainable Development Goals that include eradicating various forms of modern slavery, forced labor, and human trafficking. The goals call on member states to "take immediate and effective measures to eradicate forced labor, end modern slavery and human trafficking and secure the prohibition and elimination of the worst forms of child labor, including recruitment and use of child soldiers."

2017   A research consortium including the ILO, the Walk Free Foundation, and the International Organization for Migration releases a global study indicating that 40 million people are trapped in modern forms of slavery worldwide: 50 percent in forced labor in agriculture, manufacturing, construction, mining, fishing, and other physical-labor industries, 12.5 percent in sex slavery, and 37.5 percent in forced marriage slavery.

2019   Congress passes and President Donald Trump signs the Frederick Douglass Trafficking Victims Prevention and Protection Reauthorization Act of 2018 and the Trafficking Victims Protection Reauthorization Act of 2017 on January 8 and 9. These acts contained several provisions to expand anti-trafficking training and education, to improve the federal government's authority to combat human trafficking, to ensure that all employees and contractors receiving federal money are in compliance with anti-trafficking laws, and to provide additional services to victims.

Glossary

Bonded labor (also referred to as debt bondage) A condition in which a person is forced to work indefinitely in an attempt to pay off a debt, which is often impossible to repay because of low wages, deductions for food and lodging, and high interest rates. This debt is frequently passed down to children or to other family members who then find themselves forced into bonded labor.

Brothel An establishment where commercial sex acts are performed. It could be a commercial building, apartment, house, trailer, or other facility.

Chattel slavery A form of slavery in which a person is considered the wholly owned property of another. Chattel slaves can be inherited, traded, bought, or sold.

Child slavery A form of slavery that occurs when a person under the age of 18 is required to engage in exploitive or forced labor.

Child soldiers Children under the age of 18 who are recruited by a state or nonstate armed group and used as fighters, cooks, suicide bombers, human shields, messengers, spies, or for sexual purposes.

Commercial sexual exploitation of children (CSEC) The commercial sexual exploitation of a person under the age of 18, for the purpose of child pornography, prostitution, or child sex tourism.

Convention A compact in international law similar to a treaty in which sovereign states agree to take certain steps to address a global issue.

Dalits The name given to those in Hindu societies who are considered below the four major castes in India and the Hindu regions of Nepal, Pakistan, Sri Lanka, and Bangladesh. Also known as "Untouchables," Dalits face discrimination, violence, and oppression and are particularly vulnerable to debt bondage and other forms of slavery throughout South Asia.

Debt bondage *See* Bonded labor

Demand-side approach An approach to abolition that focuses on targeting the demand side of modern slavery. Examples include educating consumers about the products they buy or services they use or targeting clients of prostitutes, often with arrest, fines, or educational programs.

Descent-based slavery Exists when the status of "slave" passes from mother to child.

Domestic servitude A form of forced labor in which a worker living and working in a private residence is not free to leave and is abused or underpaid or not paid at all.

Domestic trafficking Trafficking of individuals within their home country.

Escort services A business that arranges sexual transactions for a buyer, often done via phone or internet.

Forced labor Any work or services which people are forced to do against their will under deception, abuse of the legal process, or the threat of some form of punishment. Exceptions include prison labor and compulsory military service.

Forced marriage A marriage in which one or both of the individuals are married without their consent and forced into a life of servitude. Child marriage is considered a form of forced marriage, given that children are unable to express full, free, and informed consent.

Globalization   The process in which people, ideas, and goods spread throughout the world leading to more interactions and integration between the world's cultures, governments, and economies marked especially by free trade, the free flow of capital, and the accessing of cheaper labor markets.

Human trafficking   The illegal recruitment, harboring or transporting people into a situation of exploitation through the use of violence, deception, fraud, or coercion.

Indigenous (people)   Groups or tribes that are native to a particular area. In certain countries, indigenous people groups are particularly vulnerable to slavery.

Involuntary servitude   Involuntary or compulsive labor, often to pay off a debt, and under threat of, or actual harm.

John (aka buyer)   An individual who pays for or trades something of value for sexual acts.

Kafala system   A legal employment system in the Middle Eastern Gulf States and Lebanon and Jordon that requires sponsorship from a national entity for migrant workers to reside in the country. The sponsors, either individuals or companies, control the mobility of migrant workers through their ability to prevent them from changing jobs or exiting the country. The system has created systemic abuse and exploitation of workers and in some cases facilitates slave labor.

Non-governmental organization (NGO)   Legally recognized, independent not-for-profit organizations that operate independently from government entities. They include charities, nonprofits, voluntary groups, trade unions, professional associations, and human rights advocacy groups.

Organized crime syndicates   Affiliated groups of individuals, such as gangs, working together transnationally, nationally, or locally to commit profitable crimes.

Peonage   A system where an employer compels a worker to pay off a debt with work.

Pimp   An individual or group who controls and financially benefits from the commercial sexual exploitation of another person. Romeo pimps primarily use psychological manipulation to control their victims. Gorilla pimps primarily use violence.

Redemption   A practice that involves buying freedom for slaves by paying their slavers in goods or money. The practice, while well-intentioned, is controversial. Some argue that the financial incentives of slave redemption in poverty-stricken nations incentivize the expansion of slavery.

Restavec   Children in Haiti who are sent by their parents to work in another household as an unpaid domestic servant because the parents lack the resources necessary to support them. Most of the time restavec are not protected in their basic rights and are severely mistreated physically, psychologically, verbally, and sexually.

Serfdom   A practice similar to debt bondage that exists when workers are bound to live and labor on land belonging to another person and are not free to leave often due to threat of violence.

Sex tourism   Travel organized with the primary purpose of effecting a commercial sexual relationship between the tourist and residents at the destination.

Sex trafficking   The action or practice of illegally transporting people from one country or area to another for the purpose of sexual exploitation.

Sexual exploitation   Occurs when an individual is forced to perform a commercial sexual act, such as prostitution, as the result of force, threats of force, fraud, or coercion.

Sham marriage   A marriage in which two individuals consent to enter into a legal union, without intending to create a real marital relationship, subject to certain conditions that include an exchange of financial or other benefits in order for one party to obtain permanent residency in another country.

Slave   A person held against his or her will and/or controlled physically or psychologically by violence or its threat for the purpose of appropriating their labor.

Slavery   For the purposes of this book, slavery is defined as the condition that exists when an individual is bought or sold as property, forced to work through coercion or mental or physical threat, physically constrained or restricted in their freedom or movement, or owned or controlled by an employer through the exercise or threat of abuse.

State-imposed forced labor   Refers to situations in which citizens or subjects are compelled by state authorities to engage in involuntary work under the threat of penalty. According to the ILO Forced Labour Convention (1930), notable exceptions include compulsory military service, normal civil obligations, prison labor (under certain conditions), work in emergency situations, and minor communal services (within a community).

State party   A country whose government has signed a treaty or agreement in the United Nations Conventions or in international law and is thereby legally bound to follow its provisions.

Supply chain   A system of individuals, organizations, activities, information, and resources between a company and its suppliers to produce and distribute a specific finished product to the final buyer. Slavery and extortion are commonly found in the supply chains of certain products.

Survivors   Former victims of slavery who have overcome their victimization.

Untouchables *See* Dalits

White Slave Trade   The trade in foreign women across international borders for the purpose of prostitution.

Index

About the Author

Christina G. Villegas, PhD, is an associate professor of political science at California State University, San Bernardino, where she teaches courses in American political thought, institutions, and public policy. She has coauthored and authored several books, including *Hard Drive: A Family's Fight against Three Countries, Democracy in California: Politics and Government in the Golden State, Alexander Hamilton: Documents Decoded*, and *The Youth Unemployment Crisis: A Reference Handbook*. She has also written extensively on the American Founding, the U.S. Constitution, and public policy.